"An authentic human story of resilient, compassionate leadership. Highly recommended."

Dame Alison Peacock, *CEO of the Chartered College of Teaching*

"Wise, intelligent, humble, humorous, pithy, straight-talking, philosophical, pragmatic... Dr Vic Carr at her very best. Vic balances the 'what and how' with the 'why' on almost every page of this great read. School leaders will find this book engaging, helpful, supportive, comforting and robustly challenging. I certainly did."

Paul Cornish, *Executive Director of Education in a cross-phase MAT*

"A vivid and compelling account of school leadership: all the joys, the dilemmas, the laughs and the really tough decisions. Vic has written a book that will both move and inspire you."

Mary Myatt, *Education writer, speaker and curator, Myatt & Co.*

"Following on from 'Leading with love', an equally honest reflection, 'School Improvement – more than Ofsted!' is a story of a school and it's fight from crisis to the 'Good' life, 'warts and all', as Vic puts it. For any leader this book will give a host of tips and practical suggestions for leadership, but for someone new to leading a school out of an Ofsted RI, this book is gold dust. The comparisons to Vic's other life as an officer in the Army reserves are plentiful and fascinating. Using these, Vic Carr provides a new perspective on school leadership – it's the unknown unknowns that really get you and there were many at Woodlands when she took over.

You'll also explore the roots of our government's educational philosophy and the piecemeal production of what passes for national educational vision. Along the way, Vic puts Ofsted firmly in its place. The detail of her journey is engrossing and you'll learn so much from the educational sources she's used. Quoting from her own staff's parallel journeys is such an excellent device! A fine addition to our books on educational leadership. Woodlands is now in a fine place!"

Paul Garvey, *Education consultant and Ex-Ofsted lead inspector*

"What fun and joy I had reading this tome of wisdom from Dr. Vic! She tells her story of taking over a failing school with passion and alacrity – we can feel the sway of her influence as she turns that super tanker round in far less than the five miles it allegedly takes. Vic is the epitome of the belief that if you have faith in your teachers, have faith in all staff, have faith in your community, have faith in your children and above all – have faith in yourself, you will succeed even in the face of great difficulties! Oh yes (sorry I forgot) and work your socks off!

This book will inspire and motivate many to put cynicism and self-doubt aside and join Vic in proving that – yet again - commitment, faith and a willingness to 'dive in at the deep end' will not just 'get the job done' but will lead a now-great school out from the abyss."

Ros Wilson, *Education consultant*

"Capturing the landscape of education and leadership in its current state is no mean feat. What Vic has done here takes a lot of commitment and effort in order to produce such a fantastic resource for educators. If you are a classroom practitioner aspiring to lead, then take a look, as Vic offers a 'warts and all' account of what leadership entails. If you are an existing headteacher, Vic invites you to see education through her lens of experience, honesty and integrity. Nobody wants to make their school worse; Viv offers guidance that places school improvement in a realm of reality – from parental complaints to governance; from attendance to curriculum; and she does with typical wit and authority. One chapter alone offers a terrific history of the development of English educational policy over the last 50 years and I found it useful and compelling. We need to reflect on this stuff more so we can make the right decisions in the future. That's Vic's message, and one that you'll agree with. I like the parallels Vic makes with her side career in the military. They are useful and help the reader see how wonderful (and occasionally fragile) leadership can be. This book is an illumination for those who are seeking a light in the dark, and it will sit comfortably on any serious educator's bookshelf."

Hywel Roberts, *Teacher – Writer – Speaker. Author of*
Botheredness: stories – stance – pedagogy

"As the headteacher, and through the eyes of the Woodlands school staff, Vic provides a compelling blueprint for leading a school community from crisis to greatness! Navigating the physical and human terrain of the unknown knowns and unknown unknowns, she highlights the constraints, limitations and the decimation of systems, whilst encouraging, engaging and empowering the reader to seize the opportunity to lead with passion and make a difference.

Through the narrative of the school's journey, Vic showcases the removal of barriers and creation of opportunities through practical and impactful strategies that harness the talent of her team to make a positive impact. It provides an inspiring story of how Vic got the right people, in the right job, doing the right thing! Then, crucially, coordinating the moving parts through routines, systems and structures to secure successful school leadership, resulting in a positive impact for the whole school community.

PS: It's a great read! It gripped me!"

Patrick Ottley-O'Connor, *Collaborative Leadership Ltd. Coach*

"Loved the book. It's like a road map to success. Leadership at its best - built on relationships, vision, hard work and a genuine passion to make a difference for all involved, not just pupils. The way the book allows you to get to know Woodlands, warts and all and follow the journey with you is so enriching and leaves you feeling that anything is possible if people are at the heart of what you do."

Nichola Hill, *@Honest_Headteacher*

Authentic School Improvement for Authentic Leaders

Authentic School Improvement for Authentic Leaders charts a full improvement journey of a school from a 'Requires Improvement' Ofsted rating, through a second, to a resounding 'Good'. It reveals the impact that a school leader can have on the motivation and engagement of teachers, parents and pupils and how this translates not just to their overall happiness, but on academic standards and systemic, long-lasting school improvement whilst maintaining their own well-being.

Bringing together a wide range of accessible and relatable school improvement practices, the chapters cover all aspects of school leadership, from operational systems to academic standards and staff morale to pupil numbers. Full of strategies, takeaways, observations and anecdotes, the book illustrates that being authentic and leading with integrity is possible for all and provides tangible results that may support positive Ofsted outcomes but are not driven by them.

Including a Foreword by Ross Morrison McGill, this is essential reading for all headteachers and senior leaders in primary and secondary, mainstream and specialist, maintained and academy schools.

Victoria Carr is Headteacher at Woodlands Primary School, United Kingdom. She has been a leader in several contexts, from education to the British Army, and held a range of roles from lecturing to headteacher, research fellow to coach. Dr Vic leads with love, and this, her second book, exemplifies how and why!

Authentic School Improvement for Authentic Leaders

Victoria Carr

Routledge
Taylor & Francis Group

LONDON AND NEW YORK

First published 2025
by Routledge
4 Park Square, Milton Park, Abingdon, Oxon OX14 4RN

and by Routledge
605 Third Avenue, New York, NY 10158

Routledge is an imprint of the Taylor & Francis Group, an informa business

British Library Cataloguing-in-Publication Data
A catalogue record for this book is available from the British Library

ISBN: 978-1-032-57849-1 (hbk)
ISBN: 978-1-032-57582-7 (pbk)
ISBN: 978-1-003-44000-0 (ebk)

DOI: 10.4324/9781003440000

Typeset in Melior
by SPi Technologies India Pvt Ltd (Straive)

Louise Roberts
24.04.80 – 31.07.23

and

Helen Sharp
09.06.81 – 12.08.23

"Learn like a champion".

"It's all about community
and the ways in which
community can be
represented".

Contents

Acknowledgements

So many people contribute to the fabric of our lives, both personal and professional, that it is difficult to pick out one or two to say a particular 'thanks' to.

That said, the leadership teams of the schools in which I have led, and the body of staff that stand with them, have made my professional journey what it is. I could have asked for no better support in deputising than Sharon, Kathryn, Kev and Cath. I could not have had better SEND champions than Alice and Clare. I could have asked for no better support with finances than Sue, Annette and Jo. I could have asked for no better PTA support than Hannah, Rachel, Clare and Lou. I could have asked for no better office support than Lisa, Nicky and Jann. The work of the teaching assistants and all of the teachers has been the wind beneath my wings. For them all, I am truly grateful.

My family knows already how loved they are and how I could never have been the person I am without my mum, aunt, grandparents and children – but this is a public show of affection for them.

Staff voices

Emily: RP Lead, EYFS Lead, EAL Lead
Lottie: Year 6 Teacher, Maths Lead and Upper Key Stage 2 Lead
Roisin: ECT Mentor
Lou: Lower-Key Stage Two Lead, Phonics Lead
Sue: Bursar and SLT member
Annica: EYFS Teacher
Sioned: MfL Lead
Dani: History Lead
Pete: Art/DT Lead
Gill: RE and World Views Lead, Part-Time Class Teacher
Clare: Learning Support Mentor, Deputy Safeguarding Lead and Member of the SLT
Alice: SENDCo and Designated Safeguarding Lead
Emma: Science Lead
Jen: SMSC Lead, Part-Time Class Teacher
Arzoo: Forest Schools Lead
Mel G: Assistant SENDCo
Chris: Chair of Governors
Richard: Previous SLT

Acronyms

ASCL	Association of School and College Leaders
ASD	autistic spectrum disorder
ASIA	associate school improvement advisor
CAMHS	Child and Adolescent Mental Health Services
CEOP	Child Exploitation and Online Protection
CIF	Common Inspection Framework, used by Ofsted to inspect schools
Cojos	Commando Joes Character Education
CPD	continued professional development
EHCP	Education and Health Care Plan
EI	emotional intelligence
GB/FGB	Governing Body/Full Governing Body
GRT	Gypsy, Romany Traveller
H&S	health and safety
HR	human resources
INSET	In-Service Training for Teachers (five days per year)
KCSiE	Keeping Children Safe in Education
LA	local authority
LADO	local area designated officer
MAT	Multi-academy Trust
MHST	Mental Health Support Team
MS	Main Scale, teacher's pay
NFER	National Foundation for Educational Research
NGA	National Governing Association
NLE	National Leader in Education
NLG	National Leader in Governance
NPQH	National Professional Qualification for Headteachers
Ofsted categories	Outstanding/Good/Requires Improvement (RI)/Inadequate/Special Measures (SM)
Ofsted	Office for Standards in Education

PA	personal assistant
PM	Performance Management
PP	Pupil Premium
PPA	planning, preparation and assessment
PREVENT	government initiative for anti-terrorism
PTA	Parent Teacher Association
RMAS	Royal Military Academy Sandhurst
RoV	Record of Visit
SATs	Standardised Attainment Tests
SBM	School Business Manager
SCR	Serious Case Review
SEF	Self-Evaluation Framework
SENDCo	special educational needs coordinator
SFVS	Schools Financial Value Standard
SIP	school improvement partner
SLT	Senior Leadership Team
TA/HLTA	Teaching Assistant/Higher Level Teaching Assistant
TLR	Teaching and Learning Review
UPS	Upper Pay Scale
VUCA	volatile, uncertain, complex and ambiguous
WRM	White Rose Maths

Foreword

Ross Morrison McGill

Vic Carr has offered a book I desperately needed when considering headship. Sadly, the by-product of accountability and the unintended consequences simply put me off taking that next step. The reasons are **threefold**.

First, I've witnessed two examples of what accountability can do to leadership teams. The former was in the early days of academisation, where chief executives danced between the 'not-yet-firmly-in-place' financial regulations and lighter-touch accountability rules. Looking back, early academisation felt like the Wild West, with terms and conditions literally ripped apart. During this period, I took voluntary redundancy and started @TeacherToolkit before eventually returning to school leadership six months later. The **second** happened in between this career period when my family found itself on the brink of life and death, with no career or income. This initial period of adversity, with hindsight, provided me with what I believe is the autonomy we all strive for as human beings. 'Life gets in the way of teaching', and sometimes, it can make any of us have to take a U-turn or choose another unfamiliar pathway. Teaching, and in particular leadership, really does prepare you for these life-changing moments and career headaches.

My **third fateful moment** came after three years of financial, personal and professional recovery, plus a career move to another disadvantaged context; the 'sharp end of the accountability wedge' found me once again! With an ever-evolving inspection framework and an international news story, the spotlight was on the school. After three years of professional joy being a stand-alone academy, the school was re-brokered to multi-academy trust with an influx of leaders offering all the solutions! Within six months, almost the entire leadership team disappeared, with countless staff members to follow.

The critical points (or fateful moments) are defined as playing 'a part in mapping and theorising … individual responses, timing and chance' (Holland and Thomson, 2009).[1]

Today, all of the above is water under the bridge, but for me, a part of my leadership DNA is still stuck on a rock under that bridge, unable to dislodge itself back into the free-flowing currents of the water. With various gagging orders in place, having been bitten once, I spoke out and jumped ship, stepping away from 25 years of school leadership to meet the demands for teacher training across the United Kingdom. I write this here because I now know I am not alone. My single story represents some difficult aspects of leadership, and I know countless others are living these fateful moments today. There were, of course, thousands of brilliant moments, but those pinch points that end one's career leave deep scars.

I am 99.9% convinced that if it were not for the circumstantial accountability frameworks used, being in the wrong place at the wrong time means I would still be in the same school or, more likely, in the hot seat. As a result, today, I speak up for our brilliant school and colleague leaders like Vic(!) and have spent the last eight years researching anything and everything on accountability, particularly inspection, multi-academy transfer, discovering legislation and ensuing injustices, using my platform to help others.

These reasons are why I wanted to write this foreword for Vic's book.

Vic has unpicked the significance of school leadership and the important work headteachers do in our communities. The book delves into systemic issues in education, such as accountability pressures, recruitment challenges and the mental health concerns of our school leaders. Vic also shares the good, the bad and the ugly and how school leaders can support one another. If you are searching for ideas on cultural development, financial planning and building collaboration, this book you now hold has this advice in abundance. It's raw, authentic and heartwarming. Equally, it highlights the highs and lows of what makes a school leader today; it is so much more than just teaching students concepts, rules and facts across the curriculum.

Vic writes, 'There has always been accountability, and rightly so'. However, there is an abundance of academic research that suggests that accountability can stifle innovation. So, how do teachers and leaders find the perfect balance?

Brilliant people like Vic lead our schools and transform our local communities. Whether a school opts for local authority control or to switch the 'freedoms' of academisation, accountability remains. The challenges they face in an ever-evolving education system is how do we encourage autonomy at a school level, without competition, exam results or parental choice becoming the dominant accountability forces at play? This accountability takes 'a number of forms which may be at odds with many teachers' personal philosophies of teaching' (Knight, 2020).

In 2018, I was part of the National Association of Headteachers' Accountability Commission, which outlined a good alternative for the sector.[2] Together, we looked carefully at the education systems in Canada, Finland and Singapore,[3] which do have school inspections, but their reports are **not** published externally to the public. These countries have been known to perform better than England in various Programme for International Student Assessment tests.

In the last 24 months, we have observed Esytn in Wales abandon graded inspections, and SIAMS (Church of England schools),[4] responsible for 1 million students, have also abolished grading in the last 12 months. Are any of these schools now failing due to one-word gradings being removed?

In its quest for simplicity, the current Ofsted grading system reduces the multifaceted nature of schools to a singular, reductive label, overlooking the nuanced dynamics of educational environments and the diversity within student bodies. Despite recognising the uniqueness of each school, Ofsted's one-size-fits-all methodology appears incongruent, leading to a skewed focus where grades overshadow the depth of qualitative assessments. This approach, akin to a 'football manager syndrome', often results in headteacher attrition following poor inspection grades, with schools compelled to prioritise reputation over genuine educational quality. Grading not only limits teaching to a prescribed curriculum, such as the EBacc or SATs, but also perpetuates bias and inequality, disproportionately affecting disadvantaged schools. Furthermore, the grading system inadvertently fuels the housing market and local media narratives, which can vilify educational leaders, especially in schools labelled as 'stuck' or 'coasting', trapping them in a cycle of disadvantage! Worse, one could assume that the grading machine perpetuates inequality across the sector and in our communities. These 'stuck' or 'coasting' schools, often graded lower, need help to face challenges in attracting quality teachers and resources, and exacerbating existing issues; where does this help come from? What makes these brave leaders step up, and how can we protect them in a plethora of accountability matrices?

The subjectivity and inconsistency of accountability, especially in the inspection process, raise questions about the reliability and validity of assessments as an accurate indicator of educational quality. Additionally, factors crucial to student outcomes – such as parental involvement, peer influences and community support – are not comprehensively accounted for in these evaluations. Ofsted inspections, perceived as exhausting, stressful and demoralising by teachers, do not capture differences in school quality that matter for students' individual outcomes. They are 'weak predictors of students' achievements and well-being (von Stumm, 2021)[5] and school quality! The current inspection framework's sporadic nature, sometimes leaving schools uninspected for over a decade, poses risks to pupils, suggesting a need for a more continuous and holistic approach to evaluating school performance.

However, my perspective has widened, and I now champion intelligent accountability. You won't often see me write this down, but I now believe (despite my scars) that **we do need** Ofsted! An improved and collaborative inspection system can provide a crucial benchmark for parents, providing a transparent and objective picture to gauge the performance of schools and colleges. A new inspection system can help parents make informed decisions when selecting schools, with areas for improvement signposted, enabling schools (and parents) to target their strategies and training more effectively.

This book provides a critical perspective on how the aforementioned factors impact teachers, leaders and our students and families, advocating for a more balanced and humane approach to system leadership. Inside, Vic does not just provide an account of school improvement; it's a comprehensive exploration of leadership, providing a glimpse into school leaders' working lives with stories that will keep you gripped to the pages.

We should never underestimate the significance of any teacher, leader or head-teacher involved in school improvement. The need for an analytical yet pragmatic approach centred on students and staff (rather than compliance) can also provide strategic steps to address weaknesses. These barriers range from tangible issues like financial constraints and insufficient infrastructure to implicit skill sets, such as dealing with a lack of confidence and imposter syndrome or having the ability to juggle strategy and switch to mundane day-to-day implementation tactics.

Looking ahead, Vic envisions a future where schools overcome barriers like competition and mistrust, fostering a culture of shared knowledge and cooperation; anticipating what changes in leadership will be needed. This book is not just a narrative of school improvement; it's a comprehensive exploration of the multi-faceted nature of leadership, providing practical insights, personal reflections and critical analysis for current and aspiring educational leaders. My only hope is that our education policymakers pick up a copy!

This book is important for anyone searching for a comprehensive insight into school leadership and how to balance the modern challenges of education. It is full of classroom soul, offering a rich tapestry across all aspects of school life. I just wish I had read it years ago.

Ross Morrison McGill
Founder of @TeacherToolkit

Notes

1 https://www.researchgate.net/publication/340514662_Fateful_Moments_As_A_Micro-Celebrity_An_Autoethnography.
2 https://www.teachertoolkit.co.uk/2018/06/11/accountability-commission/.
3 https://www.teachertoolkit.co.uk/2018/09/23/nfer-accountability-research/.
4 https://www.teachertoolkit.co.uk/2023/03/20/inspecting-church-of-england-schools/.
5 https://acamh.onlinelibrary.wiley.com/doi/epdf/10.1111/jcpp.13276.

Introduction

> If I was to move to a different school and encounter the same type of issues as in Woodlands, I would take time to observe the strengths and weaknesses, make small changes informed by research and best practice over a period of time, invest in CPD, put in a rigorous monitoring schedule and foster a culture that is committed to reviewing practices to improve teaching and learning for all children. In other words, I would repeat the model used at Woodlands.
>
> *– Emily*

In 2023, as I write this book and reflect, there is no conventional way to become a headteacher in the United Kingdom, nor is there a conventional way to actually do the job. Indeed, there are even several names given now to what was once a very conventional role, these include principal, head of school and headteacher, amongst them.

I successfully applied for my first headship in June 2012 and yet did not start at the school until January 2013. I had been a non-class-based deputy head in a different Local Authority (LA), with the added responsibility of special educational needs coordinator (SENDCo), yet upon arriving as a head, I knew I still had A LOT to learn. Starting mid-year from out of the locality – as a 'newbie' – is an interesting endeavour, more of which we will unpick.

Subsequently, I was seconded to my second headship starting in September 2018 following an 'interview' (unexpectedly conducted in my red Birkenstocks after a shocking start to my professional week, again more of this later) in July 2018, leaving my other school in the capable hands of my then deputy headteacher. This time I was experienced; life (a divorce, single-parenthood, double mastectomy) and the trials of a first headship had toughened me, and I was ready for the rigours of this new challenge – but had no experience of taking on a struggling school – I am reliably told that few do, and maybe this ignorance is why I did it.

This book will take you, the reader, on a journey – the same one I went on. It will hopefully enable you to visualise and understand the experiences I had. Not only was I in a school in a challenging situation but in a time in history where there was

DOI: 10.4324/9781003440000-1

global and national unprecedented volatility, uncertainty, complexity and ambiguity (VUCA for the military minded). I did not just survive all of that but thrived whilst tackling it – and as a result, so did the school and all who learned within its walls. In many ways, we continue to.

As with my previous book, this one will be punctuated with true stories and lived experiences from my career, but this book also has lots of testimony from the staff of the school where I currently work, who have been alongside me for the last half-decade, dug deep and turned the fortunes of our school around with me. Whilst I can talk about my own leadership vision, drive, determination and success, what I cannot do with any authenticity is talk about how that felt as a member of my staff – for that, you can hear their voices sprinkled throughout the book. First up was Emily. Now, you have Lottie, who, when asked what she felt like before I got to the school, said this:

> It was a shock to the system. I was in my NQT year in my first teaching position (Y3). Within the first term at the school, the Headteacher had gone, and we had an OFSTED inspection in which they turned up in the car park at 8:00am (no preparation) which took the school from Good to RI. The overall feeling was one of fear and uncertainty.

Why do I do it like I do?

The abridged version of my life to date can be caught up on with a simple 15-minute journey on YouTube to watch my TEDx Talk or by reading the first chapter or two of *Leading with Love*, so I won't bore you with my history or philosophy, but it is important to note that I do have my own style of doing things, for my own reasons, and this includes not just how I am as a human being but also as an educator and leader. This underpins everything, but it is not for everyone – no offence taken if you just don't 'get me' whilst you read this book; it will usefully burn on your log burner and probably be more use to you as a heat generator.

Anyway, each of you will have survived your younger years, developed your own way of 'being' and 'doing' – and you are all here ready to 'deep dive' into my experiences of school improvement because something I have said or done has resonated, or the journey I have been on has similarities to your own. Some of you will have a backstory similar to mine, others will have had a fairy-tale life. What matters is not necessarily how you got here, what you endured or what you enjoyed, but the fact that you are here now and are actively involved in supporting young people to embrace the next stage of their lives and want to develop and enhance your repertoire of school improvement knowledge and strategies for their benefit, and that of the staff you are lucky enough to lead. Read this book and absorb it as it is shared, not as a manifesto of how things *should* be done, or what *you* should do, but more of a book about what I did, given the circumstances, and to what degree it positively affected lives. I am not the be-all and end-all of school leadership.

It is hard to talk about one school without inadvertently coming across as such. If you can, liken what I tell you to trying to open a jar where the lid is immoveable. Several people might try, one after the other, and the one who finally opens it may get a cheer – but they are the one who finished the job of several before. Steal what you want, or ignore it all and enjoy it as a funny read (except Chapter 1, which is not funny at all) – it is up to you!

Role modelling

I want to tell you something really obvious before I begin, though, especially if you are new to this gig – you will be a role model, whether you know it or not. When you can see it, you can be it and the young people you work with will be looking around them at the adults they can emulate and learn from. You are one of those adults. You are far more though. If you are a leader, you are a role model to your staff and to the parents of the children for whom you are responsible. The staff you employ and the standards you set mean your example and influence are therefore potentially amplified. Pause now and take on that responsibility. I have said this before, but that is because I truly believe it:

> [E]very decision you make, every chance and opportunity you grab, every person who supports and champions you, and who you support and champion, builds and co-creates your legacy – that which you will eventually leave behind for and with others. Your decisions and behaviours are not meaningless, they will be like keys, opening doors that you didn't even know existed with endless opportunities on offer to you, and crucially, others, so you need to be aware and ready to seize and signpost those opportunities as they crop up. One thing I know for a fact now is that, if you are open and aware, you can see that life is constantly bursting with opportunity, so stay alert to it!

I say this because one day, 20 or 30 years from now, one of your pupils may be standing in front of a room full of people and might be talking to them about their experiences and how those experiences have shaped the course of their lives, them as human beings, them as leaders in their fields. They will be considering where it all began, those who influenced and affected them and thinking about each of the key events that led them to that particular moment in time in the distant future.

You could be part of that narrative. But here is the terrifying reality – this could be for positive or negative reasons! Twice in the last couple of years, I have been contacted by serving headteachers WHOM I TAUGHT IN YEAR 8 ENGLISH, not one but two decades ago!!! Not only does this make me feel terribly OLD, but it also tells me that I have made an impact on generations to come. That blows my mind somewhat and makes me feel terribly humbled. Each of us will be having that impact, whether we ever know about it or not.

When I was young, I never considered that I would have the humbling and amazing privileges that I have had – could never have dreamed that I would be a headteacher one day, with all of the responsibility that this involves for the lives of others; for me, that is nearly 600 children and over a hundred staff!

Let's start 'big' with the UK national picture

We all know that humans like a good grumble about their jobs at times – perhaps this is simply human nature. For me, I explain to my children that work is just that, 'work'; it isn't called 'leisure' or 'pleasure'. However, that being said, in the United Kingdom, there has been a growing dissent, a real dissatisfaction in the education world that goes deeper than superficial grumbles about early starts, late nights and workload.

Leaders in education have never been under so much pressure (and if you read Chapter 1, you will know that there have been some tough times for the giants upon whose shoulders we stand!). The 'fear culture', an inevitable side effect of high-stakes accountability in a market-dominated system, has perpetuated recruitment shortages, increases in the poor mental health of educators and many leaving a profession that they once loved unduly early. Whilst this has been exacerbated by the pandemic, in reality, systemic issues related to political interference, chronic underfunding, breakdown of the social-support infrastructure for the vulnerable, increased workload and a lack of professional respect in society are key reasons for many being disenfranchised.

To be honest, this is even reflected in the United States, with teacher job satisfaction in one survey at a 40-year low of 12%.[1] This growing sense of dissatisfaction also seems to be spreading throughout Europe.[2] Perhaps this disillusionment is a global issue; perhaps it is deeper than just education, but for now, for this book, the focus is on education.

Undoubtedly, in the United Kingdom, there is a great deal to lament in the education system, as exemplified by Izzy Garbutt, the youth member of Parliament (MP) for Wigan and Leigh, in 2023 in her parliamentary speech. She highlighted just one of the constraints we face in terms of the never-ending conveyor belt of academic testing: in her talk, she mentioned young people, when they leave school, do so with a detrimental lack of understanding of the world, which is directly influenced by the current formulaic and compartmentalised curriculum (see Chapter 1 to discover how that curriculum came to be and Chapter 14 for how we, at Woodlands, manage it).[3]

When this articulate young person said what we all know (in education at least), that young people are not defined by school percentages of A*– C grades, evidence in an Ofsted inspection report, or simply passes or fails, she shed light onto the failings of what could be considered the 40-year experiment into marketisation of education that has seen it reduced to nothing more than statistics and numbers which can impact so many stakeholders in so many ways. The most appalling way is in the destruction of leader self-esteem and mental health, schools and communities as schools shrink and close, but not far behind is the wholesale dismantling of respect for, and appreciation of, the teaching profession in general.

There has always been accountability, and perhaps rightly so, but the negative impact of the fundamental imbalance in the current agenda is evidently taking its toll, not just on system leaders, but on the people the system is intended to serve, not least our children. For me, there are three extreme manifestations of the current education system on our children. The first is pupil anxiety (and deterioration of mental health) as a result of high-stakes tests in primary schools. Of the seven years a child is in primary school, they are tested now in four of them, previously it was five. The second is strike action, something that we have all navigated as leaders (and which I support as a legal action for staff to take), but for pupils, this causes disruption. Finally, the tragic loss of leaders such as, most recently, Ruth Perry, who champion their communities and schools, care for their staff and pupils and strive for innovation and social transformation.

Commiserate or celebrate

Whilst there is undoubtedly a great deal to lament, and much of it out of our day-to-day control as educational practitioners, there is, however, also a great deal to celebrate!

For me, never before has there been such an opportunity for innovative thinking! This began technically only a couple of years ago when, as a profession, we comprehensively embraced virtual teaching and learning as a result of the pandemic, but it has since grown momentum. Some of the changes implemented during that time remain in place. Improvements in the way things were done before (that may never have been considered viable had it not been imperative) are the legacy of the pandemic in the education world, and for which we are grateful. The swift step-change into the use of online learning tools meant that a generation of teachers, myself included (for whom technology was only partially embraced), suddenly had to learn to accept and implement contemporary methods, bringing them right up-to-date (ok, I accept that some of us are not necessarily conversant with TikTok just yet, and I was thrown for four days looking for, and not finding, my 'Twitter' app on my phone before I was told it had changed to X – but you get the drift!).

Whilst the pandemic response unquestionably showcased (on an international scale) the capability of educators and educational leaders to embrace and use change as a fuel for ingenuity, like war does for the military, it did so much more. It also demonstrated unequivocally the dedication of those in education to see young people achieve success – even to their own detriment at times. In the United Kingdom, this was key to at least try to redress the balance (albeit temporarily) in the acute lack of respect that our profession tends to suffer and to exemplify the extent to which we all plug the leaks and fill the gaps created by the destruction of so many other over-stretched services, combined with multiple manifestations of deprivation, poverty and lack of agency.

We might be a long way off rediscovering professional respect, but in a world of click-bait and capitalist focus on profit margins from media sales, I find it reassuring to remember that we are not alone, and public sector workers (including police, ambulance drivers, doctors and nurses) are also fair game when it comes to being lambasted in the press for monetary gain, so at least we know it is not personal!

I am someone who has always been in awe of our educational leaders, and I remain so on a daily basis. Despite being a serving headteacher for over 11 years in some pretty challenging circumstances, I still don't feel like I am yet a 'grown-up' in the world of senior leadership. I certainly do not class myself as an expert and remain focussed on personal and professional improvement wherever possible. I am not only learning from myriad experiences every day, but I am still able to be surprised by the gamut of circumstances that we, as educational leaders, are regularly faced with at the visceral interface of education and educated.

Right people, right job!

There remains, as ever there has done, an existential place between educators and those being educated, a transactional space where anything is possible and magic really happens when the right people are doing the right job, with the right resources and the right environment. It is in attracting, training and recruiting the right people (and supporting their ongoing professional development) that we ensure, as system leaders, that we have the right people doing the right job – and fundamental to this in my view is effective coaching and mentoring, from pupils to student teachers to trained staff at all levels. Everything about my practice, establishing systems, challenging conversations and pursuit of excellence is underpinned by a philosophy of coaching and mentoring, so it will frequently crop up as you progress through the book and is why I am so committed to collaboration with organisations such as CollectivEd.

Excessive accountability, recruitment and retention, then, might be three of the key barriers to the future of education and look likely to remain so for the foreseeable future. But there are others, both school and, therefore, context specific, that I will talk to you about as we journey through this text.

The pandemic showcased the resilience and tenacity of many leaders; their ability to manage the challenge of the political arena (in which education firmly sits) is nothing short of miraculous. We are all subject to overbearing accountability instruments, the fickle court of public opinion, vilification in the national and local press, conflicting parental and governmental expectation, the systematic destruction of social infrastructure and centrally funded LA support networks, austerity and funding cuts, union action and the legacy of capitalist ideology. All of this against a backdrop of uncertain future expectations and requirements of leadership in both the global village and our national society, alluded to, for example, in portmanteau research such as that of Jacob Morgan in his book *Future Leader*.

Given the rather bleak contemporary landscape, then, as those inherently devoted to the legacy we will leave and to our future leaders, we should all be engaged at some level in seeking knowledge and understanding – asking the 'so what' questions in our individual settings but also about the educational direction of travel in general. Thinking through the implications of policy, and challenging it when we disagree, will be critical. I feel sure that even the well-meaning Conservatives of the 1970s (you will come to this later on in Chapter 1), who dreamed up the idea of neoliberalism and marketisation would have put the brakes on had they realised the way their ideology would become weaponised and so toxic four decades later.

It is funny to think that when the world stopped for a time during Covid, the magnitude of the work undertaken by educators as a matter of course was unveiled, from feeding students, to finding homes for them, washing clothes, to preventing them from being trafficked and everything in between. Although perhaps quickly forgotten in the desire to kick start the economy, now exposed, these facts can never again be hidden and could have provided food for thought for all policy-makers and an opportunity to embrace the knowledge of those in the profession. Let's end this section upbeat: I wonder if incremental changes are happening – after all, even the new king gave an unexpected and unprecedented shout-out to educators in his 2022 Christmas Day speech, so there is hope that our considerable contribution to society is beginning to be recognised and I genuinely feel that the national pressure of strikes and growing calls for reform in Ofsted are gathering momentum. There is hope, at least, and hope not only floats but can keep us afloat.

The REALLY BIG thing

There is a single vital ingredient which will, in my humble opinion, be the foundation of all future educational leadership survival and development activities, underpinning any thriving academic and scholastic environment and culture. It is why I offer things like free phone calls to leaders I don't even know through social media, and free group TEAMS sessions to support those new to leadership who might be struggling. The ingredient?

The ability of leaders to work collaboratively.

This is something that has been impinged in the last two decades in the United Kingdom by the divisiveness and polarising impact of the academy agenda, built on the foundations of competitiveness between schools and de-centralisation by the government. The divide between academies and state-maintained schools, promulgated and promoted by successive governments and media outlets in order to meet their own agendas (not those of educators), will eventually subside as more and more schools do become academies (through choice or political manoeuvring).[4]

The removal of perceived or actual barriers to collaboration could serve to promote further active links between organisations and strengthen once again the ability of educational leaders to work together effectively cross-sector. Overcoming the significant barrier of competition and the resulting mistrust will be fundamental if leaders of the future are to be encouraged to accept the mantle of responsibility we currently carry.[5]

Aspirant leaders in the current climate may have little knowledge or understanding of the requirement of a variety of roles that even five years ago simply did not exist. Who knows what the *next* five years will bring in terms of expectations of leaders, but I believe research – not politics – and a diverse, growing repository of knowledge created from within the profession, and those invested in it, will facilitate discussion, dispel misunderstanding and encourage people to become educational and *educated* leaders of the future, as a result. Needless to say, rather than the perpetual 'traditional versus progressive' educational debate, I choose to look at things a little more pragmatically, something that has served me well.

Education, like all other aspects of life, is affected by the society it serves and draws its requirements from. To embrace the perpetually changing requirements of society, it is imperative that successful organisations collaborate and work in partnership both within the sector and beyond it. Schools do not operate in silos, nor do Multi-academy Trusts (MATs). We should not be in self-made bunkers for our own survival, and yet this is the reality for some people. We can learn from and with colleagues if we are prepared to open up and share our journeys. Hence the premise of this book.

There is an enduring interest in leadership for improving good practice and outcomes in schools, and myriad books exemplify this. However, this often compartmentalises aspects of what makes schools good or better (putting teachers first in one book, zero tolerance for poor behaviour of pupils in another, for example). There is an argument to suggest that the best leaders are as familiar with their leadership narrative and moral purpose, their perspective on the fundamental components of leadership and school improvement, as they are with their own school story and for me, it is in the combining of the two that makes for success. This book is therefore less conceptual academic theory and more practical application, but just so you know, I don't stand on my own soapbox, I will give you some references and some suggested reading as we go in the takeaways at the end of each chapter!

Any leadership narrative originates from worldviews, biases, experiences and beliefs and is the combination of thoughts, words, examples, stories, assertions and guidance that one accumulates and communicates as a leader through intentional, and unintentional, behaviour. It is the purpose of this book to demonstrate, mainly through the story of one school and its development, that in engaging in topics of leadership, ethics, organisational and personal growth, research and systems, for example, it is possible to bring nebulous leadership and improvement practice into focus, coalescing that practice into systems that have intellectual and emotional legitimacy and proven impact on well-being (as well as standards).

I believe that in demonstrating how it is possible (despite personal fear and potential for reputational harm) to take over a school that has a complex cocktail of financial, academic, systemic and cultural issues which place it in Requires Improvement (RI)/Inadequate/Special Measures and then lead it towards good and better – others may find resonance with their own experience and perhaps find the courage to do the same.

There is no other book currently which gathers authentic and varied experiences of members of a school in crisis as it fights for life and then recovers: from caretakers to teaching assistants, newly qualified teachers to senior leaders, administrative assistants to school bursars. This book gathers it all in one place.

Many people may not have time to read books in their entirety to find and extract the good practice that can be applied to their own setting or role (primary, specialist or Pupil Referral Unit (PRU) settings, whether they have issues with teaching and learning, curriculum design, finances, for example), this text should bridge that gap and therefore can be read in chapters if necessary, or front to back.

School improvement – down and dirty!

To that end, the book! There is no chronological thread throughout the book. Part of the reason for that is there was no linear model to improvement for me at this school: the disparate parts were like a 5,000-piece puzzle in a box that needed to be put together. Each of us would choose to do this in different ways.

Chapter 1 deals with the broad history of why we are where we are today, outlining the momentum and impact of cumulative government agendas over the last 40 years. I then get specific and discuss my information-gathering strategies in Chapters 2 and 3, including some of the considerations people should make before taking on a school in a difficulty. How the varied and complex areas of school were transformed over the last five years is compartmentalised in Chapters 4–15, from external to internal threats, what limited us and why, what is implied in our roles as educators, what is explicit and more besides. Finally, in summary, I focus on the future (now we are judged as a 'GOOD' school) in Chapter 16.

I will share, within the main body of the book, some overarching thoughts about individual mental preparation for taking on a school in difficulty, our five-year school improvement journey across everything from finance, to human resources (HR), special educational needs and disabilities (SEND) to subject leadership and development areas to illustrate the realities of what politicians can only hint at. I talk less about Ofsted and more about profound and inclusive improvement for *all* in school – staff and pupils. There is no disconnect between practice and research in our school because our practice is situated within contemporary research and based on the lived experience of practitioners engaged in critical analysis of what works for us and what doesn't.

The only thing we can plan for is change

Empty political rhetoric, egotistical desire to create a name for oneself and lack of policy contribution from educators are the outcomes of ways of working that have left the legacy that now frames our educational reality. We see this in terms of national curriculum design (from Early Years through to A Level), in terms of restrictive examinations (from Early Years through to A Level), in terms of Ofsted directing the avenue of approach for education and in terms of significant misunderstanding at national levels about effective funding, and how it should be spent.

As leaders in education, our collective mission should be, and by and large is for most of us, the impact we can all have on children and young people and thus – by extension – the communities that we and they live in. But I think we should all go one further and extend this overtly to the impact we can also have on our colleagues to ensure they remain motivated and committed. Finding innovative ways to motivate colleagues, enhance their careers and aspirations and develop their skill sets and knowledge are all real barriers to educational leadership and school improvement when so many talented individuals leave the profession before they even step on the first rung of the leadership ladder.

In working collaboratively as leaders, we can be the voice of change but also the risk-takers and the ones who set the conditions for success for our colleagues to embrace learning that may lead to change within our own organisations and far beyond. Giving licence to our colleagues to strive for answers – to probe, question and innovate – and then ultimately to challenge themselves gives them a voice. At Woodlands, that collective voice is the one I ask for in order to challenge me and in doing so ensure that I remain high functioning and versatile, agile in my leadership. We should all perhaps be craving the respectful and informed challenge of our peers and colleagues. Creating cultures where this is commonplace will in effect create successful microsystems where our children and young people can thrive and will facilitate leadership by example at all levels.

In a world where thinking outside of the box, and routinely preparing for change, has yet to become normalised, we need to be able to adapt quickly. The only thing we can plan for is change, and therefore our business as leaders perhaps should be in research-informed, evolving leadership practice at its best, perpetually collaborating, innovating and problem-solving.

What does that look like?

I was asked about my views on change management and school improvement in 2022 in order to speak at the World Education Summit. I think the initial expectation was that I would be able to give a decisive and brief response. I didn't. The only definitive thing I could say was that change is a certainty, and perhaps the secret to thriving in light of that certainty is embracing the fact that things will unlikely remain static no matter our organisation, the country we live in or what we do for a job. Having spoken on the topic for an hour, I didn't even scratch the surface. To be fair, how could I condense my views on this complex and often contested concept into a few short sentences? Whole books have been written on change and its management, what drives it and why – everything from society to war, from pandemics to policy. Change, and thus its management, is contextual and influenced by internal and external factors and drivers – and it is no different in a school. Therefore, the caveat to what I share here is that it is simply what **we** have done with our combination of people, complexities and drivers.

We all know that every school is unique – and yet in England, every school serves the same Ofsted masters on one hand and wonderful children and staff on the other. Somewhere in that dichotomy lies the sweet spot of school improvement where staff well-being and a positive culture can be created and preserved – but, trigger warning, it is not easy, and there are no easy, quick fixes.

Big picture

I am one of those people who begins with the big picture first – my mind works that way, and it helps me to see things in context – to understand the contributory factors that might affect something, someone or an organisation. Funnily enough, in recent Intelligence Corps training we conducted something called Intelligence Preparation of the Environment (IPE)[6] and (newsflash) the military has something that is EXACTLY the same as that which I do when I arrive in a new school!

At first, what I do can appear to some people like inertia because I am not creating tangible products if I arrive in a leadership role and simply begin by 'observing' and talking to people. I have spoken of this before, but I read a book about a year after arriving at my current school called *Turn the Ship Around* about a US naval submarine commander who was forced unexpectedly to command a sub he was not familiar with. He had no other choice than to break the mould and go and ask people on the sub how things worked and why they did things the way they did – the outcome was that he took over the worst performing sub in the US fleet and literally 'turned the ship around' ensuring that she became the best performing one within the year.

The way that I counter the negative assumption that observation and conversation in order to understand are synonymous with inertia is by being explicit and literally telling everyone at the outset that I will seek to make few immediate changes (unless I feel practice compromises safety). Instead, I will take time to get to know the systems, the personalities and the culture with a fresh pair of eyes before making suggestion about where **we** could make changes that will save time, create an efficacious and productive staff or make things easier, for example. Usually, I want to maximise 'bang for buck', and a single change made will hit two or three targets if I do it correctly.

Find a way to protect the organisation from external harm, whilst building the internal capacity for improvement

I have done this twice now in the last 11 years as a school leader in two very different schools. Twice, it has worked very well for me. Twice it has made school improvement partners (SIPs) nervous because the external narrative of improvement is often situated in seeing rapid difference, equated to 'impact', and the rhetoric that people are often professionally beaten with is that in order to show dedication to improvement and change, it must be conducted with 'urgency' and thus outcomes must be immediately visible.

Because I am in the habit of creating effective and sustainable change in a particular and unique school for the right reasons, with the buy-in of all stakeholders, it is not lack of urgency that prevents my immediate action. The truth is that I am usually feeling highly anxious and trying to manage and mitigate for that anxiety because I can see the external threats of organisations (such as Ofsted) circling around in what many school leaders feel (and know) is a *very* threatening way. Simultaneously, I can see the internal organisational issues (if not the causes of them), and I know that I have to try to find a way to protect the organisation from external harm whilst building the internal capacity for improvement and a healthy culture – all of which we will explore later. Easy business, obviously!

For me? It has often been a case of 'holding the line' (and managing my own impatience, one of my less favourable character traits, and one that I continue to work on!) because I prefer to work in an informed way and am always thinking on a number of time frames – long, medium, short and immediate and taking into consideration a number of factors, staff capacity, finances, fabric of the building, resource requirements, reputation, pupil need, parental engagement, academic provision, culture, behaviour, external pressures, health and safety – the list goes on.

Associate school improvement advisors

My LA operates a system where experienced headteachers can support others by applying to become and subsequently becoming associate school improvement advisors (ASIAs). ASIAs usually meet with headteachers throughout the year, depending on their school category (linked to published data and therefore performance and/or Ofsted) and the place they are in the cycle of inspections. They can also be asked to do bespoke work, such as conduct Teaching and Learning Reviews (TLRs) as they are known in our LA, and their own schools are paid for their time. This is a mutually beneficial role and part of the multi-million pound, money-making machinations of education in 2023.

In July 2018, I was part of a five-person ASIA team tasked with assessing progress against improvement objectives in what is now my current school, Woodlands, improvement objectives which had been set two years before.

The LA had stepped in to support and put a very experienced headteacher and Ofsted inspector into Woodlands as an executive headteacher for the remainder of the 2016–17 academic year. The following academic year another very experienced headteacher and national leader in education (NLE) was asked to be executive headteacher for the academic year (2017–18), and it was at the end of this year that the LA asked us, as a group of experienced headteachers and ASIAs, to come in and assess the situation before the re-inspection window began in the 2018–19 academic year.

At this point, I had no intention of becoming the third executive headteacher in three years nor of applying for the substantive post if and when the situation with the substantive headteacher was resolved. I knew that the following academic year, Ofsted would be conducting another inspection, as it had a schedule to work within and a school in RI was routinely inspected within three years. Whoever took it over, I decided, would be essentially in a 'no-win' situation; that person ended up being me, but we are jumping ahead (as usual!)

In being embedded in the school for four days, what I knew was

- two different part-time, very experienced headteachers, inspectors and NLEs were interim executive headteachers in post in the two years before my arrival;

- the school had received a RI judgement from Ofsted two years before my arrival;

- the school had suffered significant deterioration of published academic standards since that inspection, and it is widely known that this adds a vulnerability;

- the school was working on a hybrid of pedagogical methodologies; and

- it had lost over 10% of its pupil numbers.

At that time, before, during and for a few days after that TLR, I did not know that the person who would take on all of this would be me. After five years, this is what we now have:

> Our school culture is exceptionally positive and will leave a legacy for many years. We are a huge family; we always have each other's backs, are hugely supportive and teamwork is what drives us to success. There are many visitors that I have met across the last five years who have all said what a happy, nurturing and welcoming place our school is, and they are right! Roisin.

Takeaways

- Even before considering change, seek first to develop 'situational awareness'; in other words, seek to understand the situation from a range of perspectives (more about this in Chapter 2).

- Take special care to acknowledge that you may have at least one blind spot and therefore may need a degree of input from others who may see things from a differing perspective to help you out.

- There will be immediate and obvious, obscured, purposefully hidden, complex and simple considerations that you will need to know about before effecting change (more about this in Chapter 3).

- Exposing all you need to know can take a little time, is based on increasing trust or mistrust, and evidence of how you react when, as a leader, you are surprised or shocked by information that is unexpected and might be unpalatable.

■ How you react at the uncovering stage is vital on many levels but sets the conditions for success if, rather than get frustrated, you remain focussed on simply information gathering without judgement and problem-solving without blame.

Notes

1 https://www.ny1.com/nyc/all-boroughs/news/2022/09/14/teacher-job-satisfaction-lowest-in-decades-edweek-survey-#:~:text=The%20Merrimack%20College%20survey%2C%20which,varies%20widely%20by%20demographic%20profile.
2 https://www.euronews.com/next/2023/02/02/teachers-pay-which-countries-pay-the-most-and-the-least-in-europe.
3 https://www.youtube.com/watch?v=VKrpYo9N5hs.
4 https://repository.uel.ac.uk/item/85472 https://www.tandfonline.com/doi/abs/10.1080/02680930802660903   https://www.tandfonline.com/doi/abs/10.1080/02680939.2017.1402959.
5 https://books.google.co.uk/books?hl=en&lr=&id=A6qsBwAAQBAJ&oi=fnd&pg=PP1&dq=school+academies+and+capitalism+barriers+to+collaboration+UK&ots=bJCAvw4G1G&sig=yra9rnu5xPSZztOlmYtWQJKyGII&redir_esc=y#v=onepage&q&f=false.
6 https://www.ihatecbts.com/cbts/2022/9/7/jko-joint-intelligence-preparation-of-the-operational-environment-jipoe-cui#gsc.tab=0.

Good reads

Clear, J. (2013). *Atomic Habits: An Easy and Proven Way to Build Good Habits and Break Bad Ones*. Random House Business.

Hewstone, N. (2023). *The Unhappy Headteacher: Navigating Headship and Finding Joy in the Role*. Authors & Co.

Marquet, L.D. (2013). *Turn the Ship Around! A True Story of Building Leaders by Breaking the Rules*. Portfolio Penguin.

Morgan, J. (2020). *The Future Leader: 9 Skills and Mindsets to Succeed in the Next Decade*. Wiley.

Mukherjee, P. & Davies, M. (2020). *A Few Wise Words: Inspiring Stories of Success and Hugely Valuable Advice from a Unique Collection of Famously Successful Individuals – How to Plan Your Journey Towards Success and Fulfilment in Life*. Amersham Publishing Limited.

Vainikainen, M.-P., Thuneberg, H., Marjanen, J., Hautamäki, J., Kupiainen, S., & Hotulainen, R. (2017). *How Do Finns Know? Educational Monitoring without Inspection and Standard Setting*. Standard Setting in Education, (pp. 243–259). DOI:10.1007/978-3-319-50856-6_14

External drivers
Impact of neo-liberalism on schools over 40 years

Our School Improvement Partner has always been positive in their feedback, and it was helpful to have a 'mock' deep dive. I found the LA's SLE feedback on planning and the monitoring of books most useful and productive. Our ASIA has supported us in realising we needed to overhaul the curriculum in places. All have had a positive role – some more intense than others. Ofsted, I feel, is just a 'snapshot' of the intense work we have undertaken but they 'drive' and contribute to a lot of the extra work we do.

– Gill

External drivers

I write this chapter with a few asides and a little commentary to make light reading of what can be heavy material. I am often asked who dreamed up Ofsted or why we have the systems we have, and I am sure that there are many of you reading this who wonder the same thing. Well, search no further; I have a wee potted history of why we have the systems we have, and happy reading it will make too! (If you want to skip this potentially nightmarish chapter, I don't blame you, but it's good to be 'edumacated' right?!) It won't help you plan school improvement things, that is for the following chapters, but it might help you understand the landscape we find ourselves navigating, and it will help you gain a **balanced**, politically neutral view and understand that it isn't *all* the Conservatives' fault – because it isn't!

Neo-liberalism and Margaret Thatcher

In a word, and it is only one, as it is hyphenated, neo-liberalism is the reason we do things the way we do around here! This is a complex term, and for those of you reading it for the first time, do not panic; it may take a little wider research

DOI: 10.4324/9781003440000-2

to understand it. Now, we don't have a DeLorean (well, I don't, you might), but to understand where we are today, we must travel back in time to a dim and distant past, a time when faces were not contoured and lashes were not permed, a time before oat milk latte, when your milk was actually delivered to your door on a float – a time when Margaret Thatcher ruled the United Kingdom. Under her leadership, Conservative legislation sought to place neo-liberal principles at the heart of *all* public policy, including that of education. The outcome of this was a form of governance in which market principles were advanced at the same time as central authority was strengthened – this socio-political experiment continues (and some may argue it is the root cause of all the issues we currently have with our society, incidentally).[1]

Random, you might think, a marketplace ideology for education? How? Well, the origins of this policy can be traced back to 1955 and the establishment of the Institute of Economic Affairs, which was a right-wing think tank. By the time Margaret Thatcher came to power, its influence was such that it had persuaded the Conservative Party to abandon post-war welfare drivers and instead embrace policies championed by a man called Stuart Sexton, who was a key adviser to Thatcher's first education secretary, Mark Carlisle. Those policies were based on 'free-market anti-statism' which would eventually affect both social and educational constructs as we perceive them today. 'Anti-state?' you question. 'Doesn't sound like the Maggie T we know!' some may exclaim. I know! I know, the dissonance is palpable, and yet....[2]

In my best 'Scooby-Doo' impression – Zoinks! Sexton, in his Black Paper, said,

> Obviously we get rid of the 1976 Education Act for a start. We remove all other political constraints and directions which seek to distort the pattern of educational supply and demand.... Local Authorities would no longer allocate children to schools: The parent should be able to apply to any secondary school; there should be no zones, no catchment areas.... The educational market would not be entirely unregulated: there would be an independent inspectorate, minimum standards and a minimum curriculum....The exercise of parental choice is the key. The very exercise of that choice, and the response to that choice, will produce the schools which the parents want and the children need.... They will be different, school to school, country to town, just as children are different. They will be good schools or they will close.[3]

Ahem, no words needed, right? I think we know where Ofsted was formed: the copulation between marketisation and Sexton's drive, but there were many other things that came before the Ofsted we have come to know and love which set the conditions.

In a style that we have become accustomed to in recent years, there were several education secretaries during the Thatcher reign: Mark Carlisle, Sir Keith Joseph, Kenneth Baker and John MacGregor.

Mark Carlisle, bless him, freely admitted his discomfort in post saying, 'I had no direct knowledge of the state sector either as a pupil or as a parent'.[4] He also admitted that Thatcher 'didn't much like teachers, and she didn't seem to like the civil servants she encountered at the DES'.

Keith Joseph, erm, standby to be shocked, but he was quoted as having said to prolific education researcher Stephen Ball,

> We have a bloody state system I wish we hadn't got. I wish we'd taken a different route in 1870. We got the ruddy state involved. I don't want it. I don't think we know how to do it. I certainly don't think Secretaries of State know anything about it. But we're landed with it. If we could move back to 1870, I would take a different route. We've got compulsory education, which is a responsibility of hideous importance, and we tyrannise children to do that which they don't want, and we don't produce results.[5]

As far as raising the infant that was Ofsted, Joseph believed that 'a market solution could only proceed (and succeed) in conjunction with a paternalistic Inspectorate', with the view that there was little value for money evident in the education system. Yep, value for money – how you measure this in terms of human growth is anyone's guess.[6] As if this situation could have been any worse, Joseph, with the longest tenure of secretary of state (SoS) for education during the Thatcher era, reportedly had an extremely low opinion of teacher unions and did not remain impartial when he told Clyde Chitty, 'You don't understand what an inert, sluggish, perverse mass there is in education. The teacher unions were ... perverse, perverse'.[7] Funnily enough, Simon, in 1991, nailed it when he said that Joseph's almost five years in office was 'a disastrous period for education, culminating in a crisis almost reaching the proportions of a Greek tragedy – and having similar characteristics'. I am not sure whether, almost 40 years later, I should laugh or cry at the accuracy of this statement or the fact that some could argue it is the same today.[8]

Anyway, on a brighter note, next came Sir Kenneth Baker, a man perhaps principally remembered for what we call In-Service Training for Teachers (INSET) days, or maybe it was the controversial 1988 *Education Reform Act*... Trevor Fisher discusses in more detail the shift in power relationships, the politicisation of education in the following two decades and the increasingly rigid control of politicians over education policy and processes in his treatise,[9] but make no bones about it: 1988 saw a momentous change that we can feel the echoes of today, and Sir Ken was only in post a couple of years!

Finally, the quieter tenure of John MacGregor. His time as SoS education might have been short (16 months) and some may even say, unremarkable, yet his words leave a lasting legacy – although quite what his qualifications were in education or child development to make such remarks, I have no idea:

> I have always been critical of the way educational thinking developed in the late 1950s and early 1960s under the influence of the teacher training institutions.... I feel that some of the ideas about child-centred learning

which were so influential during these years have a lot to answer for with regard to the lowering of standards which has taken place in too many of our primary and secondary schools.[10]

Foundations laid

The 1979 Conservative election manifesto contained a brief section on 'standards in education' declaring,

> We shall promote higher standards of achievement in basic skills. The Government's Assessment of Performance Unit will set national standards in reading, writing and arithmetic, monitored by tests worked out with teachers and others and applied locally by education authorities. The Inspectorate will be strengthened. Schools will be required to publish prospectuses giving details of their examination and other results.[11]

Enough said, right?

School effectiveness

Research in the 1980s sought to identify elements in a school which were most likely to affect its effectiveness – to be honest, lots of research has gone into this, but if we are outlining the last 40-odd years, then this is a key time to focus on as it was 'of the time' and related to the political storm that education found itself sitting within. Of note, Murgatroyd and Morgan came to the conclusion that

> the most critical variables in determining what makes a difference between a high performing school and others is not teacher:pupil ratios or per capita expenditure, but: (i) the climate or culture of the school; (ii) the nature of leadership within the school and the system of schooling; and (iii) the support of parents for the work of the school.... Notice something important about these three variables: they are all about ethics and processes, about school culture and the way in which the experience of this culture shapes action and performance in the school, about the dynamics of leadership at every level of the school as a system and about the nature of the relationship between the school and its primary stakeholders – teachers, students, administrators and parents.[12]

This research brought into sharp focus the role of leaders in shaping vision and strategy, communicating that vision to all stakeholders, engaging stakeholders in the work of the school, engendering commitment and sustaining performance outcomes associated with this strategy – over time.[13] This is naturally no different from the expectations of today's leaders, but clearly, today's policy can find roots in the 1980s, and it is interesting that school culture and ethics were so overtly positioned in the 'improvement' narrative even back then.

Thatcher's reforms, which were, according to some, 'piecemeal and hesitant' at first, became 'hectic and continuous', culminating in the 1988 Education Reform Act.[14] This legislation changed the institutional make-up and methodology of education, substantially modified the way it constructed social interactions and reshaped values, meanings and objectives.[15] To put things more strongly, it annihilated the educational culture which had developed between 1944 and 1979, and began the work of creating one in which old 'social actors' were marginalised and new ones, those of the marketplace, were rendered much more powerful. The coercion and social control it created was successful: it established enduring ground rules for schooling in the 1990s and beyond.[16]

John Major and more of the same

John Major inherited an education system from his predecessor that had suffered a significant decline in investment, with an unsurprisingly corresponding increase in inequality. His government were equally as hard as that of Margaret Thatcher and could be considered equally confrontational towards the teaching profession. For such a quiet and unassuming man, this is a bit of a surprise, I know, but there it is.

The education department was twice renamed during the Major government (no idea why!): the Department of Education and Science (DES) became the Department for Education (DfE) in April 1992, and subsequently, the Department for Education and Employment (DfEE) in July 1995.

The SoSs went under similarly transformational handles (funnily enough, making no difference to their overall effect): secretary of state for education and science: Kenneth Clarke. SoS for education: John Patten. SoS for education and employment: Gillian Shephard.

Kenneth Clarke, now then, was perhaps most notable for a hat trick: the implementation of the National Curriculum testing regime in 1991, The Three Wise Men Report and Teacher Appraisal.[17] The first, we all know as SATs. Although he claimed to be a 'fervent believer in testing',[18] apparently, he was a little underwhelmed with the legacy of testing ideology introduced by Kenneth Baker (him and I both, but what do I know!).

> I tried to make some sense of those wretched SATs...but it seemed to me that we had gone far, far too far down the track for me to try to change that. But the actual nature of the SATs and the way that they were conducted left a lot to be desired...whoever devised them...had not had a very good understanding of what it was really like to conduct a class of 7-year-olds.[19]

You're telling us, Ken! Anyway, because he had such little regard and respect for them, a year later, in 1992, the second round of Key Stage 1 tests was implemented; the first league tables were produced, and the rest is history. Deep joy.

And finally, Ofsted (happy 30th birthday!)

1992 Education Act

The Conservative government, under Margaret Thatcher, had begun huge reforms, the hangover of which would last generations; it still gives me a bad head now. Having implemented the National Curriculum, its accompanying testing regime and the resulting league tables, the government under John Major focussed on 'the inspectorate' to really tighten up school accountability and place the spotlight on schools starved of funds and their inadequacies. From 1992 onwards, school inspections were conducted by privatised inspection teams (overseen by the Office for Standards in Education – Ofsted was born). The 1992 Education Act made provision for the appointment of 'Her Majesty's Chief Inspector of Schools in England', basically the head of Ofsted, who would inform and advise the SoS about 'the quality of the education provided' by all schools in an annual report.[20]

Although Ofsted was inaugurated on September 1, 1992, under its first chief inspector, Professor Stewart Sutherland, inspectors did not conduct the first round of school inspections until September 1993. Astonishing that, as I write, it is 30 years of Ofsted – 30 years of what Gillard said so succinctly:

> The establishment of Ofsted did little to raise teachers' morale. They quickly discovered that an inspection involved huge amounts of paperwork and form-filling; they were suspicious of the motives and abilities of some of the private contractors; they found the week of the inspection itself extraordinarily stressful; and they had concerns about the accuracy and fairness of some of the published reports – which was understandable, given that their careers were at stake.[21]

I feel like, given the first few pages of this chapter and what you have just swallowed, we should attempt to skip happily over the somewhat shocking impact of John Patten, but it is so toe-curlingly bad to read about that the only thing for it is a summary.

The editors of *Forum*, Clyde Chitty, Liz Thomson and Nanette Whitbread, basically wrote what thousands of educators collectively thought at the time as they breathed a sigh of relief:

> There will be few who regret the eventual fall from grace of the former Secretary of State for Education, John Patten. The most amazing aspect of his tenure was that he managed to stay as long as he did. He will be remembered for his vanity, his arrogance and above all his inability to listen to the advice, wisdom and experience of others. His successor, Gillian Shephard, at least looks as though she is listening and has lost no time in making contact with teacher unions and other groups who had either been ignored, derided or insulted by Patten.[22]

Moving swiftly on then to Gillian Shephard! Shephard's time as education secretary was busy! In 1996 alone, there were five education acts, another Dearing Report and two white papers! It was, however, ostensibly a period of consolidation, and she acknowledged that the teachers needed it early on in her tenure (I wonder if it was because she had been a teacher).

> [A]t this stage, and for my time here, we've got to do a lot of listening, we have got to devote a fair amount of time to consolidation, to stability, to getting the reforms thoroughly bedded in and refined where we need to, so that they can actually flower. That is a rather dull thing to say, because of course it's always more fun to say, 'I want to turn this or that upside down'. But as far as schools are concerned, I believe we want a period of consolidation and stability, and I believe that's what teachers think too.[23]

Labour landslide – now we are getting somewhere, right?

Well, hold your horses now! Let's just take a quick moment to review what's what. In just nine short years (1988–1997), the Conservatives had deconstructed the fabric of the education system established by the 1944 Education Act. Responsibility for a school, as a result, was something shared between the government and the nebulous 'market forces' rather than the tripartite team of the government, the local authority (LA) and the school itself. Power had definitely been wrested from schools and LAs.

The Conservative commitment to increasing diversity of school provision in an increasingly competitive 'education market' had resulted in huge polarisation and division of extra resources (which were usually diverted to schools that were 'doing well' – and those were most often in 'favoured conditions and favoured contexts', we might call those favoured contexts 'affluent areas' perhaps).[24]

They had widened the poverty gap, with significant implications for society as a whole but, importantly, schools that served the most vulnerable. Within state education, poverty and educational underperformance were strongly correlated; as a 1997 Ofsted survey reported, state schools with heavy concentrations of 'poor children' were by far the worst performers.[25] Now, a quick pause for thought: was that post-code, poverty or school related?

During this period, the promotion of traditional (also known as right-wing) education had caused significant and prolonged national controversy about a number of topics based on what we now call inclusion and diversity – for example, relationships and sex education, religious education, homosexuality and race, amongst other aspects of educational life such as teacher militancy and what constituted 'British' history.[26]

Aside from being busy doing all of the above during their 18 years in office, the Conservative Party had

- removed teachers from any curriculum development;

- alienated and insulted teachers;

- diminished the influence of the teacher unions;

- all but destroyed the power of LAs;

- introduced a National Curriculum;

- introduced SATs;

- introduced an empowered inspectorate; and, woefully,

- dramatically cut education spending as a percentage of gross domestic product.

In the end, the government destroyed itself, imploding when John Major's government was swept away in the general election of May 1997 as Tony Blair's 'New Labour' Party scored a landslide victory.

Many of the ideas which underpinned New Labour's education policies were heavily influenced by the Institute of Public Policy Research (IPPR), which had been launched in 1988 by Labour-supporting businessman Clive (Lord) Hollick.

In his foreword to the 1997 Labour manifesto, Tony Blair declared that

> Education will be our number one priority, and we will increase the share of national income spent on education as we decrease it on the bills of economic and social failure. [27]

Derek Gillard, legendary English educational historian, illustrates the reality, however.

> During the campaign, he said his government's priorities would be 'education, education, education'. It was unsurprising, therefore, that many teachers hoped – some even dared to believe – that the first Labour government for eighteen years would usher in a new 'golden age' in education. Tests and league tables would disappear, Chief Inspector Chris Woodhead (who had become something of a hate figure) would be sacked, Ofsted scrapped, and grant-maintained schools would be brought under local authority control. No such promises, however, had been made during the campaign.[28]

Sadly, it would quickly become evident that 'New Labour's' education ideology was synonymous with that of Thatcher and Major, including both endorsing 'parental choice' and also competition between schools in a diverse and unequal school system.

Anyone who today *only* blames the Conservatives for the system of education we have is actually ill-informed. Given New Labour's predisposition to advocate for neo-liberalism, few were surprised that not only did Chris Woodhead keep his job as chief inspector (head of Ofsted), but he and SoS for education,

David Blunkett, appeared to share the same enthusiasm for vilifying teachers. Former Labour deputy leader Roy Hattersley said, after Blunkett named and shamed 18 schools in his first 3 weeks in post,

> [A] Labour victory should have heralded a new age of cooperation and consensus. But the psychology has not changed. Schools are to be frightened into improvement by the threat of exposure. The blame is again heaped on teachers, not the conditions of deprivation in which their pupils live or the inadequate and under-funded buildings in which they are required to teach. Bullying teachers is the cheap as well as the easy option for a Secretary of State who genuinely wants improvement but has not been provided with the resources essential to bringing it about.[29]

Special advisors and SoS (almost literally SOS!)

Interestingly, during New Labour's reign, SoSs for education were far less important to policy than were the 'specialist advisors', with the most influential being Andrew Adonis, Michael Barber and David Miliband. The SoSs were David Blunkett, Estelle Morris, Charles Clarke, Ruth Kelly and Alan Johnson.

Well, what do we credit Andrew Adonis with, taxpayers? Yep – the academy agenda and crippling student debt! Adonis exerted a powerful, and as it transpired toxic, influence on New Labour education policies, producing a constant stream of policy and eventually successfully persuading Tony Blair to allow universities to charge 'top-up fees' – a policy he subsequently regretted, in retrospect, particularly given what has happened since.[30] Not only did he come up with some 'great ideas', but he also spent time exerting power over several SoSs for education, many of whom said they suffered as a result of what government insiders called 'The Adonis Problem'. The most notable casualty was Estelle Morris, who, it was widely believed, resigned because she felt undermined by Adonis.[31]

David Miliband has been credited with contributing to the 1997 white paper 'Excellence in Schools', which was the precursor to the 1998 School Standards and Framework Act, and this was the start of the National Professional Qualification for Headship (NPQH), amongst other things. Oh, and at this time, after the green paper for SEN had also hit the education system in 1997, good old David Blunkett announced that schools Ofsted judged to be failing would have two years to improve – **or be closed**.

Another Scooby moment – it has been 20 years since Every Child Mattered!

In September 2003, the chief secretary to the treasury, Paul Boateng, published the green paper 'Every Child Matters', which 'provoked a huge debate about how best to integrate children's services to ensure that no child ever again slipped through the net'.[32] I seriously wonder what he would say now. Let us not even dip a toe into Serious Case Reviews (SCRs) and actual children who have more than slipped through the net over the years.

Ofsted – vertically challenged?

Under New Labour, in their third term in office, a new Ofsted inspection regime was introduced. Inspections would be shorter, and schools would be told only two days before inspectors arrived. Bell described the changes as 'the most radical since Ofsted was set up in 1992' in the *Guardian*, the month before they were introduced and two months before Christine Gilbert took over as head of Ofsted.[33] To be fair, I was at university that year, so there is a little memory loss about that time, which means I could not point Gilbert out of a line-up if my own life depended on it, but she must have been influential!

New Labour legacy: the Blair years

Professor Maurice Galton comprehensively reviewed research evidence from the Blair decade in *Forum* in the summer of 2007, concluding, surprisingly, that New Labour were less successful in raising standards than they had suggested to the proletariat. Mike-drop moment.

Gains, if any, were limited. In fact, teachers claimed that they suffered excessive working hours in an attempt to deliver a broad curriculum in a climate of professional distrust, disrespect and Ofsted fears. Simultaneously, the increasing pressure of league tables, targets and Ofsted inspections resulted in some 'perverse incentives' for schools to 'offload' pupils, many of which we still see today.[34]

Peter Mortimore, in his summation of a decade, expressed the collective disappointment many felt. He acknowledged that there was a lot to do when New Labour came into office in 1997. He further said that many teachers wanted to help improve schools and make society more equal. He illustrated what we have come to know as 'the norm': instead of the formulation of a long-term improvement plan based on big questions and collaboration, schools receive top-down policy created in silos by successive ministers and their advisers, who (despite being distant from the role), think they know 'what works'. They cherry-picked research, suppressed evaluations that gave them answers that did not fit preconceived ideology, and compounded the already significant mess they had inherited. Trusting teachers – which is what ministers do in the best-performing countries – was not on the agenda.[35]

Gordon Brown

Following Tony Blair's resignation, Gordon Brown became prime minister and leader of the Labour Party on June 27, 2007. On June 28, 2007, the day after, he appointed Ed Balls SoS for children, schools and families.

So, what are we to make of the legacy of education in England from Gordon Brown and Ed Balls? To be fair, it is worth remembering that the Brown government was only in power for three years (a lot of stuff went down during that time, and it all ended quite badly). Despite their limited tenure, the duo had enormous energy, commitment and abundant ambition. Subsequently, they produced several policies, reports, and both green and white papers all committed to improving life for the nation's children, and especially those from poorer families.

However, the contradictions were manifold. Ed Balls continued the policy pursued by previous governments, undermining the role of LAs by increasing the number of academies. He compelled schools to use a particular method of teaching reading – 'synthetic phonics' – against the advice of internationally renowned experts, yet extolled the virtues of returning decision-making to schools.

Whilst he may have appeared to be concerned about England's testing and league tables regime, and rightly so, he remained resolutely committed to maintaining it, despite widespread hostility from parents and teachers; despite clear evidence of the damage it was causing, not least to the children themselves; and despite the fact that all other parts of the United Kingdom had abandoned the practice.[36]

Coalition

With the arrival of David Cameron and a coalition government, there was further scope for pragmatic education reform that eluded our country and, actually, as it happened, eluded the coalition. I could speculate as to why, but for now, let me tell you this. The only changes in education were a change in name (from the Department for Children, Schools and Families (DCSF) to the DfE) and the appointment of Michael Gove as SoS for education. To be fair, that was more than enough.

Academy agenda

Two successive New Labour governments had opened 203 academies and despite the controversy surrounding the ones that had been opened, they had planned to increase that number to 400 had they retained their government. Michael Gove decided early on that 'go bigger or go home' would be his mantra and was determined to go much further than a mere 400. He hastily created his 'Academies Bill', which was published a mere fortnight after his appointment! It demonstrated the direction of travel and decisively removed both LA power to veto a school becoming an academy and parent/teacher legal rights to oppose academisation. During that time, in his first month as SoS, he also wrote to all English schools, actively inviting them to become academies. He went on to say that he had 'no ideological objection' to businesses making profits from the new generation of academies.[37] There we are then.

The dark ages – the changes

It is irrefutable that the coalition government changed almost every aspect of education in England, and this against a socio-political background of welfare cuts and rapidly rising poverty levels. In order to effect such profound change, Michael Gove focussed on weakening his 'enemy' – a collective of invested educators that he unfavourably described as 'The Blob'. His strategy of rapid and all-encompassing change destabilised education in its entirety, thus making it possible for him to create an alternative system based on neo-liberal policy.[38]

The changes included, but were in no way limited to,

- the role and power of the LA as custodians of education;

- removal of barriers to the rapid expansion of the academy programme;

- introduction of a new and highly controversial National Curriculum;

- changes to SATs tests, including phonics testing and published league tables;

- a new system and expectation for special needs assessment and provision;

- dramatic changes in funding of higher education;

- the provision of teacher training and expectations within it;

- abolition of the obligation for teachers to be 'qualified'; and

- changes to teachers' pay and conditions which were comprehensive: abolition of the national pay scheme, introduction of performance-related pay, pensions decimation.

It was a torrid time, marked by experts, such as Michael Bassey, as led by a dangerous man leaving a disastrous legacy.

> It needs to be recognised that Michael Gove, as a government minister, was dangerous. With outstanding energy for reform, but severely limited understanding of education, he imposed half-baked ideas on the millions of young people in our schools and their teachers. At last the prime minister realised this and sacked him, but his legacy looks disastrous.[39]

It is disastrous.

I now recommend a lie down in a darkened room!

I think this chapter, as difficult as it might have been to navigate (and trust me, this is literally a brief dusting of information about what has gone down in educational history in the last 40-odd years), has outlined the overarching drivers of the school improvement agenda and reasons for them. It has dealt with the more negative influences on school leaders and their school improvement agenda, including the aims of successive national governments, despite political leanings, and their unrelenting congruence with the international focus on employability, underpinned by accountability, neo-liberalism and western cultural ideologies.

Most importantly, I think, as you sit stunned, is to consider this:

There has been change, a lot of it, all due to political interference. It can happen in a heartbeat. It can upend the world as you have come to know it. But teachers teach, pupils learn, schools run. The end.

A lot of what you have read about is still in place today. Even so, there are ways of working so that you don't need to feel irritated with your LA: they have been underfunded and robbed of any agency, just like schools and their leaders have. We had lots of support from our LA, lots, and in many ways, we could not have made the changes we have or have become the school we are now without them. But this isn't the only way.

My friends who are CEOs and those who are heads of school in Multi-academy Trusts (MATs) tell me that support structures are in place in those organisations and can be equally as valuable. You don't need to feel pressure or feel the effects of divisiveness that have been perpetuated between LA-maintained schools and academies. It is all part of the educational edifice, and behind it sits **people** who, by and large, don't even get to make their own decisions because they have political constraints preventing them from doing so.

Anyway, moving on from these external drivers, let's talk internal drive instead. Turn the corner over to mark your place. Have a rest, then grab your notebook and pencil to steal ideas if you like, and prepare for an insight into the work we did!

Takeaways

- Don't let all of the political stuff that can come at you like a tornado blow out the candle that is burning within you for teaching and for children.

- Teaching is a social concern, first and foremost, and is based on the desire of the profession as a collective to support social mobility and improve life chances and outcomes. Someone has to do it, so why not you?

- All you need to do is understand which aspects of the external agenda apply to your own school, influence you as a leader and need your attention. This is what helps inform the creation of your range of 'to-do' lists, which then inform the strategies you use to achieve each element on the list.

- Understanding the political arena of the time is as important as understanding the policies you don't yet have in place.

- Whilst you need an appreciation of the complex aims of government and, by extension Ofsted and their shifting intent, you can absorb their aims in a positive way whilst not letting them define the heart of your school.

- If you allow Ofsted to dictate direction in school, a whole new re-culturing would need to take place for every iteration of the EIF or every new white paper. Unthinkable.

Notes

1 Jones K (2003) *Education in Britain: 1944 to the Present*. Cambridge: Polity Press. p. 107.

2 Chitty C (2009a) *Education Policy in Britain* (2nd edition). Basingstoke: Palgrave Macmillan. p. 47.

3 Sexton S (1977) 'Evolution by choice' in CB Cox and R Boyson (Eds.), *Black Paper 1977*. London: Temple Smith. pp. 86–9.

4 Ribbins P and Sherratt B (1997) *Conservative Secretaries of State and Radical Educational Reform Since 1973*. London: Cassell. p. 55.

5 Ball SJ (1990) *Politics and Policy Making in Education: Explorations in Policy Sociology*. London: Routledge. p. 62.

6 Knight C (1990) *The Making of Tory Education Policy in Post-War Britain 1950–1986*. London: Falmer Press. p. 152.

7 Ribbins P and Sherratt B (1997). p. 80.

8 Simon B (1991) *Education and the Social Order 1940–1990*. London: Lawrence & Wishart. p. 488.

9 Fisher T (2008) 'The era of centralisation: the 1988 Education Reform Act and its consequences' *Forum* 50(2).

10 Ribbins P and Sherratt B (1997). p. 129.

11 http://www.conservativemanifesto.com/1979/1979-conservative-manifesto.shtml.

12 Murgatroyd S and Morgan C (1992) *Total Quality Management and the School*. Buckingham: Open University Press. p. 98.

13 Murgatroyd S and Morgan C (1992). p. 40.

14 Jones K (2003). p. 121.

15 https://www.education-uk.org/history/chapter15.html.

16 Jones K (2003). pp. 130–1.

17 https://dera.ioe.ac.uk/id/eprint/4373/1/curriculum_organisation.pdf; https://www.legislation.gov.uk/uksi/1991/1511/made.

18 Ribbins and Sherratt (1997). p. 156.

19 Ribbins and Sherratt (1997). p. 156.

20 https://www.legislation.gov.uk/ukpga/1992/38/contents; https://journals.openedition.org/osb/1771.

21 https://www.education-uk.org/history/chapter16.html.

22 Chitty C, Thomson L and Whitbread N (1994) 'Editorial' Forum 36(3) Autumn. p. 67.

23 Ribbins P and Sherratt B (1997). pp. 204–5.

24 Benn C and Chitty C (1996) *Thirty Years on: is Comprehensive Education Alive and Well or Struggling to Survive?* London: David Fulton Publishers. p. 226.

25 Jones K (2003). p. 113.

26 Jones K (2003). p. 120.

27 http://www.labour-party.org.uk/manifestos/1997/1997-labour-manifesto.shtml#:~:text=as%20a%20country.-,The%20vision%20is%20one%20of%20national%20renewal%2C%20a%20country%20with,its%20place%20in%20the%20world.

28 https://www.education-uk.org/history/chapter17.html.

29 Hattersley R (1997) 'Spare them the rod' *The Observer* 25 May.

30 https://www.theguardian.com/education/2017/jul/07/tuition-fees-should-be-scrapped-says-architect-of-fees-andrew-adonis.

31 https://www.theguardian.com/politics/2002/oct/27/publicservices.schools.

32 Chitty C (2009a) *Education Policy in Britain* (2nd edition). Basingstoke: Palgrave Macmillan. p. 220.

33 https://www.theguardian.com/uk/2005/aug/30/schools.ofsted.

34 Galton M (2007) 'New labour and education: an evidence-based analysis' Forum 49(1&2) Spring/Summer. pp. 157–77.

35 Mortimore P (2009a) 'Missed opportunities and mad ideas: the government's legacy' *The Guardian* 7 July.

36 https://www.education-uk.org/history/chapter18.html.

37 https://www.theguardian.com/politics/2010/may/31/michael-gove-academy-schools-profit.

38 https://www.education-uk.org/history/chapter19.html.

39 Bassey M (2014) 'Goodbye Michael Gove' Forum 56(3). pp. 417–20.

Good reads

https://www.cipfa.org/policy-and-guidance/articles/academies-article

https://www.theheadteacher.com/school-procurement/health-and-safety/take-a-strategic-approach-to-risk-management

Conkbayir, M. (2022). *The Neuroscience of the Developing Child: Self-Regulation for Wellbeing and a Sustainable Future.* Routledge.

Roberts-Holmes, G. & Moss, P. (2021). *Neoliberalism and Early Childhood Education: Markets, Imaginaries and Governance.* Routledge.

Scott, K. (2019). *Radical Candor: Fully Revised and Updated Edition: How to Get What You Want by Saying What You Mean.* Pan Macmillan.

Vandenbroeck, M., Lehrer, J., & Mitchell, L. (2022). *The Decommodification of Early Childhood Education and Care: Resisting Neoliberalism.* Routledge.

2 Gaining situational awareness
The creation of the 'to-do list'

The biggest factor in our school improvement success, in my opinion, is the headteacher getting everyone on board right at the beginning, being open and honest and leading from the front; ensuring that there are systems in place for all staff to follow and know are there to protect them; understanding staff worries and concerns and supporting them, providing opportunities for staff to challenge and better themselves with appropriate coaching.

– Lou

Gaining situational awareness

Although I had a good grounding of information with which to begin as executive headteacher at Woodlands, I knew the 'ground in general' as the military say, because I had spent a little time lifting up the proverbial rocks and carpets to see what was beneath them – the knowledge was pretty superficial. In four days, as part of a team of associate school improvement advisors (ASIAs), what else could it be? I did gain evidence of the 'atmospherics', however, the intangibles, whilst I was at the school as an ASIA in the summer of 2018, and this information was enlightening in itself.

I knew that the follow-up inspection would be due, 'Schools judged as 'Requires Improvement' will be re-inspected under section 5 usually within 30 months after the publication of the section 5 report'.[1] I knew that as executive headteacher, the incoming leader would have to prepare everyone for the potential outcomes of the inspection (based on information they would need to gather quicky, more about this in Chapter 4) and also simultaneously gel and galvanise the team of almost 100 people before their arrival.

I did not know that person would be me when I was there as an ASIA, but I did know something of Ofsted at that time.

DOI: 10.4324/9781003440000-3

Ofsted 2018

'Inspection is above all about human judgement'.[2]

As headteachers of the time, under Amanda Spielman, we were familiar with the previous chief inspector, Sir Michael Wilshaw, and his intent. He said that he was keen to 'listen to professionals' in order to continually improve the inspection regime. We were assured that the Common Inspection Framework (CIF, as it was called then) would provide 'consistency' so lacking previously so that everyone would share the faith that inspectors' judgements would 'mean the same things'. However, leaders in 2018 remained anxious about the inspection process, with good reason. This was no different in 2023.

As long ago as 2015, the idea of discarding the 'outstanding' judgement was mooted, recognising that it is complex and subjective, with the additional and arbitrary reward of exemption from subsequent inspections.[3] Naturally, then, as headteachers, we concerned ourselves with reflections about how inspectors were meant to accurately interpret words differentiating the 'Outstanding' and 'Good' grade judgements consistently (school to school) during the short, intense and highly pressurised atmosphere of an inspection. Words such as 'unwaveringly', 'substantially', 'uncompromising', 'deep', 'incisive' were littered throughout the outstanding description with little commonly understood exemplification and consistency. However, for Woodlands, the main concern was how to avoid the 'Inadequate' and look to retain the RI assessment – for very good reason.

At that time, just as now, the political stance of the government posed a threat to the status of a school judged to be in a RI category – relying on Ofsted to identify schools for forced academisation. Just as now, there were potentially irreversible consequences of a RI judgement – and as for two consecutive ones.

Not only that, but in 2018, leaders were still grappling with the hangover of the national changes in how schools were measuring attainment and, given that outcomes for pupils were always key judgements influencing how the inspection would evolve, understanding this in a school and being able to tell the story were key because the familiar metric that had underpinned initial inspection conversations (nationally comparable, if flawed, data) had been discarded. To be graded Good for what was then called 'achievement', schools needed to demonstrate that children's progress was 'above average'. Without clarity and consensus in relation to what 'average' now represented, it was virtually impossible to do this.

In 2015, Sir Michael Wilshaw said that HMI would ask a number of questions about school leaders during subsequent inspections. Despite him leaving, we were still using the same framework in 2018 and therefore expected the questions to be the same. One of these questions was, 'Are they focused on what really benefits children and young people, rather than wasting their time endlessly preparing for an Ofsted inspection which could be years away?'

Pragmatism

Interesting question, Sir Mike. As a serving head who knew and had first-hand experience with an inspection system that had (and has) the power to impose severe sanctions on a school and therefore the lives of the people within it, I knew that heads like me must be pragmatic and provide a 'yes' response to *both*. Until Ofsted accepts that it is culpable for the compliance it demands of school leaders, we must be pragmatic! Central to this pragmatism is an acceptance that school improvement does not go on in Westminster or Ofsted HQ but in schools and class-rooms up and down the land – driven by school leaders and practitioners work-ing relentlessly with children and their complex families. An inspection is only a glimpse of this work, but its outcome is unparalleled in terms of impact.

This was the reality – and remains so despite the end of Sir Michael Wilshaw's ten-ure and indeed the end of his successor, Amanda Spielman's tenure, despite two itera-tions of the framework used to evaluate schools since the time I took over at Woodlands (in only six years!). Who knows what the future holds? If we look back at history and the establishment of the current regime, which (for interest really) I did with you light-heartedly in Chapter 1, then we can almost predict the direction of travel – but not with certainty. What I know is, although this book – and the work it is predicated upon – acknowledges Ofsted, it also favours focus on what *really* benefits children and their families yet suggests that the two things do not have to be mutually exclusive.

Given this background, some said at the time that it was 'professional suicide' for me to take on this school; more of this in Chapter 3. Those who know me will agree, however, that I am guilty when someone tells me the reason why it *can't* be done of doing it anyway.

The first thing I did?

Set the scene. We still do it now: hold a session where our staff – in its entirety – come together on the first day of the school year and the autumn term. We realign our values, discuss our year ahead, share our summers and our personal experi-ences and refocus. More about this in subsequent chapters, but I explained in the first whole staff and governor training day environment that none of us work in isolation, in a vacuum, and that much of what happens to make things go wrong, and to right them again, is inextricably linked to two things:

■ the quality of relationships between people and

■ the culture created from those inter-relationships which facilitates effective management of challenge and change.

There, you need read no further! You have the answer!

Oh, fancy a bit more meat on the bones? OK, then, I will tell you what happened next.

The main effort

I said my priority number one, **the main effort**, would be to look at what the most obvious weak points were in our Ofsted defences as they were the immediate threat to our organisation, and to do that, I would need information. I would look at our organisational vulnerabilities – at that time, there was a very obvious one – standards of attainment, to be precise, and in tackling this, everyone would see how I worked.

In creating a system, together, we would then apply and use this to set a routine way of working in all areas of school so that everyone would know what to expect – I didn't mention expressions like the 'psychology of organisational safety'; I didn't even have that language then (have a look in the "Good Reads" section at the end for an accessible book about this), but I knew intuitively what was needed.

I needed to know and to understand the areas that needed to be addressed. That is impossible without time, honesty and open analysis of what was being done, why and whether it was working. I wanted to create firm foundations for the future – for whomever eventually got the substantive post. Me – as it happened.

I said I would allocate an experienced senior leader to each aspect of academic improvement we would make, devote time and money to training, follow up with guided coaching in planning, preparation and assessment (PPA) time, have a rigorous monitoring schedule that told us if we needed to tweak practice for consistency, and thus constantly improve, just as we would expect children to improve.

I also explained that as headteacher, I was responsible for at least two different teams who had to work as efficiently as each other if we were to remain protected from external harm. The educational team, and the administration and support team. I explained that once the academic plates were spinning, I would leave the daily oversight of the education team to the allocated senior leaders. I would then be working with the administrative team to work out how (and what) we communicated with parents, how we purchased things and budgeted for the future, as well as ensuring the website was compliant for the looming inspection and the record-keeping for things like safeguarding, were also on point. Additionally, I would ascertain our ability to improve infrastructure and conduct cyclical maintenance of things like the five-year electrical tests, for example.

Sounds easy, right? I would like to say it all went swimmingly just because I did that little speech. Erm.

Everyone loves a list!

My tick list of jobs for the first term sounds very simple. It wasn't. Many things were happening concurrently, so some days, I worked an exhausting 20 hours. I will share some of that tick list next so you can see just what I **was** aware of before I tell you what I **wasn't**! Stand by for lots of head-nodding because I know I won't be alone in having done this, or in having such a list.

What I knew I needed to do:

■ Source and install a digital tracking system and train staff how to use it consistently and effectively, both for them and me, in order to enable me to manipulate data and see where to focus resources across a three-form entry, two-site school. Also, in order to share data effectively and honestly with the governors to ensure they knew what was happening in school, and reinforce the improvement narrative related to data when it arrived.

■ Review, rationalise and refine teaching in all core subjects so that the understanding of teachers was robust, the planning was thorough, the delivery effective, the assessment and next steps easy to establish and the feedback loop for children proved useful for them to make rapid, significant and sustained progress. I also had to challenge the LA about the suitability of the specialists they had allocated to the school and review the provision accordingly.

■ Find suitable and appropriate texts to engage and challenge children, enthusing them to want to read. Go through all of the class and main library books to ensure that they were all relevant and supportive of contemporary thinking, sourcing books to ensure that children had a rich reading diet at age-appropriate levels.

■ Review early years to confirm quality provision both internally and externally, to ensure that children were nurtured and their needs catered for, and also that their learning offer was within the landscape of national drivers for change in this area. Ensure that we were compliant as a minimum and better than that to give children the start to their schooling that they deserved. This also involved evaluating the preschool and nursery provision and their financial viability.

■ Build capacity in staff for excellent teaching and also emergent leadership – proactively seek potential, capitalise on it, train it, enthuse it and support it. This involved substantial time and financial investment, which I had assumed, and also strategic understanding so that we were not throwing money like buckshot at a wide range of unrelated and disparate ideas or pressuring staff who would benefit from more training to perform at high levels in order to lead effectively.

■ Review, rationalise and refine tracking in the provision for and funding of children who were disadvantaged and ensure the information was shared appropriately with parents, school governors, teachers and the world on the website. This was needed to prove what was useful for those children in terms of making rapid, significant and sustained progress, and to discard what was not. This also involved sharing information with nearly 1,000 parents about who could access that funding and how they could do it. Not only was this a legislated expectation, but doing it also ensured the money received was spent appropriately and that relationships between parents and school improved.

■ Review, rationalise and refine provision, support and funding for children who had special educational needs and disabilities (SEND) and ensure the information was shared appropriately with parents, school governors, teachers and external agencies in a timely and effective way. This was needed not only to gain funding but also to understand the needs of the children so that they could be planned against. It had the second order effect of requiring us to source quality staff to work with those children, training them effectively and ensuring they were adding value.

■ Speak to every single staff member to find out about them: their aspirations, family make-up, previous jobs, reasons for working in our school, barriers to their individual success, what they contributed, what they felt they could offer, what they felt about the journey of the school thus far, what they thought I could do to make healthy and productive changes to how things worked, etc. This was to support my endeavour to stabilise staffing, recruit for gaps in experience and skill and plan for training needs, alongside talent spotting and future planning for deployment of staff.

■ Review, rationalise and refine Performance Management (PM) and appraisals in school for ALL staff – format, conduct, practice, staff understanding of role and job description, governor review and how this related to budget setting, pay policy, human resource (HR) legislation, etc. This also involved looking at staff training, significant amounts of continued professional development (CPD), rigorous monitoring of the impact of that training and its benefit to both practice and pupil outcomes – informing us as part of our cost-benefit analysis of where we would spend money in the future.

■ Review, rationalise and refine governance, following a governance review recommended by Ofsted, ensuring that governors knew their role in terms of challenge and support, the difference between strategic influence and operational delivery, that clerking was done appropriately, and that minutes and agendas demonstrated challenge. This also involved organising for governors to come into school, be trained and briefed on progress regularly (warts and all) and be appraised about what we were doing to tackle issues with transparency and integrity.

■ Review, rationalise and refine behaviour for learning expectations, policy and practice – simplifying both rewards and sanctions. Being clear on reasons why we do things and communicating those expectations to all.

■ Create a healthy challenge culture and team ethic across both sites to remove the urban myths that staff on one site were inferior to the other, that parents felt the systems were better in one phase than another, that the headteacher never visited one site and so on.

■ Be human.

- Review the entire curriculum that children were exposed to and ensure it made sense, that there was joined-up thinking across all aspects of it, that it was covered by staff in terms of expected content, assessed and resourced appropriately and consistently.

- Engage with parents, open clear and effective lines of contemporary communication and be visible, accessible, approachable whilst also holding firm on school ethos, standards and behaviour expectations.

- Model expectation and behaviour at all times, supporting staff mental health and ensuring that anyone for whom the journey had taken a toll was supported to either remain or find alternative roles, as the job of improvement was going to be very challenging, at pace and with high stakes attached.

- Manage all staff, parent and governor expectations of being inspected imminently and what the impact of that would, and could, look like.

- Actively gather evidence to create an authentic, effective and honest Self-Evaluation Framework (SEF) so that I could share it with governors, staff (and, yes, Ofsted).

- Manage the volume and quantity of external support, the feedback and next steps given, and whether those next steps were congruent with our developing ethos and direction.

- Manage and balance work-life expectations whilst driving all of the changes needed – for all staff and, indeed, for myself!

- Empower, entrust and manage the staff at every level.

As you can see, that brief summary (and the real one was far longer!) contains some of the *known*, the observable, the tangible that I knew needed to be tackled and that I also knew would involve a great deal of systematic and profound change – from thinking, to understanding, to enacting, to reviewing, to perpetuating. I knew that those changes would be in the **how** of what we did, which I will come onto, and key to that would be communication.

What I did not know!

What I did not know, and what was not – therefore – on a tick list to start with, was the school's financial position. This information came after applying for and being successful in becoming substantive headteacher of the school.

Deep diving

I apologise for using some inspection vernacular that may invoke a negative physiological response, but for me, from the big picture, with some situational knowledge, comes the impetus for deep dives and shallow paddles. I am planning to share the deep dives first!

In January 2019, the academic plates were effectively spinning when I became aware of the financial situation. What this meant was that I had no choice other than to switch fire to focus on the financial administration systems whilst other senior leaders focussed on the academics. Let me outline why.

Once I had the information about academic standards, not least from published data, but also from having spoken to staff and ascertained the barriers to effective planning, teaching and assessing; looked in books and spoken to children; and observed lessons whilst as an ASIA and as a headteacher in the autumn term, I could progress our longer-term, strategic planning. I know that my predecessor would likely have done exactly the same had she remained in the role. Having asked the difficult questions about the products we were using, we discarded what we knew was not working and asked individuals to do some research using the internet, consult colleagues in other schools and use their professional opinion, and then also ask numerous consultants; we were clear on what we planned to use for all four key areas we planned to focus on in that academic year: maths, reading, writing and phonics.

I won't discuss the products, each to their own, but we were satisfied that for our school, in its current state, with the staff we had and the external driver of Ofsted, alongside the internal driver of children who needed a progressive programme that we could track and add to, the products we chose were the right ones. They must have been because with simple adaptations since (a key text here, some modification during 'lockdown' there), they remain effective in providing the skeleton, the core business, of what we do, and they provide results for pupils that are tested by internal moderation, external moderators and standardised tests alike.

Normalise excellence

With the team decisions made about the products, the next phase focussed on devising and implementing a cyclical training plan for staff. Train, plan, do, assess, find gaps, feedback, follow up, train, plan, do. This needed to be manageable because I didn't want to burn out, nor did I want staff to. So, we chose writing and phonics, maths and reading – in that order. The training was delivered by consultants and followed up by our senior leaders, our external LA improvement advisors, the staff themselves in peer moderation and from an ASIA that I had brought with me from my previous school (more about that in Chapter 5). This ensured that we had 360* vision about our progress and practice and minimised the blind spots we might have had – albeit at times, it proved painful. We had people in school almost weekly.

Children's books and behaviour were showing positive evidence of this way of working, and with each successive visit from external scrutineers, the feedback positively reinforced the messages that I was giving and proved to be a force multiplier, motivating staff and thus helping them to find their equilibrium and improved mental health in order to rediscover some of the joys of the job. It needed careful handling, but it was essential; I knew that. Everything was slow. Anything that did not add value to our main effort was discarded as energy and time wasting, so I was reinforcing my messages of wanting to focus on what mattered, not extraneous practice for nebulous reasons or Ofsted inspectors. Our culture, how we did things, was being formed, decision by decision. I have since come across a term for it, and it isn't new, called 'Informed Enquiry'.[4] An example of this in the first term was the tracking system, which was previously done by hand for almost 600 pupils.

I had convinced the very able deputy head to engage with National Professional Qualification for Headteachers (NPQH) within the first month of arriving and (as part of that qualification) to research and take ownership of implementing an electronic tracking system in school, which she did. This was despite the pressure exerted upon me to simply 'get a system'. Resisting that pressure was hard: I needed to work with useful data and to understand where children were. I was trying to write the SEF. I was expecting a call from Ofsted at any minute. I did not have what I needed and just had to breathe through it.

Although I was familiar with the system I had used in my previous school, I wanted to be sure that the investment of money, time and effort to implement and train staff, and then iron out inconsistencies would be well worth it for the right product for **our** school. Eventually, we got an intuitive and effective product and spent a term on implementing it appropriately. This subsequently saved hundreds of hours of staff time and produced useful information that staff members were able to utilise to inform many aspects of their work with children – rather than simply switch off after submitting meaningless data for 'the head' and any visitors.

This sounds like something insignificant, and perhaps it is if you work in a healthy and high-functioning school, but staff, being empowered to go out and find options, bringing back information to discuss and deliberate over before purchasing and implementing as part of a carefully considered strategy is not necessarily common practice everywhere!

We selected a few things to focus on at that time but chose to do them well and with fidelity, and to this day, I genuinely believe that the *follow-up* to any successful initiative was and is the most important part of its success. Interestingly, I spoke on this topic recently at the Schools and Academies Show and was told that what I do is 'Normalise Excellence'. What I consider as the 'routine' and 'foundational' is perhaps just normalising excellent behaviour and practice; I leave that to the reader to decide and judge, but the magic of what we do is definitely in the routines and systems we have created.

No blame!

Once staff saw that uncovering a difficult truth, or an ineffective way of working, would not involve blame, punishment or negative repercussions, but conversation, exploration and a mutual commitment to agreeing that the issue would not crop up again once rectified, their confidence increased to be able to share ideas and challenge the status quo. Spotting inefficiencies and offering solutions to issues became almost normalised. Time spent on pupils and educating them was maximised as we revolutionised and simplified ways of working as a team.

I had ideas, of course I did, but those ideas were brought to the team with the caveat that they were just ideas, and I would prefer them to be challenged and improved upon rather than just accepted because I was 'the boss' and then fail (I still keep some of my ideas that never saw the light of day in the vague hope that one day I can convince the Senior Leadership Team (SLT) of the sense in some of my madcap – hosting a festival on the school field, opening a coffee shop or building a two-story play den in one of the classrooms). Again, when staff saw that this was legitimate and authentic because it became integral to how we worked, and still is, they were empowered, and this multiplied our creative influence over decisions we made.

It's all about the 'how'

I focussed on school improvement. But in focussing on the **how**, this facilitated a cultural change and a way of working that embraced all aspects of what we do so that any change followed the same system.

- Identify the issue, or be open to having it brought to my attention.

- Remain curious.

- Find out as much information about it as possible, or empower someone else to find out.

- Get someone different to look at it to make sure nothing is overlooked.

- Research methods and products that could be used to address the issue – use a range of sources and apply comparisons between those sources and our school.

- Decide as a team, once the information has been collated and shared, which direction the school will take it.

- Ensure there is finance and HR to manage its purchase, training and implementation, with capacity to follow up and embed.

- Routinely plan-in evaluation of the efficacy of the product or method and make informed changes as appropriate, sharing outcomes with governors and other stakeholders.

This is change management, but within a healthy organisational culture that we were building in the ashes.

Slow and systematic wins the day!

And thus we followed the same systematic way of working with all four key subject areas simultaneously. Naturally, we had no choice other than to focus on core subjects – when *everything* needed to be done, and very little time was being spent on foundation subjects anyway, anything that we did to improve would be better than what had been happening, so I just had to prioritise and focus on chipping away. I believed that the turnaround would take three years, and to be fair, had Covid not happened, it is highly likely that it would have taken a term shy of three years. As it happened, the pandemic only delayed the full inspection that we needed to re-grade us, not the work that went into us being re-graded. Four years and a term after I took over as head, our school was graded as GOOD across the board. But it wasn't the destination; it was the journey that made the school what it is and helped build us up, ready for exponential growth (which I will share later on in Chapter 16). The grading came and went, we were the same school the day before as we were the day after, with the same way of working and the same sense of passion.

In the background, simultaneously with the day-to-day work in core subjects that was beginning to bear fruit, I had asked staff to begin to explore the wider curriculum they should have been teaching (and sadly were not) in light of changes to the curriculum and inspection framework that would come in autumn 2019 but which would influence us all in terms of direction of travel after the impending inspection (due before the end of summer 2019). There would be no slowing down after the inspection; we would have work to do if what I thought was going to happen did happen, and at that time, I was hoping against hope that we would retain an RI.

I wanted to know how confident staff felt teaching all aspects of the curriculum, what resources we might need to consider on a whole school basis, what planning tools we may need and where the expertise lay in staff knowledge and skill so that we would have effective subject leaders in place who could work with me to implement and drive change across the entire curriculum. I also asked them to consider their level and pay grade, what additional work they felt able to take on to support the leadership element of school long past that first year and what training they felt they needed. I then stepped away and allowed the senior leaders to oversee the weekly monitoring, planning preparation and assessment sessions, external scrutiny from visitors, meeting routinely with them for an update. Meanwhile, as a result of establishing all of the above, I was able to turn my attention to the admin team out of necessity.

> On the first INSET day when Vic explained the job we had in front of us as we were due an inspection, I fully appreciated the scale of the work needed in my particular area. Also, when Vic talked those of us who were on Upper Pay Scale about whether we could help, the penny dropped.
>
> – *Annica*

Show me the money!

I had inherited a personal assistant (PA). I had never had a PA, and whilst at school, I have not had one either! The inaccurately titled PA very quickly became, and remains, an exceptional member of the SLT and, as she thinks so differently to me, is the perfect foil to some of my more inventive ideas. Anyway, we began from scratch in the area of finance, as we did across the board, as any new headteacher might. Anything is possible, however, and nothing is ever perfect in any school, so we looked at the two in-depth financial audits, and we 'set to' (more of this in Chapter 13).

Of course, with this came extensive scrutiny from the LA. There is nothing unusual in this; the LA needs to be able to see where their investments and the budget are being spent and that they are accounted for effectively. Inevitably, we worked long hours, and it was a time fraught with anxiety and stress – I was managing people, money, curriculum, progress, morale, having to make difficult choices and make changes which had very real implications to an already very difficult antecedent situation. I think any headteacher feels this way taking on a school, but especially one that is in an Ofsted category.

An example of this is when we looked at finances and realised that although the school once had three full classes of 30+ in each year group, this was no longer the case. The implications of this were both financial and organisational. In the region, 60 children had left prior to my arrival, and this exodus took with it their funding. That also meant two full classes of children – so in effect two teachers. This is the horrid maths of the school leader.

We needed to work on creating mixed classes in some year groups whilst managing the impact of this on curricular matters (when we were also trying to raise standards and keep class sizes small) and also on parents' morale.

My chair of governors at the time was an absolute salvation, as she led alongside me with pragmatism and a desire to learn in order to support the regrowth of the school. Tenacity and honesty, transparency and training were the keys to forming healthier Governing Body (GB) relationships with school. Inevitably, some governors left. I also knew that parents would be deeply unhappy. They had, for the most part, been supportive in staying and keeping their children at the school and the class restructure and subsequent changes could potentially just be another factor, and final straw, in them losing faith in us. Nevertheless, it had to happen.

So, how did I set about managing the expectations of all stakeholders, maintain standards, set a budget and implement effective financial practices?

With a team I had empowered over the term before and building upon our way of working, and the creation of our culture.

We had addressed the financial systems overhaul, trained the governors and implemented effective practices as a result of the oversight of the LA finance team.

We had a financial recovery plan, and we put it into action, one aspect of which was the restructure. I explained the rationale (based on the facts and actual numbers) to the governors. I shared it then with the senior leaders and asked for ideas of anything I may have overlooked. As a team, we could think of nothing. We therefore formulated a warning communication to parents and sent it out indicating that due to myriad reasons, we would be restructuring some year groups.

We worked with teachers to plan for children in new classes and the new structures and then called the parents of each child who would be moving into the mixed classes and explained to them why. We also wrote letters to each parent about their child's class for the following year, placing senior staff in mixed classes (as we also try to do now).

We then dealt with any individual complaints as just that. Individual complaints. By now, we had received our inspection and thankfully retained the RI judgement with leadership categorised unusually as 'Good'. This helped parents to have faith in our decision-making as leaders and minimised issues I know that we could have had relating to forced academisation – this indicated capacity for improvement. We just needed time. That and the way we had worked for two terms sharing improvement as it happened, being transparent about the rationale for any changes, making personal calls when needed and appropriate, having tricky conversations when required and an open-door policy all helped.

We managed change by making changes in light of our way of working: seeing an issue from all sides – with external help if needed, researching what we could do before making informed decisions about it – and then sharing information in accessible and appropriate ways (so there were no shocks) before following up and making amendments if needed.

There are many examples I could share and will share throughout the book, but I think you get the message – whether it is academics or finance, managing changes can follow a simple formula. Once everyone is accustomed to the formula, then it becomes less emotionally and mentally taxing to navigate the change – for all concerned. The process becomes predictable and almost comforting, depersonalising it and giving all stakeholders a sense of psychological well-being.

Shallow paddling

The shallow paddling, or quick wins, can be satisfying (and also give you something to hold onto) when managing change manifests in difficulty.

For me, the simple and superficial changes could be informed by others, with the specific oversight of our team. These are the things that do not need maximal input from senior leaders. One example I could give is that I asked one of our Parent Teacher Association (PTA) members to conduct a website-compliance checklist and make some suggestions about how we could make it easier to negotiate and more user-friendly for the layperson. The list of actions they suggested we sent to the new website company, and hey presto, a workable website for the people who most needed it!

For accessibility and visibility, I set up a Twitter (now called X) page and tweeted (posted?) photos and soundbites of what was happening on a daily basis; I wrote a long weekly blog that guided parents through the changes in an informal way and also spoke to them of my own parenting pressures, aspirations and life. I stood on the gate every day and greeted people so that they could vent and ask questions before they became complaints.

To save money but triangulate my views and reassure governors, I built on networks I already had; for example, I asked a colleague in the LA to conduct a Safeguarding Audit to assure me that our systems were as robust as I knew they were and find any weaknesses in our practice. I painted my office and moved around furniture. Quick wins in the shallow end.

Change management is more than managing change, and school improvement is simply managing change effectively within a healthy culture

Change management is about emotional and situational intelligence, courage, trust, belief, culture and the team of people you have with you. Anyone can come into an organisation on day one, make cuts, change policy and practice, shake it all up, but this should be tempered with an understanding of whether that organisation needs such ruthless and immediate action, what is gained and also lost in managing change in this way and the implications longer-term.

For me, successful change management is more than managing change and should be situated within the culture of an organisation, done in alignment with its ethos and values, and with an unstinting dedication to relationships and communication at its core. This is what enabled me to sleep at night – knowing that what I had done, I did genuinely in the best interests of the pupils, staff and parents and that many people had shared the decision-making process.

But what got me there in the first place? What would encourage anyone to do it, given the barriers to success they will face? Read on, dear reader, Chapter 3!

Takeaways

Much of what happens to make things go wrong, and to right them again, is inextricably linked to two things:

- the quality of relationships between people and

- the culture created from those inter-relationships which facilitates effective management of challenge and change.

Whether it is academics or finance, managing changes can follow a simple formula. Once everyone is accustomed to the formula, then it becomes less emotionally and mentally taxing to navigate the change – for all concerned. The process is depersonalised and becomes predictable.

Notes

1 https://assets.publishing.service.gov.uk/government/uploads/system/uploads/attachment_data/file/723268/School_inspection_update_060718.pdf.
2 https://assets.publishing.service.gov.uk/government/uploads/system/uploads/attachment_data/file/723268/School_inspection_update_060718.pdf.
3 https://www.sec-ed.co.uk/best-practice/the-common-inspection-framework-an-analysis/.
4 https://www.tandfonline.com/doi/pdf/10.1080/13674589900200062 p. 118.

Good reads

Ainsworth, P. (2021). *No Silver Bullets: Day in, Day Out, School Improvement*. Independent.
Allen, B., Evans, M., & White, B. (2021). *The Next Big Thing in School Improvement*. John Catt Educational LTD.
Edmondson, A.C. (2018). *The Fearless Organization: Creating Psychological Safety in the Workplace for Learning, Innovation, and Growth*. Wiley.
IMPACT – the Journal of the Chartered College of Teaching.
Tomsett, J. & Uttley, J. (2020). *Putting Staff First: A Blueprint for a Revitalised Profession*. John Catt Educational LTD.

3 Barriers to success
Why do people become headteachers?

As a student, arriving at a Requires Improvement school made me feel a great amount of fear. I was completing my final teaching placement. I researched the school. I felt let down by my university and instantly thought this meant I was going to fail my last placement. There were so many questions that went through my mind. What does requires improvement mean? Why are my university sending me to a school with an RI grading when I am learning to become a teacher?

Yet, from being a final year student, through to a well-established teacher, I have always felt passionate about Woodlands. Mainly because of the support I received from Vic through the loss of my dad, and the grief process, Sharon being the student mentor lead and popping her head in most days with the simple yet very effective question 'Is everything ok?', Laura being an inspiring mentor at a time where I was at my lowest to Andrea who supported me through PPA cover in my final month on placement. These are the key people from the start of my Woodlands journey that made me realise I could do this. If they could support me as a student while being scrutinised by the LA, SLT members and outside representatives then they could do anything.

– Sioned

Barriers to success

There is an overabundance of barriers to meaningful school leadership, both conceptually and literally, from the phase where you are applying for a leadership role all the way to being fully immersed in doing the job.

Those obstacles can take obvious forms, such as lack of money, lack of infrastructure, a hostile team, legacy cultural issues, individual ego, the list goes on. They can also be more subtle: lack of confidence, inability to shine in interviews, imposter syndrome, menopause brain and limited support networks to name but a few.

DOI: 10.4324/9781003440000-4

If multiple barriers exist for leadership in general, then there are almost overwhelming barriers to leadership of a school in difficulty, or one in a challenging area. This is because, in my view, added to the generalised list alluded to earlier are the more specific complications discussed in this chapter.

Why choose to take on what some people call a 'problem school'?

Firstly, I should caveat the rest of this chapter, which will expose some of the barriers that I feel face leaders who are prepared to take over a school in difficulty, with the statement that it is not right for everyone, nor is it a judgement on the quality of the leader if they deem it inappropriate to take on such a school. Equally, someone overcoming those initial barriers may face further barriers once in situ which prevent them remaining; there is no shame in this. Instead, without judgement or shame, I will expose how I intentionally created a positive narrative for the reasons why I did it, and in doing so, hopefully, show how these barriers can be psychologically, physically and, perhaps, practically overcome. I should also say, in terms of personal reflection about preparedness to take on a school in difficulty, this chapter is important, but as an aside, in terms of advising others who may be considering taking on such a school, it is important as part of our moral obligation to others in our profession, to ensure they also reflect on themselves in order to know if they are in the right space to do so. If you are in an influential position, telling someone to 'go for it', without understanding whether they should, can be catastrophic.

Personal appetite for challenge

I have never been one to shy away from a challenge. In many ways, I thrive on taking on a challenge and successfully executing it (a psychologist will no doubt see why in about 30 seconds of meeting me and understanding my back story, but that isn't the point). As a recently qualified teacher, I moved to Kenya and both established and ran a school for the children of ex-patriot farmers. My friends and peers thought I was barking mad because not only was I moving to another country, and continent, but I was moving three hours from the main city and into the foothills of Mount Kenya in order to set this school up. This was at a time of limited access to the internet (dial-up modem, anyone?). I had no telephone, and ordering anything from the United Kingdom was quite a palaver. And yet, I did it, and I have testimonials that I recently found when spring cleaning that illustrate the success of that little school (which has since become something much bigger!) and its positive impact on the children we served.

It taught me a lot as the leader of the future I would become. I learned about planning ahead, about taking care of personnel, about curriculum oversight, about pay and conditions, about integrity, about nurturing children and adults and also about overcoming adversity. But I also learned about connectivity and collaboration.

Harnessing people in the locality to support my efforts with children, considering local context and opportunities – it brought home to me the adage 'it takes a village to raise a child', and that has stuck with me.

A healthy personal appetite for challenge is, I have to admit, not something that everyone is born with. Some people develop an unhealthy appetite for risk-taking, which isn't the same, as a result of life experiences or genetic make-up. Largely, though, when we as humans are tested in life, we learn so much about our strengths – not just what they are, but how they evolve, are fostered or damaged. As we self-reflect, sometimes with the help of others or based on mistakes we have made, we are more able to understand our motivations for challenge, as well as our capacity for it, 'we are able to extend and apply knowledge of positive human functioning in the face of challenge – in other words, the capacity to flourish under fire'.[1] In turning around the negatives of my earlier years and building on their outputs, I am able, it seems, to cope with a degree of challenge in a healthy way and maintain the resilience to do so without it having an adverse impact on me.

My challenge has not been my own resilience but creating a culture where the entire team generates and relies upon a pool of resilience that we contribute to, maintain and draw from at various times. I am often found saying that I cannot do the job alone. Indeed, I could not have done the job alone. I have relied upon the differing skills and knowledge of my diverse team who both encourage my appetite for challenge (whilst holding their breath sometimes) and also rein it in when necessary.

As long ago in history as 2006, the government acknowledged in its National Audit Office report 'Improving Poorly Performing Schools in England' that

> [t]he range of leadership tasks...cannot be done successfully by the Head-teacher alone. The National College promotes 'distributed leadership', where the management and leadership of the school are shared among a mutually supportive and collaborative team of people, guided by the Headteacher. Especially in larger schools, having a wider team responsible for developing a positive culture and ethos for learning helps build expectations of teachers and pupils throughout the school more readily than if the responsibility is vested mainly in the Headteacher and Deputy. A school with distributed leadership is also less vulnerable to the departure of its Headteacher.[2]

The problem is, you have to create that team when you get there – you arrive at a school (in crisis or not) not knowing if there is anyone there who will co-create the team and take on distributed leadership tasks with you. Or I did.

Stepping into the unknown, then, is very much a case of utilising your appetite for challenge and accepting that for a while at least, you could well be on your own.

Health and personal circumstances

There are points in recent years where I can see, with hindsight, I should and could not have taken on extra responsibility – and I am glad that I did not or that opportunity never presented itself. Occasionally, I ignored any red flags in my life and applied for things that were not right, which interested me, and I am glad I was not successful at the time (hindsight is a wonderful thing).

Had I been a new parent, adopted a child, fostered a child, if I had been recovering from breast surgery when the opportunity to take on the job I have now presented itself, I would never have been able to do it. My body, post-pregnancy and post-surgery some years later, needed the time to heal, and I needed the time to recover, and it was right that I had no additional stress and anxiety whilst I did so. I am not saying that parents should not take on challenges, nor that women who have had babies should not as a result of their bodies needing time to recover or anything else – we are each individual, after all. What I am saying is that reflecting on *your own* current personal circumstances is key to understanding if you feel you have the physical and mental strength to take on a school (more specifically one in difficulty) with the demands that it places on you. Because it is a certainty that leadership of a school in difficulty will place demands upon you that you didn't even know existed.

As someone post–breast surgery and as head in my previous school, although recovering well at home, with the successful systems and team I had established functioning effectively, when the first secondment opportunity came up for this job, I wanted to apply. I didn't and was disappointed not to be able to do so, but the timing was not right. The following year, I had to have more surgery, and the second secondment was advertised. I said out loud that I wanted to apply, my family advised me not to, and I listened: but not everyone has trusted adults who will offer advice if they are not certain about what to do. If I had been physically able, I would, I am sure, have felt robbed of the opportunity immediately, but I came around to the sense of not taking such a big job on, safe in the knowledge that it wouldn't have been for me and what is for me will not pass me by (as they say in Bonnie Scotland). I am blessed that the third time the secondment came up, by pure chance, I was in the right place at the right time.

Upon taking up my first headship, only a few months into it, I went through a divorce. This had a huge impact on my physical and mental health, inevitably, and made the job of leading a school a lot more difficult than perhaps it would have been. I know that I cannot be certain, as I don't have a time machine or a way of testing this hypothesis, but logic being what it is, I feel that had I not had my attention and energy divided between solicitors, upset children, family, school, staffing, Ofsted, curriculum, I would have fared better in my early months as a new head (I know I would have slept more!).

This is just an obvious fact, I know, but sometimes we refuse to see this logic or simply ignore it.

Taking a long, hard look at your health and your personal circumstances before taking on a challenge of any kind is self-preservation rather than procrastination or avoidance. An individual who is going through a marital break-up, the death of a parent, a house-move or personal illness will not operate in the same way as they did before that circumstance manifested, and will likely operate again following its resolution. Very little in life is actually forever.

The same goes for additional study or professional development/accreditation; there is no way that I could have taken on a doctorate (which I did the year later) when I arrived as a new head at my last school in January, in other words, mid-year. I had a big job at hand that I needed to do, and I had no capacity or bandwidth to take on the academic work despite being recommended to do it. I took a year of simply focussing on the school, its needs, the staff and their abilities (and, as it transpired, my divorce) and the children and what would work for them. The following year, when I was ready, I took on the doctorate and additional study and could give all of those activities the attention they deserved.

Reputational harm

Nobody wants to 'make a show of themselves' as my nan would have said. Not in any circumstances, but definitely not in a professional sense. So linked are our identities to our professional roles that when we feel we may have embarrassed ourselves in any way, we can spend days, weeks and months pondering on the shame and humiliation of it all – even long after others have forgotten about it. The thing about Ofsted is that our names, as headteachers, are on the front of the report, which is in the ether FOREVER. There is no getting away from that stigma once it is there. This can be catastrophic.

Academics at the Institute of Education (IoE) a decade ago, as I myself began my headship journey, reinforced the narrative that is well-known amongst educators (in England at least) and which was summarised in the outcomes of the Association of School and College Leaders (ASCL) annual conference in 2013. General secretary at the time, Brian Lightman, explicitly stated that taking on headship of a challenging school can become a long-term career risk. One ASCL member went a step further, however, and claimed doing so can be 'career suicide'. The main reason why is career-ending Ofsted judgements.[3]

But this fear it is not just in England. The IoE University of Central London Institute of Education and Economic and Social Research Council (ESRC)-funded study of Generation X school leaders offered insight into the very similar experiences of headteachers and their deputy headteachers (all of whom were under 40 years old) in three capital cities around the world (London, New York and Toronto). During their interviews, participants discussed their strategies for choosing leadership posts. Underpinning decision-making was an acknowledgement that their first and second headships carry huge influence, certain they will 'make or break' their career. Leaders in England specifically are acutely aware of the implications of Ofsted, with one stating, 'You are only as good as your last Ofsted. So why take the risk?'[4]

One of the ways in which I have been able to deal with the failing school narrative was, and is, to maintain a strong sense of myself as a good practitioner, committed to the professional development of teachers, pupils and myself. I have a teeny ego. I am focussed on altruism, the overwhelming 'greater good' of the job, the legacy-building aspect and the sustainability so that the school ticks over successfully when I am long gone. I am also focussed on my self-worth not being directly linked to the output – rather, the input and the effort I exert. Incidentally, this is not dissimilar to the findings of the team at The Harvard Business Review in 2016 or Biott and Gulson all those years ago in 1999 when they studied '[h]ead teachers taking over failing schools: tales of good stewardship and learning at work'.[5] Have a read, surprise yourself.

Location

I have known headteachers relocate for a prize job, a move in the right direction, a promotion or a happy occurrence that facilitates personal growth or enhances family dynamics. There has to be incentive, of course, and as coined by a popular TV show, the phrase, 'Location, Location, Location' can be all the incentive you need (I had better not mention now that my dream location is the West Coast of Scotland).

But moving to a new place and simultaneously considering taking over a school in an Ofsted category can be an unpleasant cocktail. I already had links and a small supportive network when I moved to my current LA, thankfully. This meant that when I needed a name, a number, a resource or targeted support, someone in that small network knew the answer. I did not feel isolated, despite moving into the area and being also new to headship.

During the six years I spent at my previous school, I needed specialist help from a number of services: the Gypsy, Romany, Traveller (GRT) services at the LA; the Exclusion (or Inclusion, depending on how your LA presents itself) Team; the Special Educational Needs and Disabilities (SEND) Team, Keeping Children Safe in Education (KCSiE) Team, Social Care (iART for us), governance support, virtual school, School Improvement Team, Team Around the Family (TAF) advisors, etc. By the time I was considering taking on a school in an Ofsted category, I already had a good handle on who was who and how to locate the people I needed. This facilitated quick and easier communication and enabled me to work much more efficiently when I arrived at Woodlands.

Location is as much about the physical terrain (as the army might say) as it is about the human terrain, and understanding the impact of both is essential. In terms of accessibility, at my last school, although only a few miles from Ellesmere Port, it took two buses to get anywhere. Accessibility, therefore, was an issue for services, family support, swimming, cost of trips and visits, among many other things, and that is literally the tip of the iceberg. I had to gain an understanding of the history of the place I was working in and how the socio-economic and political make-up of the place affected the school and its stakeholders. I had to understand the needs of the pupils, the staff and the parents; the expectations of the local people and the LA; and the demands of Ofsted. This was no different to my current school, or any school, with one exception: my current school was in an Ofsted category; this really does make an acute difference in terms of time frames and scope of possibility.

Location is important also in terms of commutability. Nobody needs a long drive through challenging traffic on top of a long day (and indeed a succession of long days) as you thread through the school improvement tapestry. Sounds obvious, but why would you put that additional stress on yourself? I had an 'effective range' from my home when looking for a job; essentially, it was as sophisticated as a string that would draw a circle of 45 minutes from where I lived in terms of driving commute. As excited as I might get when seeing job adverts, I wanted to be strict with myself. For me, this is super important when considering taking on a school in challenging circumstances – taking cognisance of the overall impact on your body and mind and the lack of time available for space to recover from the day if you are driving or subject to the stress of public transport and its regular cancellations.

Ofsted

There has been so much work on the impact of Ofsted on all aspects of the educational landscape. These days we rightly focus more on mental health and understand psychological safety and its impact in the workplace, underpinned by expectations of leaders having a working knowledge of emotional intelligence (EI). As far back as 1996, Jeffrey and Woods wrote about the emotional impact of inspections and on subsequent feelings and manifestations of de-professionalisation suffered by educators who were conflicted between a deep-seated child-centred philosophy and the rationalised and pitifully reductive principles underpinning inspections. It could have been written today.[6] Their work focussed on why headteachers would want to move from schools where they were 'successful' to work in schools which were labelled as 'failing' and what enabled those headteachers to cope with the relentless intensification of work required to make a difference once they were in post.

Their findings, in summary, were simple and resonate with my own views over a quarter of a century later. Firstly, those headteachers who withstood the relentlessness actually held enduring and intrinsic beliefs and values about how they should operate as professionals. Secondly, they were committed to learning (their own, that of colleagues and of pupils). The philosophy of those headteachers who have a tendency to interpret work as a series of learning ventures was what underpinned their preparedness to take on the demanding task of 'turning around' a failing school. In addition, this predisposition assisted them in order to maintain the momentum required to thrive.

Serendipity

Sometimes life simply throws you an opportunity, or you stumble across one, and it sits in the perfect time and space for you to grab it with both hands, even if you are terrified. You might wait years for the stars to align (for want of a better expression), and you might work feverishly in the background on setting the conditions for future success, but when the time is right, and you know you have the right attitude, skills and knowledge for something that crosses your path then even if it is a school in some kind of difficulty, you take it on.

The team you inherit may have the requisite skills, the timing of monitoring visits or full inspections may fall just right and sit within your expectations, and school in difficulty or not, you will thrive. Naturally, the opposite may also be true, but for me, this was my story. I had the raw materials. I had the specific ingredients. I even had the makings of the icing on the cake; I just needed to make the magic happen with them.

Unwittingly setting the conditions for future success, to be honest, is how I have operated in life. How this looks for me is taking on 'random' qualifications, or 'left-field' jobs as they have cropped up or supplementary non-paid jobs that I feel might make a difference or be interesting (but consume time!); I am always primed to take on an opportunity. My issue is knowing when to (and how to) say no to an opportunity and rationalise it to myself so I don't feel bad having turned down something.

For me, therefore, the Woodlands journey began many years before it happened. It began with my being a headteacher in my previous school and just getting on with the job at hand. Learning by baptism of fire, gaining some battle scars, gaining a lot of understanding and experience, building a reputation decision by decision, interaction by interaction. The outcome was that when it became time to find an executive headteacher for Woodlands, the third in as many years, I was a good candidate for those decision-makers. The director of education at that time knew I was right for it; he knew (from previous skirmishes we had with one another) that I would advocate relentlessly for the school and that I had the moral integrity required, as well as the determination to see it through. I had demonstrated the passion and drive I had for the pupils in our area. I had proven it, not always in a pretty way, might I add. Not everyone has the chance to 'prove' themselves in the ways that I did; in some ways, this is good! It is often the leaders who quietly go about their business and focus on their schools who are the very best leaders rather than people like me with their noses in so many things and their voices loud and getting louder. I don't think there is a right or a wrong here, by the way; I think I have just evolved into a loud voice, where maybe I didn't always have one at all. It just means that I need to be saying the right thing, in the right way, for the greater good – it doesn't mean I am better than anyone else.

Is it only me?

Whilst this may seem like my own random list, there are numerous academic and government research documents that illustrate my views are more than just personal speculation. The DfE, in their 2019 research report titled, 'Teacher Mobility in Challenging Areas', concluded that 'there are significant barriers to the notion of moving to schools in challenging circumstances. In particular, the reluctance to consider moving resulted from a set of perceptions of what working in a school in challenging circumstances would be like'. Hopefully, this book will go some way towards illustrating what that could look like, but as no two schools are the same, this is difficult to say with certainty.

> I would not go to another RI school. Twice is enough!
>
> – *Dani*

What I think I do know, from experience, is that in coaching my current staff through it all, I know I have prepared future school leaders with enough real-life and hands-on experience that they actually do know what a school in challenging circumstances is like and will not be afraid of it, as it is no longer 'unknown'. Coaching for me is key to success for my colleagues when I am long gone and put out to pasture. Whilst academic and professional qualifications in leadership and management mean that future leaders are amazingly prepared 'on paper' for raising and maintaining school standards, challenging under-performance and guiding schools through Ofsted, the lived experience of headship is an entirely different matter. It is our responsibility as custodians of our schools that we nurture future leaders effectively so that they understand some of the biggest obstacles to success that there are, exemplified succinctly by Viv Grant, former headteacher and founder of Integrity Coaching: 'Heightened Responsibility. High Accountability. Public Scrutiny and Low Job Security. Isolation'.[7]

What is the 'known unknown'?

'[T]here are known knowns; there are things we know we know. We also know there are known unknowns; that is to say we know there are some things we do not know. But there are also unknown unknowns — the ones we don't know we don't know' (Rumsfeld, 2002). Former U.S. secretary of defence Donald Rumsfeld said these words at a press conference over 20 years ago, and whilst he did not invent the concept, and may not have understood it wider than a snippet of a conversation he had a few days previously with a NASA colleague which may have precipitated its use, it has become his most famous line.

In my previous book, I did talk about the wider cognitive framework that this expression was taken from – namely, the Johari Window, which was an analysis technique developed in 1955 by two American psychologists, Joseph Luft and Harrington Ingham. They first used it as a technique to help people better understand their relationship with themselves, as well as others (an iteration of which is still freely available to use today!)[8]. The terms 'known unknowns' and 'unknown unknowns' emanate from this framework, and despite their original use being intended for personal reflection, their utility has evolved, and they have been incorporated, and actively used, in lots of project management and strategic planning situations. The 'so what' for me, as an experienced leader, is that – as a broad concept – the framework can be applied to the world of business, as well as education.

Broadly put, there are four quadrants in a risk assessment of information about an organisation that have helped me in evaluating both before and after I have arrived in a school or a situation.

Each of them is associated with a specific understanding and awareness:

- Known knowns: Things you're aware of and understand

- Known unknowns: Things you're aware of but don't understand

- Unknown knowns: Things you're not aware of but understand

- Unknown unknowns: Things you're neither aware of nor understand

Having discussed the 'known' obstacles faced by leaders before they take over a school, especially one in difficult circumstances – which I feel sure will resonate with any leader, it is perhaps worth looking at some of the unknown ones that could be faced.

Known unknowns

In both schools where I have been headteacher, I did not know about the financial situation prior to becoming substantive head.

My take on this is that you are highly unlikely to ever know the true state of the finances of a school until you are in post and have legitimate access to the information. This is for sensible reasons, really, despite the potential issues it may cause, but it is nevertheless a good question to ask and something you should seek to know as much about as quickly as possible upon taking up the role.

Secondly, I think it is safe to assume, given the global, national and educational financial climate we are all in, that there will be very few schools that are not in some sort of financial difficulty – either short term or long term – and that this will be the single biggest area in which a new headteacher will need to grow in terms of their understanding. Again, the NPQH pathway is excellent for outlining the conceptual, but until you are actually doing it for real and are both accountable and responsible, finances are an arcane art and financial management even more so. I actively grow my deputy heads in this area, as I know it is a blind spot – it was for me!

It is no surprise that the National Audit Office (NAO) discovered that a headteacher who is prepared to lead the recovery of a school in challenging circumstances will require some distinct personal characteristics. This report may have been conducted 25 years ago, but the same could be said today. Although headteachers considering leading a school in challenging circumstances are likely to need considerable presence and inner strength, for which we could read 'determination and resilience', they will likely need to help other staff to grow to such a degree that they, too, can contribute fully to the recovery of the school, what I would label 'increase capacity'. Without knowing the staff beforehand, from my experience, although a prospective headteacher may be aware that they will need to grow capacity, they may not know if it is possible to achieve with the current staff, or whether recruitment of new staff is required.[9] For me, facilitating and prioritising training both deputy heads in NPQH was key to their support; the knowledge gained in doing this course is invaluable.

Unknown knowns and unknown unknowns

Although the language is a little tortured (!), these two categories represent some of what a new-to-role headteacher may face in a school in difficult circumstances. Three-quarters of headteachers responding to the NAO survey in 2006 suggested that problems caused by previous leadership had been a major contributor to the school's earlier difficulties. Yikes. Depending on when the departing head leaves/left, there could be a number of things that have yet to be dealt with in a school or complex issues that need significant action to resolve them, which may not yet have been accomplished. A thorough handover is always preferable - but not always possible. Therefore, although the views captured by the NAO may have been subjective, the NAO did put them to the test, sensibly concluding that 'the critical importance of the headteacher's leadership and management to the success of a school is beyond doubt'. As a headteacher in any school, particularly a school in a challenging situation, you will be faced with legacy issues you're not aware of but understand when they present themselves and also things you're neither aware of nor understand when they surprise you (remember that when you go, you will also likely leave some!). Of benefit to me when this happened was utilising the hive mind and corporate repository that the staff body epitomised to try to help my cognitive processing and healthy responses; you may not have that luxury. However, I also sought external expertise, and everyone these days has access to the hive mind of sites such as X.[10]

I have asked a diverse range of colleagues about their own experiences of this phenomenon; the following is a snapshot of the lists they recalled (despite Ofsted and its glorious inspectorate, none of these things were even hinted at in the inspections):

■ Relationships between staff, including family and relations within school the, unforeseen cliques and clashes

■ Massive issues with the site: subsidence, sinkholes, cracking alongside floods

■ Leased land: losing half the outdoor space in the school as it is leased from the LA/private provider, and the lease is up. The new terms are non-negotiable and unaffordable, with an increase of 1,000%

- Policies not in place, missing or deleted by predecessor

- Impact of six to seven headteachers in the seven years prior to arrival

- HR procedures not followed

- Staff on wrong contracted hours

- Staff paid as unqualified teachers but not on a pathway to teaching

- Staff allowed to build up time off in-lieu (TOIL) and plan as a group to go out for the day, leaving school vulnerable, as it was short staffed

- Finances – huge deficit budgets to financial audit fails

- Random stashes of cash

- Being inspected very early on and going into a category

- Walking into an employment tribunal

- Falling numbers

- A folder of kinky emails from predecessor

- No Service Level Agreement for key contracts (some were 'mate's rates')

- Single Central Record not up to date

- Differences in support staff contracts

- No insurance for pre-school

- Health and safety (H&S) files empty

- No IT infrastructure

- Staff running holiday club with no qualifications

And the staff feel it too

> I was devastated to see such a wonderful school being placed in RI. However, I was not surprised. I felt so sorry for the children and staff, especially the ones who had been here when we were an outstanding school.
>
> *– Pete*

Another element to this 'unknowns' dilemma is the fact that not only are you, as the potential incoming headteacher, navigating so many knowns and unknowns, SO ARE THE STAFF! If you think about it, they do not know you other than by reputation (unless they have worked with you before in another setting). They do not know what to expect; in a school in difficulty, it is likely that the staff have already navigated some significant challenge and upheaval and will be feeling anxious at best and unwell at worst. It is unlikely that the majority of the staff will have any idea of what has caused the school to be in the situation it finds itself in as they will only be privy to certain information, and even then, not all of them. They will be speculating, hypothesising and agonising over what has happened; they will no doubt be disillusioned and, in some cases, professionally embarrassed – perhaps even looking elsewhere (actively) for a job that takes them away from the tainted reputation of the school. None of this leads to a great recipe for turning the school around.

This was certainly true at Woodlands – when I arrived at the school as executive headteacher in September 2018, I was a known unknown. They knew who I was; I had been there for the Teaching and Learning Review (TLR) the summer before. They knew me by reputation as a headteacher in the LA but did not know how I worked, what I would do to turn the school around or how this would affect them. They didn't know why the school was in the difficulties it was in, or how it would be resolved satisfactorily so that it survived into the future, never mind how it could thrive. Imagine how distressing it must have been for them, how it is for staff now in schools in challenging circumstances, for whatever reason. I think they deserve someone to fight for them. I believed that then, hence my motivation, and I believe it now, hence this book. That is not to say I want to make my reputation on turning around schools in challenging circumstances (see the earlier discussion!). This school arrived at my feet at a time when I was ready to do what needed to be done, and because of the opportunities I had taken previously, I had the skills and knowledge, the personal resilience and the mindset to do it. My friend and outgoing executive head said she was pleased I had been chosen to take on the responsibility and remarked that she felt I had the capacity to do what needed to be done. High praise indeed.

Whilst I have been headteacher, as an aside, we have discussed as a leadership team, disseminated as a staff team and a Governing Body the indicators and warnings that some leaders and leadership teams may overlook when things are not going to plan. We have done this as a result of total transparency in my approach and a 'warts-and-all' style of opening up discussion about things we have uncovered. An example of this is when I explained the Ofsted inspection narrative to the governors in my first meeting and how the indicators were that rather than a second RI judgement, the school could potentially be classified as Inadequate and, worst-case, Special Measures and would probably be brokered for an academy conversion based on published data and work in books, as well as other factors. I explained that depending on when we were inspected, we might have enough time to exemplify some of the work I planned for us to do, but without time, we would be in a hurt locker. Explaining this to parents and giving them bite-sized pieces of information to manage their expectations was also crucial to this methodology. Everyone had the same story; everyone knew what we were working on and why. The methods and strategies we used to address those indicators and warnings will be discussed further in the book. Incidentally, they continue to be addressed before they become detrimental to the overall success of the main effort of the school, and we pre-empt issues before they arise because of the systems we now have in place (thank goodness!).

Is there anything good about a poor Ofsted situation?

Well, in all honesty, very little! Again, quoting the NAO from some time ago, there is only one enduring truth about a poor Ofsted outcome (let's not split hairs about the definition of 'poorly performing', what the metric is for measurement and how this changes with each inspection iteration) if you are a maintained school:

> A poor Ofsted inspection report can be a catalyst to turning around a poorly performing school. While there are often detrimental effects on staff morale, recruitment and retention, and the school's reputation suffers, the benefits include support from the local authority, better awareness of the key issues facing the school and how to deal with them, and improvements in governance.[11]

I would argue that there are other ways to become better aware of the key issues facing a school than a poor Ofsted inspection; I would also argue that there are other ways of improving governance. I would argue that, as evidenced in the collective list of unknowns from colleagues presented earlier, Ofsted does not shine a light on policy, process, staff relationships, finances, the LA, etc., they simply do not. And on balance, whilst the LA may give additional 'support', is it really worth it when you have to tackle all of the negatives associated with an unfavourable Ofsted-generated reputation? Hmmmmmm. Arguable. What I cannot argue with, however, is the gargantuan* amount of support that a maintained school gets from the LA when it goes into a category and how instrumental this is for turning it around. I have an observation about this, however, and it is this: if we know that increased funding and external capacity in terms of consultant support (that comes as a direct result of an Ofsted grading less than 'good') helps the school make huge strides in success – why are we as a nation not funding schools adequately in the first place? Why are we reacting rather than being proactive?

I could use many vignettes from Woodlands with respect to the school improvement agenda, but to conclude the chapter, I think I need to outline the very real barrier in a very real school context to bring to life the theory and concepts that so many of you will hear about in a range of leadership courses, on social media and in the press. When I sat in a meeting with the powers that be of my (very supportive) LA and asked, in light of the sudden lack of funding available as a result of the positive trajectory of the school under my leadership, plus the second RI (and my 'good' leadership and management judgement as part of that), whether the LA wanted me to focus on academic improvement or financial recovery, as I knew that I could not focus on both together with one non-class-based deputy head, I was told, unequivocally, both. There began the most arduous year of my life, and one that required all of my wits, energy, focus, capacity and resilience and still nearly drove me to distraction. Is this what our system needs and deserves? I think not! But Ofsted was priority number one, and for me, at that time, it had to be treated like an enemy force. More about that in the next chapter!

*I just want to say I love this word. My 19-year-old daughter, when in Reception, came home crying one day. She LOVED school and her teachers, and when I asked what on earth had upset her, she told me that 'gargantuan' wasn't a real word, and she was upset because I had told her it was. Confused, I asked for more detail. She explained that her headteacher had been in the classroom with a clipboard (I leave that for your imagination) 'talking to' her teacher during a lesson on 'what word could be a better word'. During this lesson, she had made the suggestion that instead of 'big' the teacher use 'gargantuan'. Needless to say, her teacher put her in her place and told her it wasn't a word.

Takeaways

Some of the ways to deal with the failing school narrative are

- to maintain a strong sense of yourself as a good practitioner committed to the professional development of teachers, pupils and yourself;

- to focus on altruism, the overwhelming 'greater good' of the job, the legacy-building aspect and the sustainability so that the school ticks over successfully when you are long gone; and

- to focus on your self-worth not being directly linked to the output – rather the input and the effort you exert.

Notes

1 Ryff CD, Singer B (2003) 'Flourishing under fire: resilience as a prototype of challenged thriving' in CLM Keyes and J Haidt (Eds.), *Flourishing: Positive Psychology and the Life Well-lived*. American Psychological Association. pp. 15–36. https://doi.org/10.1037/10594-001.
2 https://www.nao.org.uk/wp-content/uploads/2006/01/0506679.pdf p. 35.
3 https://ioelondonblog.wordpress.com/2013/03/18/risky-business-should-headship-in-challenging-schools-come-with-a-career-warning/.
4 https://discovery.ucl.ac.uk/id/eprint/1542148/.
5 https://hbr.org/2016/10/the-one-type-of-leader-who-can-turn-around-a-failing-school; https://www.tandfonline.com/doi/pdf/10.1080/13674589900200062.
6 Jeffrey B, Woods P (1996) 'Feeling deprofessionalised: the social construction of emotions during an OFSTED inspection' *Cambridge Journal of Education* 26. pp. 325–43.

7 https://www.integritycoaching.co.uk/blog/overcoming-the-challenges-of-headship/emotional-challenges/.
8 https://kevan.org/johari.
9 https://www.nao.org.uk/wp-content/uploads/2006/01/0506679.pdf p. 36.
10 https://www.nao.org.uk/wp-content/uploads/2006/01/0506679.pdf p. 36.
11 https://www.nao.org.uk/wp-content/uploads/2006/01/0506679.pdf p. 12.

Good reads

Davis, K. (2018). *Brave Leadership: Unleash Your Most Confident, Powerful, and Authentic Self to Get the Results You Need*. Greenleaf Book Group.
Ekman, P. (2007). *Emotions Revealed, Second Edition: Recognizing Faces and Feelings to Improve Communication and Emotional Life*. Holt Paperbacks.
Greene, R. (2020). *The Concise Laws of Human Nature*. Profile Books.
Rumsfeld, D. (2002). https://www.youtube.com/watch?v=REWeBzGuzCc

4 Most likely and most dangerous

Expectation and worst-case scenario

To be honest, when the school was in an Ofsted category it felt unfair. Although, I cannot deny something needed to change, it was quite an unsettling time.

– Gill

Most likely and most dangerous

As a military analyst, and indeed a trained officer, you get accustomed to looking at a set of circumstances and trying to work out what the enemy's 'most likely course of action' (MLCOA) is and what the 'most dangerous course of action' (MDCOA) is. You try to understand the motivation and the intent of the 'enemy' based on their standard military 'doctrine' and their usual tactics, and you also try to consider their asymmetric tactics. I think the reason I am not too shabby at military analysis is because I am a headteacher, and this is how I think naturally in my workplace. (Good news, you could also be a military analyst should you wish to become one; read on!).

I don't want to demonise Ofsted. I personally know a couple of inspectors, so they are not the faceless inspectorate for me because the people I know are simply lovely, but as a headteacher, I must view the corporate 'Ofsted Machine' in terms of 'enemy' and respectfully assign them that status. Their standard tactics, for example, include a call to the school the day before an inspection for a conversation with the headteacher where the head must try to distil the entirety of their school into a 90-minute, highly pressurised chat. Their 'doctrine' is the Education Inspection Framework (EIF),[1] and the one we are currently subjected to is the 2023 iteration. You get the picture?

As for their asymmetric tactics, if we consider the political role that Ofsted plays now in terms of shaping the educational landscape, of the impact of its reports on

DOI: 10.4324/9781003440000-5

forcing schools to academise, the impact of its reports being that if a school is an academy, it must be re-brokered to another trust, the collateral damage caused to headteacher well-being and indeed in terms of catastrophic events such as suicide and so on, then it really does occupy the enemy space.

Carl Von Clausewitz wrote, 'War, is the continuation of politics by other means'.[2] Ofsted is this weaponised political instrument pitted against education providers. I know this is a bold statement but bear with me. 'Asymmetrical warfare' refers to conflicts which achieve political objectives, and implicit in this is a disproportionate distribution of power. We know that to disagree with Ofsted – to challenge it – at the macro (policy) level and micro (inspection) level is almost futile. Its role has naturally evolved to become more adversarial and is a form of hybrid warfare, and as such, headteachers must prepare for both conventional and unconventional action.

In military terms, covert action and special operations are important elements in countering asymmetric tactics. They include rapid response to incidents; this is no different in a school context (the nature of the incidents is naturally different) and includes proactive and pre-emptive activity. Many headteachers, as I write this, are united in their proactive and pre-emptive activity against Ofsted in light of the Ruth Perry tragedy, and I believe that change may be afoot depending on the outcome of the coroner's Inquest, but for now, it remains as ever it has done.

Let me give an example. When writing about asymmetric warfare and strategies to combat it, David E. Long (2008) said,

> [T]he strategic vision proposed here is not intended to be an all-purpose formula for countering all specific asymmetrical threats. Each country must create a strategy tailored to meet its specific domestic capabilities and political costs and benefits, and be flexible enough to address the specific requirements for successfully countering the specific threats facing it. With the advances in technology and the effects of continued future shock due to rapid modernization, particularly those facing but not limited to traditional societies, strategic plans must constantly be modified to meet evolving challenges.[3]

Now read that paragraph again with some substituted words which change the focus to schools (capitalised), and see if you agree with me about the similarities:

> [T]he strategic vision proposed here is not intended to be an all-purpose formula for countering all specific asymmetrical threats. Each **SCHOOL** must create a strategy tailored to meet its specific **INTERNAL** capabilities and **HUMAN/FINANCIAL** costs and benefits, and be flexible enough to address the specific requirements for successfully countering the specific threats facing it. With the advances in technology and the effects of continued future shock due to rapid modernization, particularly those facing but not limited to traditional **METHODOLOGIES**, strategic plans must constantly be modified to meet evolving challenges.

Anyway, enough about my musings, as I had been a headteacher before arriving at Woodlands and experienced an inspection from that unique perspective, I knew the way it made me feel, the way I prepared for it, the lessons I learned, how staff responded to it, what it was and what it wasn't and how we worked afterwards. It did not define us, but it was always there like a dark cloud on an otherwise unblemished horizon. It didn't stop our work, our commitment or our innovation; it just 'was' ever looming. Arriving at a new school, with that dark cloud, cumulonimbus-like, imminently upon us, decisive action needed to be taken or we would face significant casualties from Ofsted activity.

The combat estimate

This personal knowledge, this cognitive muscle memory, enabled me, on day one at Woodlands, before I had even dipped my toe into military training, to begin what I now know is a Combat Estimate,[4] an analytical tool used the world over in various domains, to help assess and plan.

For over 20 years, the British Army has used the 'Combat Estimate' as its main decision-making tool. It is not difficult to imagine that military units are inevitably more resilient than most organisations when it comes to working in high-pressure environments; they have to be, and their leaders are conditioned to work under pressure (anything from sleep deprivation to lack of food and water). Military leaders use a range of tools and 'ready reckoners' to guide their thinking in times of crisis in order to ensure they make minimal mistakes and overlook nothing, despite fear, fatigue and acute stress. Again, mistakes in a military context are often about life or death, whereas in an educational context, perhaps mistakes are classified as success or failure, so some people would argue that the two are incomparable, but for me, they absolutely are.

Naturally then, as I look back through this new lens, I can see that I focussed on Question 1: What is the situation, and how does it affect me? But Question 1 has so many components and aspects to it, both in the military world and also in the educational one (and indeed, let us not forget business world applications!). Let me share with you some of the considerations I made. I have no doubt that yours will have been, or will be, the same upon taking over a new school, whether in challenging circumstances or not:

How does the current situation affect my staff/governors/parents/pupils/LA/ community?

What is the history of significant activity, and what are the vital pieces of intelligence in general and also in detail?

Which specific aspects of the current situation affect my ability to conduct essential and routine tasks?

Which specific aspects of the current situation affect my ability to conduct essential strategic tasks to future-proof the organisation?

What are the staff/governors/parents/pupils/LA/community/Ofsted's expectations of me within my area of responsibility?

What are the school's expectations of me both within the school and externally in the local educational landscape?

What are local competitor schools doing to both offer what is expected now and also adapt to future changes in Ofsted/government expectations?

In what ways are other schools, on a wider basis, working differently from us?

How feasible is it to adapt our practice in terms of human/financial/cognitive resources and capability?

What is our current financial situation – how much cash do we have, and what is the cash flow situation?

How much time do I have?

Are there any intelligence gaps?

What are my Critical Information Requirements (CIRs) to ensure that I plan effectively and with accurate data?

Some of this information I had begun to compile before the summer from my observations and also what I discovered as part of the TLR we did as an LA team in July 2018. I spent the summer holiday making sure that my other school, where my (then) permanent headship was based, was all set for the new year and prepared for my absence through secondment. At this point, I didn't feel the sense of acute anxiety I perhaps may have felt if I knew I was to be the permanent headteacher at Woodlands from September. Who knows whether I would have felt any different had I been the substantive head from the outset.

I knew that I needed to prepare the 'day-one' brief for all the staff, to discuss safeguarding, to focus the minds and set the direction. I also knew I needed a SEF, both of which I was doing for my other school. I knew I would use the same template for the SEF and that the information I used to populate it would need to come from more than just the TLR and the published data.

The balance between working through cognitively what I needed to find out, what I knew in part, what I thought I might do and action I was able to take to prepare was all out of kilter. Even making lists of things I didn't know, lists of aspects of school I wanted to find information about and establishing the SEF template were defining moments as it meant I was doing something concrete, something other than thinking – which was already stopping me from sleeping. You begin to take control when you begin to take action, I think. Before then, you are taking stock.

In a combat situation (not that I have been in a **real** one, you understand, but I am trained to appreciate what it might feel like and how to respond accordingly), the Royal Military Academy Sandhurst (RMAS) teaches you to take a 'Condor Moment'. Essentially, a deep breath and a pause in activity (your section or platoon will be firing at the enemy whilst you are doing this, so don't panic; it isn't like a movie scene when all goes to slo-mo) whilst you assess the situation before coming up with a plan. The period before I arrived at school and for the first week, if I am honest, were my prolonged 'Condor Moment', although I did actually pause in the 'Battle for Woodlands' on a number of occasions to revisit my strategy (more on this in Chapter 8), so in effect, you don't just have one battle, the battle-rhythm and tempo are dynamic, and don't forget, we also had Covid in the mix. The importance of taking a metaphorical breath and analysing the environment rather than making any immediate and potentially ill-informed changes was key to my success, I think, as headteacher and curator of the school culture.

State of the Nation Address

The day-one brief, which I often joke is like my 'State of the Nation Address'* (SONA), is something I have always done as a headteacher at the start of a new year (September 2023 was my 12th), and I think it sets the tone of the year to come. It is good to do it in person, to stand before your peers and explain to them honestly, pragmatically and sensibly what you plan to do in order to serve them, your school and its community that year. It is more tangible than a written five-year plan or a School Development Plan (SDP) because you share your passion in words and presence in a way that a document can never do – you can be asked questions, see faces and emotional reactions from colleagues and gauge support (or not!) for what you are sharing.

In September 2018, I stood before 100 assembled staff of Woodlands, and I told them I knew that they had been through a tough time. I also said that the situation was yet to be resolved and that I knew I was asking a lot to expect them to have any faith in me, given I was the third seconded executive headteacher in three years to ask them to do so. I said that I had done before what needed to be done at Woodlands, that I wanted to seek out skills and capacity amongst them from people who wanted to invest in the challenge that I was investing in and help me love the school back to life.

I explained to them that I was a single mum, I had suffered loss, divorce, the effects of surgery. I explained that between my personal experience and that of friends and family I had supported, there was little that could shock or concern me and that I was open to staff sharing with me concerns and also passions, professionally and personally, so that we could find workarounds to the things stopping them being successful, find opportunities for them to do what they loved and therefore perpetuate a climate of success in the school.

I explained that we had a lot of work to do and not much time to do it but that regardless of how long I was there or who came after me, we were in the business of laying the foundations that needed to be laid for them and the children to thrive long term. I said that this would involve us opening all areas of the school to scrutiny, dropping some practices and introducing other practices, but none of it would be done without research and consultation. I said we would make no changes immediately, unless they were safeguarding related, and that any changes would involve decreased workload for them and increased impact on learning for children.

Clare recalls something I said in that meeting and believes that the most important aspect of school improvement in her view was based on it:

> Staff knowing the journey the school is on and knowing they are a part of it, contributing to it and making an impact. I remember Vic explaining to staff when she joined that you were either on the boat or you weren't! She effectively uses the skills of individual staff members to ensure they are working in the right subject area, and year group to have that impact.

I said that my first job would be to set wheels in motion in the office so that the Single Central Record (SCR) and websites were compliant, and I would focus with the Senior Leadership Team (SLT) on setting things in motion for curriculum review. I explained that when we did a curriculum review, we would look at a range of things, and one of them would be Standardised Assessment Tests (SATs) data, but only one. I also said we needed to find consistency across a year group (consisting of three classes), a phase and a school in all things we did and that this would manifest only when we learned to openly communicate and then buy into shared decision-making.

I said that I needed to be outward facing and inward leaning – be visible and celebratory, increase communication with parents, shaping and managing their expectations and those of the community to reignite faith in the local school, as well as those of Ofsted, as it would see our social (and other) media presence but also be there for staff to talk to and build a relationship with, to protect them from external harm, whatever that looked like. Finally, I explained that I wanted to build trust and that trust would only come when they saw how I behaved in every situation that I dealt with. I said they had an opportunity for a fresh start, that I did not know them before and would be open. They could reinvent themselves as the people they wanted to be, and this was the time to do it.

So what? Right? I bet you all do a 'lil speech' on the first day back, and it isn't that groundbreaking. I am not saying my 'lil speech' was either. What it did was put me front and centre before the people I was there to serve. It was the first tiny piece of a 5,000-piece puzzle that needed to be put down to make a start. I let my team know some personal information about me and some professional information about me, and hinted at the way I like to operate. That was enough for day one. It was important to me as part of careful staff preparation upon taking over the school and in opening doors for them to begin to co-create organisational psychological safety.

This essentially was the first step in establishing my leadership intent, how I began to acknowledge, champion and maintain morale! Early communication with all stakeholders started the process of building essential bridges and the removal of barriers that really did need to happen for us to be able to act as quickly and authentically as we needed to – and all journeys (long or short) need to start with a single step in the right direction.

*I love random facts. The SONA is based on European parliamentary tradition, where the head of state ceremonially opens the session of the 'National Assembly'. In England, this is the State Opening of Parliament, which is a ceremonial event formally marking the beginning of a session. It is focussed on a prepared 'speech from the throne', known as the King's (or Queen's) Speech, and takes place in the House of Lords chamber on the first day of a new session, although everyone in government is invited. See the similarity?

Timelines

Part of a headteacher's job is to juggle (more on this in Chapter 11). It is important to learn how to manage multiple projects and work streams as a headteacher, and more so when taking over a school in difficulty. If you are a completer-finisher,[5] or in any way a perfectionist, then you will likely struggle, as you have to split your time between strategy and tactics, planning the work, being responsible for delivery of aspects of work, and allowing delegation of the work to others to plan and deliver in ways that are potentially divergent to yours.

One thing I have accepted as I have evolved into headship from being a class teacher with a completer-finisher mentality (in the same way that I evolved into being a parent who overlooks mess when I was once childless and obsessed with cleanliness) is the Pareto principle, also known as the 80/20 rule. It is ubiquitous no matter the situation. The Pareto principle is a useful way to think about how you approach work in general and can also inform decisions about who works on what – this means you can be more efficient and not less. Equally, the well-known Eisenhower method can be deployed. This is where tasks are placed into one of four categories – Critical and Urgent, Critical but Not Urgent, Not Critical but Urgent, Neither Critical nor Urgent – thus supporting prioritisation of tasks. When you factor in cross-group dependency and your need to work between teams concurrently, the complexities can quickly become difficult to track and prioritise: these two things are key, however. Tracking and prioritising!

My strategies for successfully tracking and prioritising will be discussed throughout the book but do include, as a basis, both lists and time-blocking. Other people have come up with myriad ideas too.[6] These include anything from planning ahead, setting long and short-term goals, prioritising urgent work, effective communication, distraction avoidance, avoiding multi-tasking, avoiding procrastination, learning to say 'no', using digital and automation to support tasks, delegation (putting 'troops to task'[7]), reviewing and recording progress, managing expectations, understanding where the flexibility is. The list goes on. The secret is to find yourself in these strategies and to find what works for you, and before that (as I said in my book on leadership) is knowing yourself and your capabilities at any given time!

In an article about work-stream-efficiency and multi-group-interdependency in project management, George Pitagorsky (2015), discussed how complex projects are performed within a matrix in which the collaborative effort of several groups, each with different capabilities and expertise, comes under the direct scrutiny of different organisations (Ofsted, the LA, etc.), who may have different priorities than the actual project or programme manager (in our case, the headteacher). I think it safe to say that in schools and school teams, individuals and teams often have two lines of accountability: a project line (implementation of a new maths scheme) and a functional or operational line (produce increased maths results across the school for Ofsted accountability). An individual or team may also be working simultaneously on multiple projects (the headteacher who is working across finance, HR and curriculum improvement, for example). Pitagorsky correctly states, 'The relationship between "work streams" and projects in the matrix is a foundation for clearly identifying roles and responsibilities, managing expectations and establishing an effective project control reporting process'.[8] It is in this where the skill of headteacher as complex project manager comes in, and without experience or expertise, external support or a healthy network, it is possible to experience failure and burnout.

In a nutshell, then, is the importance of analysing timelines and prioritisation based on situational awareness gained from gathering intelligence about the context of your school from a range of sources (triangulation). In those first few weeks, prioritise gathering of 'int', or information, before you create the concrete timeline is key.

Information gathering processes

OK, how to establish the initial facts and set the conditions for finding out about the unknowns (lifting stones and seeing what lurks beneath) so that both the 'unknown unknowns' and the 'known unknowns' are discovered in a timely way. Not easy, I grant you, but nevertheless crucial.

As I said earlier, the first step, whether the journey is a metre or a mile, is the most important step because you are on your way. I did the following in the first half-term, in no particular order:

- Constructed my first-ever digital survey for parents to complete using a well-known questionnaire function. Raw information was quickly gathered in digital form and easily presented in digestible chunks.

- Went through every one of the 400+ yellow files, beautifully presented and stored in floor-to-ceiling cupboards in my office to see what was in them.

- Spoke to as many staff as I could in one-on-one scheduled interviews and made notes.

- Examined published data, asking staff who had been at the school a number of years to offer analysis on what I was looking at and why.

- Examined the support the school was getting from the Subject Leadership Experts (SLEs) allocated by the LA.

- Examined staffing experience and expertise.

- Asked PTA members to examine the website, using a checklist, for gaps to help me create an action plan.

- Asked staff what they thought we needed to change based on the TLR findings.

- Examined staff pay and contracts.

- Examined policy using a checklist to establish gaps and also compliance.

- Examined the SCR.

- Asked pupils what they liked about school, informally.

- Spoke to parents on the gate each day.

- Wrote a weekly blog telling parents about the work that week, about the direction of travel, about what I was uncovering.

- Asked about finances.

- Set up a Twitter account for school where I celebrated the good things going on.

- Had lunch in the staffroom.

- Had SLT meetings.

- Had lunch in the hall with children.

- Spoke to teaching assistants (TAs).

- Spoke to mid-day assistants.

- Spoke to cooks.

- Spoke to the cleaners.

- Looked at planning documents.

- Looked at books.

- Rearranged the furniture in my office and painted it.

So what? Well, in rearranging the room I worked in, I was able to see all the way down the corridor, and the door was most often open so people could see me.

I smile (a lot), and therefore I could greet people, smile and check in briefly as they walked by. I could observe their body language, and they could see the work I was doing and how I was interacting. This in itself gave me valuable information.

The Twitter feed and the weekly blogs invited suggestions and informal feedback from parents, which came via email and also verbally on the gate. It also came formally in the questionnaires we did and supported some of my thinking anyway. It was no surprise that parents were frustrated. Anyone who has worked in a school in RI or Special Measures will find parents dissatisfied with some aspects of school. In telling me as the headteacher why they may be disgruntled, it offered the chance for me to take considered action and then let them know that they had been listened to and that we had acted to improve our practice: 'you said – we did'.

The whole staff discussion about SLE support led me to ask for a different approach to maths support for school from the LA. It needed improving. More of this in a bit. But safe to say, there were gaps, but we definitely had a solidifying priority list forming, underpinned by hard and soft data from a range of sources, and this was good enough for me.

Leadership behaviour

Most importantly during this process, as we were gathering intelligence 'int', was how the behaviour of the SLT (and me in particular) set the conditions for the creation of a culture that was (and is) vital for our operational and organisational success, and that of the future.

I established trust and faith from and with my team not by being a hero but by doing what I said I would do. Daily.

We agreed as a team that the maths just wasn't working. We needed a different approach, so we asked the LA to find someone to support us.

I asked the LA to find someone who was going to come from a school that had been on a similar journey to Woodlands, preferably with a similar pupil catchment and therefore matching as many variables as possible with us. This would save me time in onboarding them, explaining the situation to them and then establishing their work pattern. I allocated a senior member of the team the job of researching with other schools what they used at the same time. Although I will talk of this more later when we come to core subject improvements and the *how* of it, what I will say is that much more importantly was the cultural 'how' of what we did.

I championed our school, our staff. I explained to a potentially aggrieved professional the reason why I wanted a change, and it was based on my knowledge of the school – my role as head to look after ALL aspects of school rather than their focus and passion for one method of teaching maths, and I reduced staff workload by five hours per week. Staff buy-in from simply working with integrity and in my own way? As if! And yet it really was that simple.

Establishing 'top cover'

Top cover – when used as a metaphor in the workplace, as in the military, means protection – to protect you from interference by others. I provide it to my team internally; my governors provide it to me as, possibly, do individuals, such as school improvement partners (SIPs).

There are also organisations who can be called upon to provide top cover or a layer of protection, such as HR, solicitors, unions, professional networks such as the Chartered College, and they all provide strength to the systems needed to support a school.

Making sure that all staff were in a union was key to early discussions with staff, as many of them had overlooked this personal top cover. Imagine! Making sure I sought advice from HR before taking certain actions and making certain decisions (more about this in Chapter 10) provided me with top cover, as did making sure we adhered to LA finance directives as we progressed through the first year.

I paid this forward, incidentally, and am reliably told by a group of heads I held an online 'finance' talk for (in their first term of headship, which was also during Covid lockdown!) that this was 'amazing'. Make sure you get your own top cover in place as quickly as you can to ensure you are protected as you navigate the school improvement terrain.

Key terrain and vital ground

Talking about terrain (back to the military again!), we can't escape this chapter about most likely and most dangerous without discussing key aspects of school that must be won by a leader in order to facilitate success and the potential avenues of approach that can be used.

There is a key principle of defence, embedded within doctrine and all analysis, that distinguishes between 'vital ground' (VG) and 'key terrain'. In brief, VG is the position that you must defend to the last person, and if you fail in that task, then the battle is lost, whether that VG is concrete or conceptual. Therefore, VG for me was to maintain an Ofsted RI judgement for the school. Special Measures would have forced academisation and been an unpleasant and unnecessary outcome. Key terrain (KT) includes all those areas that allow you to dominate an attacker/challenger, therefore making defence of VG that much stronger. KT for me was curriculum implementation and proven impact on pupils' learning (not just end-of-year tests and SATs, but across and within school). Ergo, if you lose control of KT, then your hold on VG is inevitably jeopardised. I worked 20-hour days for weeks, defending VG, and it worked, but I have to stress that this was unsustainable and only worked as I had the unwavering support of my team. Support from them and an escape valve for the pressure (namely, exercise and a healthy dose of childish fun – anyone seen our Christmas song videos?).

It was crucial for me to distinguish what VG was from KT with staff on a daily basis – reminding them of the end state and the main effort. In some cases,

I knew I could give up KT, and I did when I focussed on core subjects that first year, only dabbling in foundation subjects whilst we did the intelligence gathering in those areas, and post-inspection, we essentially traded work in this space for time to consolidate work in and working practice in core areas. This was not a long-term solution, but it was essential to remain focussed in the short term.

I suppose that applying the same logic, our VG now is the 'good' grading of Ofsted, and the KT remains all aspects of extant curriculum implementation (there is more KT now; however, it is easier to manage, and the VG much easier to protect and maintain!).

Communication

Flippin heck, any leadership treatise you read will tell you how important 'comms' are for success. Knock out C2 (command and control) by destroying communication, and you are in a very good position to win battles! With good communications, a leader can understand and then share information and context with a range of stakeholders in a range of ways in order to keep them informed and aware of the direction of travel and the small successes and gains along the way. I found that this was one of the most important things I had to do and very quickly establish when I arrived at Woodlands. I learned that not everyone would read an email, or a text or a WhatsApp; not everyone responded to a formally written letter or a Tweet; not everyone dropped off children and could speak to us in person on the gate; and not everyone liked a phone conversation. So, we did it all. We layered on the information in a range of styles and ways, from informal weekly blogs to formalised letters. It was all important in building a picture for all stakeholders.

Having gained an understanding of the strengths and weaknesses of the school from a range of sources (triangulating the information I had received), having worked out the people and resources that could be capitalised upon – and where this might go wrong – we made plans, prioritised and then shared who would be responsible for which element of our planning. We made them professionally accountable, yes, but also offered support, coaching and training to facilitate success. I gave freedom and a clear end state that needed to materialise and then checked in periodically to ensure that progress to the outcome was being made.

This included understanding the audience we were communicating with at any given time; asking for top cover from the SLT (inverting the power dynamics!) who read every correspondence before it went out (and still do); seeking out skill sets, knowledge and ability; and working out easy ways to communicate to access information and share information for all layers of the school (governors, leaders, teachers, TAs, parents, etc.). It also involved me constantly checking in with governors about policy, policy implementation, policy adherence, transparency and also routinely asking for their support.

In later years, we refined this practice in line with the pandemic changes that we had made and included sourcing and buying a range of equipment and resources that may not have been in place in a timely and manageable way; but by then, we had our way of working firmly established, and this rapid reaction was not insurmountable.

Evolving culture

The school culture, as a result of all of the above, was born and grew. That growth and development, based on healthy professional relationships, ensured the facilitation of authentic and accurate information gathering about Woodlands and factors that influenced the school. This grew through repetition and consistency from me. I behaved in a predictable way, so there was no fear.

When people had made mistakes, inevitable in a VUCA environment, we simply examined them as learning points and shared 'lessons learned' as we do now. We do not brush things under the carpet or hide from difficult truths. The fastest way to reputational harm in any organisation is to hide mistakes and cover them up. A school's reputation is one of its key assets and something that must be protected. There can be grave consequences for schools that do not effectively manage their reputation and take the necessary measures to protect it – didn't we all know it? Negative press and speculation, such as the school had already been subjected to, can be (and had been) hugely damaging and had strained relationships – the only way to reverse this trend was interaction by interaction, incrementally.

> Although I'd been through the process before, the scale of the journey at Woodlands was massive. I could see that turning the school round was a huge job, but only as time went on. I began full time, I took a permanent position, then a subject leadership role and then the work load and pressure began to increase (as changes were implemented). That's when the reality of being 'on the ground' actually hit home.
>
> *– Dani*

Evolving strategy

And now to what I call 'capacity planning'.[9] I am often talking about the need for capacity planning, increasing capacity in a given area is so important that it is even in the PM of every staff member, but it is crucial in multi-faceted project management with limited resources. On a short-term basis, examples of capacity planning may be in providing overtime; longer term, it is achieved by purchasing resources and investing in training staff. The key objective of this way of working is to have the capability to deploy extra resources at the right time in order to ensure a project is a success, and done well, it ensures future proofing long after the crisis has abated.

In a school context, especially one in difficulty, the additional load on any human resource (those people with a specific skill set or function) may keep changing and often increases as a project progresses and demands change. This may create a bottleneck, and planning for this bottleneck to be removed is longer term and time sensitive. For example, in Woodlands, we have one full-time special educational needs coordinator (SENDCo) – a national award winner! Two years ago, I decided capacity in this area needed to be increased to future-proof the school; otherwise, the workload would be too much, and the capacity of this excellent SENDCo could form a bottleneck. Thus, early identification and mitigation of possible bottlenecks are key to success, both in terms of productivity and output, staff well-being and morale. This is classed as capacity enhancement and has allowed us to plan new projects in school, more of which will come later.

I never stopped thinking about and paving the way for innovation and proposed plans for improvement throughout the crisis phase. Sometimes this energises staff, as they see that after the crisis has been managed and has gone, there will be something more positive and a different energy. Sometimes it freaks staff out – and this has happened in my case (more in Chapter 16).

In summary, then, the MLCOA and MDCOA need to be thought out at the outset. If the MLCOA for Ofsted is to place your school in a 'good' category, then plan against that; if, however, the MDCOA is for Ofsted to place your school in a less-than-good category, you must absolutely plan against that. If you are in a school, there will be indicators and warnings, red flags, which will inform your planning and alert you to the various pitfalls on the way that you will need to manage, including random things such as the danger of staff unwittingly self-sabotaging school improvement efforts, information misuse by disgruntled stakeholders and lack of information. It isn't just about Ofsted as an end goal; even if you take on a school in a category, it is never about Ofsted as a goal. An Ofsted grade is, for me, a gatekeeper. Good or better means you can do all kinds of wonderful things as all gates are open, less than good means many gates are firmly closed, padlocked even.

As for Ofsted, what it is, why it exists and when all of this 'accountability' started was covered in Chapter 1. In our school, we do all this analysis of what will happen when Ofsted representatives get here and plan for success when they do, or plan for the worst-case scenario, but none of us can mitigate for politics and hidden agendas, so we must focus on inside. From the external driver of Ofsted to the internal drives for effective leadership, look no further than the next chapter.

Takeaways

- The annual day-one brief sets the tone for the year to come. It is more tangible than a SDP because you share your passion in words and presence in a way that a document can never do.

- The importance of taking a metaphorical breath and analysing the environment, rather than making any immediate and potentially ill-informed changes, is key to success as headteacher.

- Early and authentic communication with all stakeholders removes barriers and increases intelligence gathering.

- Analyse timelines and prioritise based on situational awareness gained from gathering intelligence about the context of your school from a range of sources (triangulation).

- You begin to take control when you begin to take action. Before then, you are taking stock.

- All journeys (long or short) need to start with a single step in the right direction.

- The fastest way to reputational harm in any organisation is to hide mistakes and cover them up.

Notes

1 https://www.gov.uk/government/collections/education-inspection-framework.
2 War is nothing but a continuation of politics with the admixture of other means. commonly rendered as 'War is the continuation of politics by other means'. *Von Clausewitz, C. On War* (1832–4) bk. 8, Ch. 6, sect. B.
3 https://www.hsdl.org/?view&did=487275#:~:text=Covert%20action%20and%20special%20operations,against%20asymmetrical%20combatants%20and%20materiel.
4 https://www.stevejeffrey.co/7-questions-to-plan-make-decisions-in-a-crisis/.
5 https://www.belbin.com/about/belbin-team-roles.
6 https://asana.com/resources/managing-multiple-projects.
7 https://exploitingchange.com/2015/07/20/put-troops-to-task/.
8 https://www.projecttimes.com/articles/managing-the-matrix-work-streams-and-projects/.
9 https://www.linkedin.com/pulse/management-multiple-concurrent-projects-fixed-set-resources-velaga/.

Good reads

Allies, S. (2020). *Supporting Teacher Wellbeing: A Practical Guide for Primary Teachers and School Leaders*. Routledge.
Fox Wilson, D. (2004). *Supporting Teachers Supporting Pupils: The Emotions of Teaching and Learning*. Routledge.
Long, D.E. (2008). https://www.hsdl.org/c/view?docid=487275
Moxley, K. (2022). *A Guide to Mental Health for Early Years Educators: Putting Wellbeing at the Heart of Your Philosophy and Practice*. Routledge.
Pitagorsky, G. (2015). https://www.projecttimes.com/articles/managing-the-matrix-work-streams-and-projects/

From external drivers to internal drive

Why we persist, and we must persist!

It was complicated, as there were many things going on at the same time. Personally, this whole period felt like a bit of a nightmare. I was concerned, anxious, and under immense pressure due to my new role. I do remember crying at several points and quite often during this time. My mind was never off what was going on in school. It is hard not to take it personally, especially if you overthink.

– Sue

From external drivers to internal drive

A large body of literature continues to exemplify that defining effective leadership is a huge challenge to both researchers and practitioners. Leadership as a social construct has been considered in terms of 'traits, behaviors, influence, interaction patterns, role relationships, and occupation of an administrative position'.[1] After you factor in the specific field of the leaders you are studying, occupational context and role being considered, leadership can be categorised in a range of ways that are further nuanced and increasingly complex – not to mention when generational differences are layered onto the analysis. Considering what school staff of today, largely made up of millennials and Generation Z, expect of us as headteachers can be quite overwhelming. Emerging generations describe effective leadership as 'influential, results-driven, and leading by example with a servant's heart... emotionally intelligent; they prioritize their team's needs and operate with transparency and consistency in communication'.[2]

Again, sitting within this paradigm and already highlighted with the opening quote in this chapter are myriad negatives that could be present within a school in difficulty, not limited to the impact of Ofsted and shifting intent contained in successive iterations of the framework they use for inspection. Coupled with this were are necessary responses of an LA responsible for school effectiveness and

DOI: 10.4324/9781003440000-6

how, because this has been reduced to targeted improvement, this process can be perceived by teachers and headteachers as punitive and negative. I suspect that if there had not been a decline in funding from central government, making holistic support more feasible/readily available, and the inevitable challenges inherent in taking on a school in a difficult position were not so manifest, then life could have been a little easier for the team and I over the past five years. Nevertheless, it was what it was. So how do we find the sweet spot between multiple negative external drivers, multiple organisational internal concerns and our own personal internal drive? Where can we situate ourselves to be able to get on with the job, doing what is expected of us despite all of the pressures? How do we turn the negatives into something manageable? What are the steps we need to take?

Emotional intelligence

The role of headteachers is vital for the functioning of the school. I don't think we will find any argument between us in this assertion. In general, we as headteachers must have the capacity to generate results by inspiring and motivating those we serve to, in turn, inspire and teach children and young people. To do this well, as is becoming better understood, we need to know what is expected of us, feel that we can fulfil those expectations, and have the requisite knowledge of where to find support in order to do so. It requires a range of aptitudes, including a significant level of emotional intelligence (EI),[3] which (amongst other characteristics) forms the basis of internationally understood concepts of transformational leadership.[4] We now know that there is a strong correlation between EI and the effectiveness of transformational leaders, with EI conceptualised in a hierarchical model of four branches of increasing complexity: perceiving, facilitating, understanding and managing emotions. Mayer and Salvoney define it as,

> the ability to perceive accurately, appraise, and express emotion; the ability to access and/or generate feelings when they facilitate thought; the ability to understand emotion and emotional knowledge; and the ability to regulate emotions to promote emotional and intellectual growth.[5]

Despite Michael Gove once pushing the idea that headteachers do not need to be qualified teachers in order to do their jobs (as far as he was concerned, they could be business leaders as clearly, that is what he thinks the job is – I disagree, needless to say), the majority of us have been teachers and loved our jobs. We have begun to learn about some of the complex aims of society, which is where education and individual schools sit, and how we are supposed to achieve those aims and enact their assimilation in our classrooms, particularly as they change. We see how the content of what we teach is influenced by global and national events, geo-politics and changing expectations – for example, how research critiqued earlier suggests Gen Z see leaders and what is expected of them, and how school leaders we have worked for can work within those constraints, informing the school culture and curricular (whether we agree with their approach or not). We have usually seen *how* to do things and how we do not wish to do things, as we have both personally felt the effects and usually observed them in our colleagues too. This means that as leaders, we can and do build on our drives and experiences as teachers – and this is what creates the core of our job: ensuring teachers have as positive an experience in our schools as pupils do.

Scholastic published a blog in 2019 that outlined the top 20 reasons why people teach, despite it being a stressful and thankless job (get this, whilst it *is* thankless and stressful, it is randomly pegged as the third-most trusted and respected profession![6]) with a pile of challenges and long hours. I think they are essentially the same reasons (with a few additions) that headteachers lead; have a read and see if you agree![7]

For me, the ones that resonate from the list are clear:

- **To champion children** because children need advocates: as Rita Pierson said in her TedTalk,[8] *'Every child deserves a champion, an adult who will never give up on them, who understands the power of connection, and insists that they become the best that they can possibly be'*.

- **To be a mentor.**

- **To support teachers.**

- **To make a difference** in **the community** because I care deeply about the area I work in and have a strong sense of social justice.

- And, finally, **to inspire**, as I was **inspired by some AMAZING teachers**[9] who made me feel worthy.

But what, specifically, are the things that make us want to lead; what are the internal drivers that take us beyond that initial thought, and when we are in the role of *leader* keep us going when the world might be on fire around us? Well, newsflash, it isn't the headteacher standards.[10]

I call it internal drivers; you could call it intrinsic or altruistic motivation. Having a think about your internal motivations will act as a valuable starting point and useful theoretical framework when examining motivations for applying for and then staying in a school in a difficult position, and highlights some of the reality for me as head at Woodlands.

There is comparatively limited research on the reasons why headteachers choose to take on roles in challenging schools; there is equally little research on why they remain in post – although some research does point to key factors that sustain heads' commitments to their work.[11] In the case of long-serving headteachers of disadvantaged schools, their identities are shaped by their moral purpose, core values and belief that they can make a difference for the children in their care by also providing them with a sense of stability, security and continuity.[12] I wonder if, for me, the fact that school provided me with these things when I was a child is a huge contributory factor.

When considering what she thinks were the most important aspects of our school improvement journey at Woodlands, Lottie, Year Six teacher, Upper Key Stage Two lead, maths lead and millennial, said,

> A leader who works with integrity, has a clear vision for the school and drives with positivity and clear end goals. A positive, driven and focused leader – who has the support and buy-in of their team – leads to a shared vision and the whole team working together towards the same goal. We have that.

So what? I found a critical friend and made an ass(of)u(and)me!

So, armed with bags of moral purpose, belief that I could make a difference and a pretty good degree of EI, I asked for a well-known ASIA to come and join me and work as an external advisor to challenge me and be my most caring yet most critical friend. Someone who could give me 'tough love'. Someone who worked in close proximity to me in a school with similar geographical context, who knew Woodlands and its journey, and was renowned for not holding back, being brutally honest and having children's best interests at heart. I needed someone with gravitas and presence who would drive me to my limits and ensure that I was not allowing anything to slip or pass me by. Now, some folks might think that this was exactly the kind of targeted improvement which can be perceived by headteachers as 'punitive and negative', as mentioned before, but for me? I have always had the mantra, long before the Army became a thing, of 'train hard, fight easy', and my lovely ASIA offered me that opportunity. She put me through my paces (and some) and regularly did so for the staff.

In one of our earliest meetings at school she sat beside me and grilled me about Pupil Premium (PP) provision in school. I knew there was an Upper Pay Scale (UPS) teacher allocated to this role. At this point in my tenure, there was so much going on I can honestly say that I had yet to focus on PP other than to give the teacher in charge of this aspect of Woodlands the template I had used in my previous school and tell her that I knew the conversation would come up with the ASIA, as it was a glaring gap on the website. I knew the role of an ASIA was to be robust and challenge, to guide and highlight areas where more work needed to be done and to get to the bottom of what was going on.

To my shame, inadvertently, what I did was tee that teacher up for what she felt was the grilling of her lifetime, in her words:

> In terms of class teaching, there was never a question over whether I could meet the expectations. In terms of leadership, I originally felt out of my

depth, leading an area that I had no experience in, and without a mentor – Pupil Premium. I sat through a challenging meeting with our school ASIA, and found myself in tears afterwards as I did not know what to do. The feeling of relief when I was no longer burdened with that role was immense.

– Lou

The reason for this situation was me. My advice to anyone who is new to headship is never assume that leadership is enacted in the same way; never assume leaders are all like-minded people; this is not the case, and different schools require different styles and skills, regardless of the Ofsted category they may be in. A word of caution from experience: I suggest that giving a member of staff a new subject area to lead and just expecting them to get on with it is not great for them or you. I made the assumption that the PP lead, although the requisite documents were not on the website, or readily available to evidence my assumption, would have been coached through the process of leading when she was given the responsibility. This had set her up to fail. This had happened because of my ignorance and assumption (my grandad used to say never assume, it makes an ass of u and me), the result of which was the PP lead had not been able to answer key questions. She simply did not know or understand what she was being asked. Now, this was not a failure in her, she is (as her testimony suggests) very able, this was a clear failure in me as a leader. I had failed very early on, and spectacularly, I felt, in the couple of weeks I had been there.

My leadership failure (one of many!)

In terms of EI, I knew she would feel shame, embarrassment and humiliation. I knew there would be anxiety and stress about the role and decided that I needed to take this on as a task. This gave me an opportunity to model how we would do things from then on. I decided to lead by example and demonstrate how it would work in our school. That meant an apology to Lou for not knowing her level of skill and understanding and therefore placing her in a difficult situation, as well as a promise that it would not happen again. A long conversation with her, a sample of teachers, a sample of parents about what had gone before in terms of PP and then a good think about how I could, from nothing, build a body of information I needed to work effectively. It also involved me sharing this experience with our staff as a case of how not to do it. I explained to them what had happened, took the blame myself and stated that if anyone else, UPS or not, was feeling out of their depth, underprepared, ignorant or worried about their role/responsibility, they needed to grab me urgently and tell me so I could ensure that Lou's pain was not replicated for someone else.

I sat with the SLT and asked them to make suggestions about PP. I knew how I had organised this in my previous (much smaller) school, as I was the PP lead there. But how could it work in Woodlands? I wrote to parents, sharing information that some of them were entitled to apply for PP for their child and facilitated them easily finding the link to be able to do so. From there, I personally asked for, and timetabled, a meeting with every parent of a child with PP in the school to ascertain the information needed from them to inform a 360-degree understanding of their child and how we could use the money to tailor support. I set up an individual folder for each child to contain tracking information. I also shared those folders with teachers (who were primarily responsible for each child and their progress) so that they could see at a glance the performance of each child in their class, barriers to the success of the most vulnerable and strategies they had used, with evaluations, which would be passed up the school. And finally, I shared these with a governor who had been allocated to oversee this area of school spend during one of our meetings. I coached that governor about how this could and should be done to ensure transparency and triangulation. I also (some time later) asked the finance team at the LA to support us with creating a separate budget code so that we could track spend against income in this area for both reporting on the website and also reporting to governors at Full Governing Body (FGB) level. I asked for information from all sources available to produce the statutory report for the website and worked from home for a day to produce the best quality of work I could without distraction. This was all invaluable when, two terms later, Ofsted came in and spoke to the governors and me about PP spend, and also in order for us to become compliant on the website, as the report was published and minuted by the governors as having been interrogated.

What fell out of this, overtly and inadvertently, were several things. Firstly, a dawning realisation on the part of the governors that they may not know the things they needed to know (more about this later) and that I was going to lead them through this to ensure that the review of governance that they had undertaken prior to my arrival was not in vain, although I hadn't yet seen the review at this early point. This meant ensuring that the minutes were taken effectively from that point on. I sourced an external clerk and thus placed an essential (and, at that point, lacking) degree of separation between the tasks individuals were performing. I also created a very simple Record of Visit proforma (RoV) that governors agreed to complete, linked to the School Development Plan (SDP) I had worked on so that they could begin to make concrete links between their strategic role and the operational work of the school when they came in. We also digitised the minutes and stored key documents in the cloud, ensuring easy and quick filing and accessibility for all governors, whether they were able to attend meetings or not. This proved invaluable when the Covid-19 pandemic hit us, as we had already established the 'remote' framework infrastructure we would come to rely on! It initiated a training and skills matrix being completed so that we were able to see at a glance where the areas for development lay in our FGB. Subsequently, we trained the governors in finances, health and safety (H&S), safer recruitment, etc., and ensured capacity in all areas.

It also showed the governors and staff how I worked. I was genuinely sorry that a teacher in our school had felt eviscerated by our ASIA, who was simply doing her job. I felt appalled at myself as a leader that I had assumed a teacher in our school had been coached and had the requisite skills and knowledge to perform a key task in school that had ramifications for the leadership judgement of the school but, more importantly, for our ability to ascertain whether we were spending money in areas it needed to be spent and evaluating the success of that spend on outcomes for children. It showed that once I had discovered a gap in practice and a need for training and support, I would step in, show how it could be done, work with all stakeholders to get it done (which took time) and share outcomes, warts and all, with those stakeholders. I had meetings with parents, and for some, it gave them 'face time' with me, the outcome of which was that they could share how I dealt with things with other parents, beginning a narrative that I was approachable and human.

For Lou, I gave the kind of focussed and tailored support she needed, and she thankfully recovered from her negative experience with the ASIA:

> Following the personally devastating meeting with our school ASIA about PP, and with support and guidance, I learnt to believe in myself and to pre-empt information that could be asked for. In terms of speaking with inspectors, I had run throughs with the Head, school Governors, and a repeat meeting with the school ASIA, all of which allowed me to demonstrate my increased confidence and capability to lead in our school. All of this was facilitated by the Head providing opportunities for me to be professionally challenged and more importantly, coaching me. Support from Vic and coaching through difficult conversations has enabled me to grow as a leader, her professionally challenging decisions and allowing me to make decisions, not micro-managing, made me accountable for my subject and pushed me to be the best that I could be whilst supporting staff in becoming the best that they could be. My personal experiences with the ASIA drove me to becoming a better leader. It was hard at the time, but looking back, I feel that I am a much better leader because of it. I know my subject inside and out, I can support staff and have proven that I can be challenged and speak with confidence and fidelity.

Other staff talked of their experiences with the LA subject leadership experts (SLEs), ASIA and school improvement partner (SIP), all of whom provided me with challenges in differing ways, support and also top cover, as well as information at times that I needed.

Lou, as we are thinking about her at the moment, said,

> My experiences with the SIP have been mixed, there have been times when he has said that I have no points for development following an observation, and there have been times when we have professionally disagreed on the 'right way' of doing things. I now have the confidence to back myself and my decisions and do what is best for our school and our

learners. The pressure of these visitors has pushed school improvement forwards overall.

For Clare, 'SIP visits have been very useful as a critical friend'.
  Lottie said,

> Although visits from the SIP, ASIA and SLEs were often stressful, we always worked as a team to action the next steps rapidly following feedback. Feedback from the ASIA was sometimes hard to hear and felt negative, however we all knew that she was very experienced and we needed to use her knowledge of Ofsted and the new inspection framework to continue to drive the school in the right direction. Vic always made feedback from any external body clear as she fed it back, making sure we knew what was most important and why, what was a quick fix and what steps we needed to take to get to where we needed to be longer term.

Governance – effective or not?

I was wrong when I said to staff on day one that I would be a part of, and manage, essentially two teams: educators (TAs and teachers) and support staff (admin, site maintenance, mid-day and cleaning). There is a third team – the governors. As you can see from Chapter 1, the market place and the involvement of parents in that arena has not been without its issues for all stakeholders over the years – not least governors themselves. The whole topic of governors and governance has been tricky to navigate over the last 40 years, as it is complex and made more so by a shifting systemic landscape and the simple fact that they are unpaid. Volunteers for such a high profile, high stakes and important role are sometimes in short supply, not to mention volunteers who have suitable skills, knowledge and experience, and the time to devote to the role. This can mean that unless you as head are pro-active in supporting the governors and ensuring they are trained and integrated, as much as the governors are proactive, fully informed and not just well-meaning laypeople, it is a recipe for disaster. If neither head nor governors know what they should or need to be doing, then the strategic axis of the school is unworkable and leads to myriad issues.

Why would anyone want to become a governor?

Well, apart from having a social conscience, some free time and perhaps wanting the best for children and young people in the area, becoming a school governor can be a positive move for an individual's career. This is in no small part because being part of an effective Governing Body (GB) means an individual develops a range of new and eminently transferable skills, builds on skills already possessed, builds a network and gains experience in board-level project management and experience, such as financial management in schools with multi-million-pound budgets. There is a lot to commend in this.

The main role of the FGB as a collective is that it supports and challenges the headteacher in all aspects of school, from participating in setting the school's vision, to managing the school's finances, to analysing educational outcomes and establishing 'what next' in terms of focusing on school improvement. This might sound a little vague, but it isn't just financing that GB members oversee and are involved in; it is HR – in fact, it is the GB's responsibility to recruit the headteacher and performance manage (PM) them once they are in post. GB members oversee strategy decisions for the SDP, and as such, they must be analytical and evaluative. A shared role between chair of governors and headteacher (who is an ex-officio governor), who absolutely need to have a functioning and healthy professional relationship,[13] is to manage the difference between 'strategic and operational' so that the temptation for governors to become involved in the 'day-to-day' is mini-mised and the expectation that they are fully involved in the 'strategic' is under-stood. I know I mentioned 'EI' earlier; it is crucial for effective governance.

No map and compass required; the route is easy!

There are several routes to becoming a governor, from accepting personal invita-tions by school or GB members, to applying to charities such as 'Governors for Schools' that try to match the skill set of an individual with a local school that needs a governor (the application for which is online and takes no more than 20 minutes).[14]

It can really be that simple! But what then?

Firstly, you need the correct number of governors and the correct make-up of *types* of governors, something contained in the Instrument of Governance for your school (if you are not sure, the clerk could advise or the National Governance Association, NGA). If you don't have enough and cannot recruit, then this is where you might approach a charity such as Governors for Schools. The different types of governor are straightforward, and it is possible to be creative with this mixture (for example, a particularly talented parent governor whose 'time is up' can always be asked to become 'co-opted' if you have a space or an LA governor – after going through a formal process). Essentially, you have LA, staff, associate and co-opted (possibly 'foundation' in certain circumstances).

For some headteachers, managing 'rogue' governors is the biggest challenge they have; for some governors, a 'rogue' or obstructive headteacher can be a pain. Parent governors involved in governance can offer you a really valuable insight into the lived experience of parents and children in your school, equally they can focus on their own child to the detriment of their wider role. The parent gover-nor role has actually been contested in recent years, so they are in the awkward position of being on the 'inside', and there is also the fact that they may not feel wanted.[15]

There is no need to have any difficulty with governors based on their designation – the key is to have a GB handbook and ensure that everyone knows and understands confidentiality – this is the key organisational threat when sharing information about issues that crop up in school (that and ensuring there is a secondary safety mechanism of an appeals structure and therefore who has access to what information, and when, from the outset) – it is important that they all feel equally valued.

The majority of school governors, and the ratios are all different depending on the school, are co-opted. They don't necessarily have a connection to the school, may or may not share the religious nature of the school or even be residents in the LA. To be 'co-opted', the GB has to believe that the individual has the skills and experience required to contribute to the effective governance (ergo, success) of the school. Sometimes referred to as 'community governors' as, in reality, they often do come from the community the school is in and understand the needs and nuances of that community; as a result, they usually have a real sense of social justice and want the best for their locality.

What skills do we need?

A useful (if not overwhelming and terrifying) read for your governors, summarising all aspects of what is expected of them (the end state) is the Competency Framework.[16]

For the GB to evaluate the skills required of a co-opted governor to achieve the end state, they should do a 'skills matrix', and the step before that is to do a 'skills audit'.[17] There is a caveat to this, doing the skills audit doesn't mean that all is automatically well. As a general starting point, however, and in order to acquire the basic information needed about the collective and individual skills and experience you have in the GB, they are great (remember situational awareness I was talking about in Chapter 4?). As a headteacher, I have participated in them each time we have done them, annually if we have a change of governors, and here is what I know – the questions are pretty limiting and limited! As Steve Edmonds, director of advice and guidance for the NGA agrees,

> It is fair to say that most are designed with the intention of supporting boards to implement the DfE competency framework for governance into their working practices.... I am sure this has contributed to the poor design of skills audits and why for many boards they have become little more than a token compliance activity: something boards do rather than do anything with.[18]

Now, if this were teachers producing meaningless data for the head rather than meaningful data which they can use to hone planning and adaptive teaching for impact on pupils, we would have something to say! Poor governors.

Thankfully, the NGA has produced guidance notes, which signpost the GB to the NGA and other resources which can enhance knowledge and understanding to boost skills. The guidance notes which accompany their audit tools are designed to support GB members in their ability to 'clarify understanding and promote accurate and consistent evaluation'.[19] The point about skills audits is that they should be completed in as much detail as possible and lead to an action plan, which means you can train the aspects of governance you have weaknesses in and deploy GB members with appropriate skills to take on aspects of governance commensurate with these skills. That doesn't mean yet another action plan! The outcome of your skills matrix evaluation can feed into any kind of school improvement evaluation currently in use, most often in the 'Leadership' section of the SDP or the SEF next steps, but should definitely ensure clear targets in key areas.

The annual skills audit, in case you have no idea what one is or what it should offer, should be functional and should focus on

- needs or opportunities to expand knowledge or skills as identified through annual self-assessment and production of a shared skills matrix;

- evaluation and review of training needs for the coming year and developments in individual competencies since the previous year; and

- recruitment, selection and succession planning at GB or committee level, or both.

External review of governance – who governs the governors?

The governors at Woodlands had an external review of governance just before my arrival in September 2018; the summary areas for development are outlined as follows:

> Early Issues identified: chairing and Board leadership; challenge – responding to the School Development Plan, questioning and curiosity (balancing the strategic and the operational); communication; clerking; structure and skills; governor visits training, development and new governor induction.
>
> – *F. Stagg, NLG, February 2018*

I wasn't sure what underpinned the decision to conduct a review until I saw the report for the purposes of this book (which made it clear that Ofsted had suggested it in September 2016 when they said the school was RI), but it was useful. From there came the decision, once I was in post, to make changes to the clerking services, which was only one of the recommendations that had not been tackled.

I would say the triumvirate of head, chair and clerk is key to successful governance and, by that, successful school leadership in the round. If in doubt, and it hasn't been done before you take on a headship in a school in crisis, my advice is to get an external review of governance.[20] Sassoon said of clerking,

Much has been written about the role of the chair and the headteacher, vis-à-vis governors' efficiency and effectiveness; much less about the role of the clerk. The National Governors' Association has spearheaded training for clerks so that they can understand governance, develop knowledge, secure the skills necessary to service the needs of governors and governing boards and act as the governing board's trusted adviser. It is a vital role for governors to discharge their responsibilities responsibly if the governing board is to act efficiently and effectively, adding value to the school/academy.[21]

What the review didn't offer me, and nor did a change in clerk, was the information about what the governors didn't know about the school. I had not been headteacher at Woodlands long enough to gauge this effectively and was conscious that at any point we could have a call from Ofsted. I was wary of assuming any knowledge given my painful experience with Lou. Recall in Chapter 3 that I talked about the known knowns and the unknown unknowns. Thus, I began to uncover things about their gaps in knowledge – as they did – and we all needed to be open about, as per the Ofsted recommendations – this was not about blame but about a cultural shift based on honesty and transparency and all the governors bought into it (thank goodness!). An example of this is, in the autumn term, our LA published the draft (union agreed) Pay Policy.

The draft Pay Policy is a generic document and needs to be worked through (by 'people') and agreed at the FGB level because it outlines to whom, how, when and why pay is awarded to anyone in your school. It is a binding document that can be used to take you to the employment tribunal if things go wrong, and it also outlines the structure of your school so that it is understood how people can get promoted, with what metric they will be assessed, etc.

My usual practice in my previous school was that I spent time going through this document each autumn when it arrived and shared it with the Finance and Pay Committee for discussion before it went to the December FGB for ratification. Anyway, I (once again) assumed that the governors would know that this was what needed to be done. I worked on the template Pay Policy and emailed the governors for a date when they would usually meet and not only go through this document, but go over several anonymised PM documents to ensure that they were satisfied I was doing it fairly and consistently, and in line with policy.

Tumbleweed.

I then explained that some of them needed to join me and go over the PM documents and go through the policy; when they did, they **really** enjoyed the process. I explained to them why they were doing what they were doing (it was a bit funny looking at the 'anonymised' headteacher PM, but let's not dwell on this, for the first year, I wanted them to see how my targets fed and cascaded into the targets of all layers of school staff). They found the entire process useful and informative, and it helped when they were asked about it at the FGB meeting the following week.

Your governors are your greatest allies and give you the best top cover known to man. Kevlar? Nothing on governance, but they need to be 'in' and part of everything that goes on. How can your governors support you if they don't know what is going on? More about this in Chapter 15.

Takeaways

My advice on assuming anything when taking over a school as head:

■ Don't. Ask. Ask again. Triangulate.

My advice on governance in summary:

■ External review of governance

■ Skills audit

■ Effective recruitment

■ Skills matrix

■ Training, training, training

■ Inclusion at all levels – subject leadership/finance/SEND/Safeguarding, etc., named governors to all create RoVs each time they come in

■ Up-to-date information in headteacher reports each term

■ Clarity and challenge in meetings

■ Effective clerking and information management

■ Follow up on decisions

■ Communication, communication, communication!

Notes

1 https://studylib.net/doc/26149944/eighth-edition-leadership-in-organizations-gary-yukl---pd... P.2.
2 Jake Aguas MJ (2019) 'Millennial and generation Z's perspectives on leadership effectiveness' *Emerging Leadership Journeys* 1(13).
3 Forgas JP, & George JM (2001) 'Affective influences on judgments and behavior in organizations: an information processing perspective' *Organisational Behaviour and Human Decision Process* 86, 3–34.
4 Ayiro LP (2014) 'Transformational leadership and school outcomes in Kenya: does emotional intelligence matter?' *FIRE: Forum for International Research in Education* 1(1).
5 Mayer JD, & Salovey P (1997) 'What is emotional intelligence?' in P Salovey, D Sluyter, DJ Sluyter, and P Salovey (Eds.), *Emotional Development and Emotional Intelligence: Educational Implications*. New York, NY: Basic Books. p. 10.
6 https://www.ipsos.com/en-uk/advertising-execs-rank-below-politicians-britains-least-trusted-profession.

7 https://www.scholastic.co.uk/blog/Why-do-teachers-teach-38681#:~:text=To%20 share%20a%20passion,specialism%20to%20cultivate%20it%20further; https://cfey.org/ wp-content/uploads/2015/11/Why-Teach-Leaflet-Final-copy-for-dissemination.pdf.

8 https://www.ted.com/talks/rita_pierson_every_kid_needs_a_champion?language=en.

9 https://www.ted.com/talks/victoria_carr_the_power_of_language_everyday_heroes; https://www.teachertoolkit.co.uk/2018/12/26/365-good-teacher/.

10 https://www.gov.uk/government/publications/national-standards-of-excellence-for-headteachers/headteachers-standards-2020.

11 https://www.researchgate.net/publication/341097344_Why_do_Headteachers_Stay_in_Disadvantaged_Primary_Schools_in_London.

12 Towers E (2017) 'Stayers': a qualitative study exploring why teachers and headteachers stay in challenging London primary schools (Unpublished doctoral thesis), King's College London.

13 https://www.teachingexpertise.com/articles/governors-and-head-make-it-a-relationship-that-works/.

14 https://governorsforschools.org.uk/register/.

15 https://www.nga.org.uk/news-views/directory/keep-parents-governing-campaign/.

16 https://assets.publishing.service.gov.uk/government/uploads/system/uploads/attachment_data/file/583733/Competency_framework_for_governance_.pdf.

17 https://www.nga.org.uk/knowledge-centre/governing-board-skills-audit/.

18 https://www.nga.org.uk/news-views/directory/governance-skills-audit-the-way-you-do-it/.

19 https://www.nga.org.uk/news-views/directory/governance-skills-audit-the-way-you-do-it/.

20 https://www.nga.org.uk/training/directory/external-reviews-of-governance/.

21 https://governorsagenda.co.uk/2019/01/04/an-effective-clerks-responsibilities-to-the-governing-board/.

Good reads

https://www.ted.com/topics/leadership

https://www.parentkind.org.uk/about-us/who-are-we

Garvey, P. (2020). *Taking Control 2: How to Prepare for Ofsted under the Education Inspection Framework*. Crown House.

Kingsley, A. (2022). *My School Governance Handbook: Keeping It Simple, a Step by Step Guide and Checklist for All School Governors*. John Catt Educational Ltd.

Sternad, D. & Kobin, E. (2023). *Develop Your Leadership Superpowers: 50 Key Skills You Need to Succeed as a Leader*. Econcise.

6 Constraints and limitations
What hurdles must be overcome to ensure success?

Having worked in previous schools where a lot of work needed to be done to develop SEN Provision, it didn't come as a surprise what was needed: a consistent approach so staff were sure what they should be doing to best support children with additional needs in school. I was hopeful that in as quick a time as possible, new SEND practice would be implemented to get staff onboard and able to see the benefit of what they were being asked to do: support parents and enable children to succeed.

– Alice

Constraints and limitations

Where to begin? On the macro-level, this chapter will deal with the range of constraints and limiting factors that leaders have to manage in schools – not least the dismantling of several external systems, such as children's social care, the National Health Service (NHS), early intervention (SureStart) and Special Educational Needs systems, not to mention post-Covid-19, post-BREXIT and the ongoing conflict between Russia and Ukraine, which also have implications that continue to affect school finances and hence improvement.

On the mezzo-level, there is the impact of any kind of staffing restructure (financially, HR and skill set), the 'academy agenda' and its cost implications (all MATs must do 'due diligence' before taking on a school), financial forecasting for the future (especially with a huge deficit), the cost of buildings maintenance/ development (how do you regrow your school numbers without investment?) and where the responsibility lies for all of this. Essentially, future-proofing your school in light of the aforementioned – who can you turn to for help?

On the micro-level, well, this includes any kind of HR topic from managing staff in difficulty to managing underperforming staff; local area designated officer (LADO) referrals to misconduct sit beneath this heading, and although they will be

DOI: 10.4324/9781003440000-7

touched upon here, they will actually be discussed in further detail with positive and negative stories to support the range of strategies that can be used (and the systems that can be put into place to prevent negative outcomes) in Chapter 10.

Decimation of systems: social services

OK, let's go macro before I get stuck into Woodlands and the mezzo-level stuff. Big, previously valuable and useful systems have literally been annihilated for lots of reasons. I know you know this, but if you imagine a school as the hub at the middle of a bike wheel and each of the spokes is being removed one by one, and then tell me about your confidence in the integrity of the wheel and its ability to keep the bike moving in a straight line, the brakes working, and the rider safe whilst going downhill, in the Tour de France, I would hazard a guess that it would be rapidly diminishing as time went on if there at all!

On some days, all I can say is running a school when you are at the mercy of systems that are themselves broken feels like careering out of control despite how strong your legs are and how much you grip the handlebars. Politicians widely recognise the problems from social care to social services; however, reforming social care does not offer immediate vote-popularity. In many ways, it is the opposite and requires them to galvanise the population behind apolitical long-term thinking which leads to improvements the public might recognise and experience – and this takes bravery. The public cannot fail to notice the dire straits people who require social care encounter and navigate. In findings from NatCen's 'British Social Attitudes' survey, a mere 14% of people say they're satisfied with the way social care services are running, and an enormous 57% are actively dissatisfied.[1]

As for children's social care and social services, how can you make sense of it all? For children and young people who end up in emergency accommodation, sometimes likened to prison accommodation, perhaps with a bag of clothes if they are lucky – dropped off by overworked and underpaid social workers – their life chances are all too predictable. Thus, the Independent Review of Children's Social Care report from 2022[2] outlined the obvious really: the need for an urgent overhaul of the care system in England. This has yet to bear fruit; meanwhile, those in care are 'wearily familiar with the system's pitfalls', having 'seen the impact of social services' mismanagement on children's well-being and future prospects'.[3] Here is what is scary for me on so many levels: ten years from now – according to Smith – there could be

> 100,000 children in care in Britain. The care system costs approximately £10 billion per year to maintain, yet the outcomes for care leavers remain incredibly poor. This is because all too often the current system offers a binary choice: stay in a home where there is obvious risk to a child; or move the child into care at the risk of compromising their long-term physical and mental health.

I think she might be right, and yet, here is what is interesting in terms of why we are focussed on school improvement and what should drive us: the Local Government Association (LGA) makes a clear case that Ofsted directly affects outcomes for children because they influence decision-makers.

> In discussing levels of child protection investigations and risk aversion in the system, the report fails to acknowledge the role of the inspectorate, Ofsted, …it remains the case that the inspection regime drives a degree of risk aversion within many children's services departments.[4]

The LGA highlighted the impact of neo-liberalism: fragmentation of children's social care services which had been transferred to alternative delivery models and market providers, and also referenced the impact of academisation of some schools.[5] It further drew attention to the complex environment that social workers have to work within to support children and families whilst simultaneously safeguarding children. Over a decade of public sector austerity has led to the removal of early help and support from services such as SureStart,[6] which was most effective particularly in areas of high deprivation, with concurrent cuts to the NHS. If social workers must be able to refer to a range of necessary services to successfully help families, how can they do their jobs if those services no longer exist or are burdened to the point of collapse?

Well, as my daughter would say, 'Duh, Obvs!' You look to schools and seek them (amongst other mainly voluntary and charity services) to strengthen the communities they exist in rather than just providing educational support services. There is no doubt that strong communities can play an important role in supporting families; after all, the old adage 'it takes a village to raise a child' is based on something akin to truth, but it is schools that must take up the slack. Not sure where this is mentioned in an Ofsted inspection report, but that could just be me!

Finally, and apropos of what we have encountered and worked on in Woodlands, are the challenges of rising cost of living and housing costs and decreasing availability of social and affordable housing. The LGA further points to this as

> increasing numbers of families are finding themselves priced out of their local area and forced to move away from their friends, families and the local networks that can provide vital support in times of difficulty. This of course also has implications for children and families in terms of stability and stress.

Decimation of systems: safeguarding

> My role is not something that changes for Ofsted. What I do on a daily basis for children and families happens whether Ofsted come into school or not.
> – *Clare*

All organisations that work with, or come into contact with, children should have safeguarding policies and procedures to ensure that every child is protected from harm from all adults and even from other children who might pose a risk to them.[7]

Safeguarding is literally that: an action taken to promote the welfare and safety of a child, therefore protecting them from harm. But it has many complex forms and involves many complex agencies, all of whom are under pressure and most of whom are underfunded. The worry is that if you, as head, are not 'all over' the safeguarding practice in your school, then a child ultimately could die, and any combination of things that sit behind that, from abuse and maltreatment to trafficking and mutilation of their body parts. This is such a huge responsibility that no matter how many systems you have in place or how good the people you work with are at putting them into place, you sometimes go home at night and are unable to sleep. For me, an additional layer to safeguarding pupils is safeguarding staff, and for that, we have supervision.

If you are new to headship, and grappling with it all, then this is a rabbit warren that is vital to get to grips with. Safeguarding involves everything from creating a culture where children feel able to disclose to training staff to observe potential signs of abuse or neglect, from empowering children and giving them language and a voice by working with charities such as the National Society for the Prevention of Cruelty to Children (NSPCC) to working with agencies such as Child Exploitation and Online Protection Command (CEOP),[8] from educating parents about internet safety to asking governors and new staff to do online learning and training about Female Genital Mutilation (FGM), PREVENT and antiterrorism.[9] The issues are not necessarily with what YOU do as a head but rather with the services outside, the external agencies that you may need help and support from, which are slowly dwindling. My advice is don't give up and use networks – people out there always have suggestions that you haven't considered, capitalise on them.

Decimation of systems: special educational needs and disabilities

Ok, stand by for ground-breaking news: SEND is on the increase and has been (demonstrably so) for over five years.

According to the government, in 2022–3,[10] more than 1.5 million children in England have special educational needs (SEN), which is an increase of 87,000 from 2022 and is actually sitting at around 17%+ of ALL PUPILS. The percentage of pupils with an Education and Health Care Plan (EHCP) has increased to 4.3% from 4.0% in 2022; in real terms, this is 389,171 children (in fact, since 2016, the number has increased by two-thirds). The percentage of pupils with SEN but no EHCP (SEN support) has increased to 13.0% from 12.6% in 2022; in real terms, this is 1,183,384 children. The most common type of need for those with an EHCP is autistic spectrum disorder (ASD), and for those with SEN, support is speech, language and communication needs. So what?

Don't panic; the government has a plan.[11] Some may say it is underwhelming, as it contains things for the future that make little impact on the now, and others may say it is not ambitious enough, nor is enough money being dedicated to it, given that we are not far off one-fifth of all pupils having SEND in our schools. That remains to be seen (and as for how it relates to us, see Chapter 16). For the context of this book and my focus on Woodlands, there were a large number of children who had SEN, and we needed to properly assess their needs so they were fully understood. This would ensure that they, their parents and those asked to teach and assist them were properly supported.

In a nutshell, again, I could not have either improved the situation with SEND, safeguarding and early intervention in our school, or future-proofed it without two key individuals. Commonly referred to in school as 'Clarice' (they are Clare and Alice), they move around the area as a 'fire team' and are a perfect example of professionalism and dedication to the most vulnerable. Let's face it; there is a reason Alice won a Pearson National SENDCo of the Year Award, Silver in 2023!

How have we arrived at such award-winning practice?

Clarice – SEND

> I tend to do what I feel is right for the schools I work in, focusing on the children and families not specifically doing things for Ofsted.
>
> *– Alice*

The first thing to look at for me was the lack of time-saving (and any other) systems! As I became **substantive** head, in a way neither I could when seconded nor the previous two seconded heads could, I had the autonomy to make decisions on operational matters in school. The leading name for me then, as now, for an effective system of recording actions and tracking outcomes whilst keeping everyone who needs to know in the loop, no matter their location, is Child Protection Online Monitoring System (CPOMS), and whilst we elected to investigate the different academic tracking systems on offer for our school, I made the leadership decision to buy in CPOMS immediately. It quickly became the backbone for recording any and all interactions between pupils, parents, staff, external agencies, etc., and has literally saved my bacon on more than one occasion in terms of things such as creation of a chronology when we have been accused of not doing our jobs and not supporting pupils (more about this in Chapter 15).

You know the army has an acronym, 'CAKE', which I just adore for anything that shows effective use of time – it stands for 'Concurrent Activity, Anticipation at All Levels, Knowledge of the Grouping System, and Efficient Drills'. Anyway, concurrently with looking at systems – don't you love that word – I was looking at the capacity of the SENDCo. Now, the SENDCo lived an hour away from school and thus was travelling two hours a day to and from work – and by her own admission, this was affecting her life as a single parent and her children's lives, as well as wasting two hours of her day that could be better spent on her work. (Remember my views on barriers to working in a school in crisis in Chapter 3?)

Innovative thinking

The SENDCo from my previous school was randomly travelling an hour a day three days per week in the *opposite* direction to my SENDCo (in fact to *her* town!) to be SENDCo at my colleague's school, a school in Special Measures which was really suffering and needed support from her as an executive head who was also 'seconded-in'. In what would appear to some a '*radical move*', I firstly ascertained the possibility of swapping roles as a mutually beneficial career and family pathway move for both my SENDCo at the time and the one from my previous school, and I also spoke to my headteacher colleague in the school in Special Measures (sure, weren't we both like twins, almost!). Both SENDCos were on temporary contracts for three days per week. Both SENDCos were happy to literally switch to gain back two hours per day each! Both had worked with innovative leaders (I know I am bigging myself up here, Annette, you're welcome!); both knew the pressures of the job of working in a school in crisis in very similar situations. It was (logistically anyway) a no-brainer. The SENDCo from my previous school had the added advantage of working with the devil she knew (me), and the SENDCo at the time in Woodlands hadn't yet formed any kind of relationship with me so was happy to make a move based on family circumstances and improved work-life balance.

Having spoken to my headteacher colleague and both of these members of staff on a number of occasions (taking time out of a busy day, naturally) to talk to them about what was in 'the art of the possible', we then moved towards a more formal agreement with the support of HR. This may appear radical to some people, and perhaps it was, but to me, if we go back to Chapter 3 and reflect on work-life balance and having the predisposition to take on challenges, I felt that if two passionate and committed people who were effectively doing the same job were travelling in opposite directions for two hours a day and literally crossing each other on the motorway could change their work location and still have a huge impact on the life chances of the most vulnerable and staff in two challenging schools by saving those wasted hours, then I wanted to try to facilitate that! Structurally, this made no change whatsoever to the time and money given to SEND in either school, but imagine the carbon footprint, fuel saving, time and energy saving and saving on child care that it offered the two SENDCos.

It meant that the SENDCo who came to join me (the -ice in Clarice), who was also the part-time SENDCo at my previous school, travelled less and therefore could spend more time in school, supporting me with after-school meetings with parents, with training and coaching staff, in setting up systems and so on. From there, we established a direction of travel for SEND in our school (naturally, she was part of the SLT and soon began working full time – soz Kev!). We looked at classes of children and spoke to staff about what they were observing and the reasons they thought they were seeing this behaviour. We spoke to parents. We looked at potential needs. We had a lot of difficult conversations with a lot of people.

Tracking and recording – the irrefutable value!

With CPOMS firmly established as a system for recording behaviour, we were able to track the classes where the behaviour issues lay, and we noticed patterns with individual pupils that we were then able to observe. We spoke to their parents and discussed with them whether they observed similar behaviour patterns in the home. We discussed with them ways of supporting them and the children both inside and outside school, and we began to track their behaviour using the SEND profiles (the format of which has been overhauled in the last five years – we never get complacent). From there, we set up calendars and diaries to make sure that statutory assessments were done on time, were of a very good quality, and therefore, professional paperwork was completed and submitted in a timely way.

This meant that we began receiving funding for children, which then enabled us to be able to employ teaching assistant (TA) support for those children. Behaviour issues decreased; academic development increased, and although it cost more money (we are not funded for a full TA salary even if a child is awarded an EHCP, a situation that may change in light of recent information I have come across), it was very much worth it for the children and their classmates and the learning that could take place once their behaviour was regulated as their needs were met. I elected with the governors to appoint a SENDCo full time, which, to my joy, Alice chose to take on! Having a full-time SENDCo, which obviously has cost implications to your budget, I was also able then to plan carefully for the children whom we had identified as urgent (based on them breaking windows, running through school and hurting themselves and others, for example) and begin to overcome the backlog of a whole host of other needs in our student body. Staff and parent morale rose as we tackled each situation in the same calm and pragmatic, supportive (but professionally firm) way. We then built on this to establish early intervention practice.

Naturally, this did not take place for a year, by which time we had already had our Ofsted inspection, and we were progressing into that second year as we felt able to assess pupil needs in reception, preschool and nursery from September 2019. Thankfully, I had established this key part of our puzzle because that September, my LA-funded SLT evaporated. Naturally, when Ofsted said we were on the right trajectory and wrote to me about my good leadership, the LA decided quickly that they needed to divert their financial support from our school to other schools in crisis. Whilst I had only been there a year and felt saddened that I would now be bereft of support, I understood the rationale. Their gift to me, for a year, I think because I broke down and cried in June 2019, was they paid for my non-class-based deputy for a year. It was a new deputy; the previous one had successfully completed NPQH, helped me through Ofsted and then been seconded to a newly formed MAT (as she was, and is, brilliant). My new deputy and I knew we had a tough journey ahead, and we were far from 'out of the woods', but in the year I had worked with her as a member of the SLT, I had been routinely and regularly impressed with her and her professionalism, which she has only built upon over time. So, the core of the leadership team was growing and evolving. One newly minted Bursar, one newly appointed full-time SENDCo, one funded newly in post-deputy head, one headteacher made up the SLT as we headed towards our second year. There is just one more to add, and you will meet her in the next section, where we will round off the SEND journey.

A big sort out – how long is a piece of string?

In all honesty, it was a year in a furnace. That is how long it took to establish the correct people, in the correct role, doing the correct job, with the correct tools at hand for SEND. It was no quick fix. We needed cohesion, leadership, management and vision. By the way, it goes without saying that this is the case equally for children. There are no quick fixes; as we know, the current system means we have to pay for support for children for at least two terms to show that they need that support in order to access education and then complete copious paperwork to apply for the formal funding, and hope it is accepted despite the increasing need and burden on the LA finances.

This is far from ideal, and with increased external provision, we could make this a quicker and much slicker process. If teachers were more trusted, if professionals had more time, if the NHS wasn't so under pressure and community paediatricians had more availability. If. If. If.

Anyway, the SENDCo in that year revised our practice and created both the SEND register and the Early Alert support register, which meant that we could track very closely children who may need some support for a small period of time. Perhaps their vision was impacting their ability to make progress; they would go on the Early Alert, and once they had seen an optician and had glasses, they were able to access learning and begin making progress again, and then they would be removed. Fluidity enabled us to track and show actions that we had put in place for children below the SEND threshold but who were nevertheless overcoming barriers.

It also meant that we were able to report statistically to governors on a termly basis and interrogate attainment data. My SENDCo produces a part of my head-teacher's statutory report each term to the governors, and she will tell them not only the children who are being supported in various ways in terms of education and special needs but also (as another one of her roles is in terms of safeguarding as designated safeguarding lead (DSL) for school) in safeguarding. In fact, she works with Clare, our deputy DSL and learning support mentor (LSM), who is the fifth part of the core SLT.

Having a full-time SENDCo means that we can talk about provision for children and our TA support needs. We can recruit the correct TAs for the job and manage their performance through appraisal. We look at the needs of the child, and then we search for a TA who can best support that child. We look for resources that can support that child. Finally, we look at the learning space that each individual child occupies within our school. We try to future-proof school in terms of the resources that we buy and in terms of the permanent things that we put in place for all of our pupils, as we have a range of special needs in our school which goes from very specific rare diseases which have life-limiting complications, all the way through to dyslexia; we have children who have got Down syndrome all the way through to ASD and so on. The range is vast, and none of us in school are experts.

Therefore, we rely upon specialist services (which are few and far between), most notably speech and language therapy, but also occupational therapists, educational psychologists and community paediatricians, just to name a few. Without a SENDCo doing that coordinating full time, I certainly would not have managed, and we would not have been as successful as we have been. Why? We have such a big school. As was noted earlier in the government stats, the national rate of SEND is hovering around the 20% mark, so imagine in a school of 600 what 20% might look like. We would be looking at a considerable number of children, in fact, including our Early Alert; we are there or thereabouts now and our SENDCo manages all of their needs. Not only does she line manage the TAs, coordinate with external SEND staff from the LA, advise internally for staff who seek suggestions for strategies, coordinate paperwork, conduct reviews with parents and report with me to governors (the list is endless), but she also heads up our Neurodiversity Parent Support Group (more about this later!). She said of those early days,

> Work life balance was difficult to manage due to the sheer amount that needed to be done in a short space of time. However, I had realised it would be a challenge so wasn't surprised by this. Luckily with the support of my husband and family I remained positive and worked hard to ensure I still spent valuable time with them. Vic helped in talking through the SEN children that needed support the quickest. A lot of the staff were willing to complete SEN tasks asked of them as they saw the value in what they were being asked to do.
>
> – *Alice*

She was right.

Clarice – pastoral support

I wouldn't be able to talk about Clarice without talking about the role of Clare, not just Clare's role, but Clare the human.

Clare is one of the kindest, most patient people I have ever met and worked with. Her sensitive dedication to the most vulnerable families comes from somewhere deep inside her, and it's a well that I tap into on a regular basis. At my worst, as a result of the passion I feel for children and their care, I can get quite frustrated with parents who do not support their children (for any number of reasons). I suspect because I was once a vulnerable child and only made a success of my life because I did have support from school and from family members, but nevertheless, the way that Clare supports and champions parents, who – she reminds me – are perhaps as vulnerable as their children, as they have not always had the guidance they needed themselves, (thus often choosing to lead them by the hand to support networks or supporting them herself), is second to none.

When I arrived at Woodlands, Clare was part of a different two-woman team who dealt with things like mental health and counselling children. I could see that she was a person who lacked confidence, who may perhaps have been in the shadow of others and who needed to have that confidence brought to the fore. That came through in one of my early conversations with her, conversations I had with all staff to get to know them, trying to establish what they brought with them to the table and what could be built upon to facilitate future successes for them and the school. Those meetings are among some of the most influential in my leadership journey and the journey of Woodlands.

Clare proved to me that she was not only committed to our school and to the children but also committed to making the workplace better for her colleagues. She initiated, along with her '*oppo*' at our school at the time, mental health well-being days which weren't just for children. I could see that there was some creativity in her that needed to be expanded upon and I knew she would absolutely love the staff mental health and resilience training I bought in, both through Thrive in Five with Christina[12] and also Inner Armour (as was then) with Al. Certain staff, who had lived through the years before my arrival, really took something from these sessions. I knew they would, and it gave me great joy to see the personal healing that took place, how colleagues opened up and supported one another and how that then reflected in the professional work in our school. Regulated adults are able to co-regulate effectively with children.

Naturally, as I quickly realised that we needed more capacity in terms of the pastoral side of school, I knew I needed to build on what Clare brought to the party. We were working on SEND; we were also working on considerable safeguarding issues. She was the perfect person to tackle the gap in our defences that was safeguarding when the previous deputy left on secondment – be that Child in Need (CiN), Child Protection (CP) Team Around the Family (TAF), etc. Clare, once established in her own room within the heart of our school, with a movable wall between her office and Alice's, naturally began to see a lot more children. Clare and Alice, Clarice, as you already know they are affectionately known, began to establish ways of working that I think have built a really strong community of care in our school; something commented on as a real 'stand-out' strength. Pupils and staff know they can knock on either of those doors and sit in the area outside the joint offices if they need to talk to someone, if they're feeling anxious or, simply, if they just want to spend quite a few moments reflecting. Whether it's on the beanbags or the sofa that is there now, the small space that's been created by those two wonderful humans, 'The Nurture Club' as they like to call it, is a godsend to some of those children (particularly those for whom being outside in large open spaces gives them anxiety).

Clare's role, day-to-day, is to manage parents and their needs, manage social care interaction and communication, liaise with the police, oversee CPOMS as part of the core SLT, manage interactions with social workers, manage interactions with family support workers, manage interactions with local charities and projects such as passion for learning/RAGE fitness and other local organisations who offer support for vulnerable children and those who are borderline/on the poverty line with their families, such as the food bank. She helps parents find accommodation. She liaises with financial support networks. She basically goes out of her way to try to ensure the pupils and families are provided for.

Not only that, but she goes over and above and is the interface between warring factions of different families, trying pragmatically to model how to heal wounds that have been caused by harsh words, separation, divorce and so on. She's always smiling. She's always loud. She always spoils everybody around her, particularly the school dog, Gus (more about him later in Chapter 12). The dog loves Clare because Clare gives the dog lots of treats (he also needed a diet as a result, but we won't go there). Clare has done emotional literacy support assistant (ELSA) training and is one of three trained ELSA staff in our school, coordinating with Alice as to which children are supported on this programme, working with the other two pastoral ELSA TAs to ensure that we target as many children who need it as possible.

The way that we work and build capacity means that we are constantly looking to enhance and develop the skills and the pool of talent that we have. This year, it has been supporting a teacher to complete the SENDCo course (I have also completed it in the past), and next year perhaps another teacher will do it. In the coming year, we will obviously look to develop ELSA and other pastoral aspects of our work further, but for now, Clare is the fifth and final part of a very proactive, dedicated, core, non-class-based SLT.

She is also a staff governor. Her confidence has grown as she has been recognised for her considerable impact; she takes great care to meticulously read policy documentation and to highlight any inaccuracies and discrepancies. She makes thorough notes on **everything**, including when I share some of my 'pearls of wisdom', as she calls them. The one that made me chuckle the most was when she wrote down when I said in a coaching session, 'Why are you telling me this? Would you like me to take action? Would you like advice on how you can take action? Or are you just offloading and you want me to listen?' She often quotes that to other people without me saying a word, which I find hilarious. In her own words, she said,

> Initially, I was not confident at all that I could meet expectations as I didn't feel I had a 'place' within the school to make an impact or improve

outcomes for the children. I felt that I had been sitting in the shadows of others for a long time. My confidence grew in the past two years when I finally accepted that SLT had every faith and confidence in me and encouraged me to have self-belief. Nobody had ever allowed me to develop my role or empowered me to believe that the work I was doing with the children was having a positive impact. My role has changed significantly in the past two years. I have a good work-life balance and my mental health is good. In fact, being happy in my job and being kept busy improved my mental health as my role gave me more to focus on. I am able to prioritise my tasks by using a basic to do list! If I cannot complete my jobs during school working hours, I choose to complete them during the evening time, ensuring I still make time for my family. I am never afraid to hold my hands up and admit that I have made mistakes.

Supervision – if you know, you know

Safeguarding Supervision with the Safeguarding Children in Education (SCIE) team is extremely useful.

– Clare

If you don't know, then you don't know. I was SENDCo in my school when I was a deputy, and I also supported the head there with safeguarding issues. When I became a head in my last school, I did the majority of the safeguarding stuff, and I found it tough, as there was so much of it. What helped me was the SCIE team and one individual in particular, who we will call VT. She, as innovative as she was and is, decided she would establish in her diary a series of supervision sessions and team us up with other schools in our deprived area.

I cannot tell you the support I felt when I cried about the plight of children in those sessions, when we explored (as a non-judgemental team) the opportunities open to us as school leaders in this crucial area, and discovered things in a collaborative and mutually supportive environment that we did not know, to our advantage.

When I moved and became head at Woodlands, I simply brought supervision and the team with me. I also included my replacement in my last school and therefore broadened the scope to include Woodlands, where it was not included before I got there (it also means I get to see the lovely Kev periodically and check in with him – bonus). Despite the Safeguarding Team that I established at Woodlands growing quickly from being only me, as it was in my last school, to a minimum of three people at any given time, there can never be too many people in a school trained in safeguarding and informed. There is a hive mind in our SLT and corporate knowledge of virtually all scenarios we could possibly come across, as well as the inherent psychological support of working in a group, and yet – external supervision is **vital** in my book. I would never be without it. If the LA implodes and VT is no longer able to offer it, I would buy it in, preferably from her; it is that important to me to protect the minds of my staff, who are dealing with the most horrific things that humans can do to one another on a daily basis, alongside all of the other wonderful stuff they do and offer.

Protect and care for your staff, and watch that proliferate and ripple throughout your school. Righty-ho, what's next? Oh yeah, curriculum!

Takeaways

■ Don't give up on SEND or safeguarding, even on the darkest days. Use networks – there are always suggestions that you haven't considered; ask your networks, capitalise on them.

■ Access or create supervision – it helps support staff when they are dealing with social care issues in school.

■ Protect and care for your staff – physically, emotionally, professionally, mentally.

■ Train as many people as you can to create capacity in core aspects of school – this includes safeguarding and SEND.

Notes

1 Schlepper L (2023) 'The British public are clear-eyed about the problems in social care'. Nuffield Trust blog https://www.nuffieldtrust.org.uk/news-item/the-british-public-are-clear-eyed-about-the-problems-in-social-care#:~:text=Low%20pay%2C%20years%20of%20stagnating,care%20in%20England%20last%20year; https://www.theguardian.com/uk-news/2022/nov/02/state-of-social-care-in-england-never-been-so-bad-social-services-boss-warns.
2 https://www.gov.uk/government/news/fundamental-shift-in-childrens-social-care-set-out; https://www.gov.uk/government/groups/independent-review-of-childrens-social-care.
3 https://www.spectator.co.uk/article/who-cares-the-real-problem-with-britain-s-social-services/.
4 https://frg.org.uk/policy-and-campaigns/the-care-crisis-review/; https://www.local.gov.uk/parliament/briefings-and-responses/independent-review-childrens-social-care-case-change.
5 https://www.communitycare.co.uk/2020/10/09/childrens-trusts-lessons-outsourcing-failing-local-authority-services/; https://epi.org.uk/wp-content/uploads/2017/07/EPI_-Impact_of_Academies_Consolidated_Report-.pdf.
6 https://www.theguardian.com/politics/2019/jun/16/sure-start-numbers-plummet-as-cuts-hit-childrens-services; https://www.suttontrust.com/wp-content/uploads/2018/04/StopStart-FINAL.pdf.
7 https://learning.nspcc.org.uk/safeguarding-child-protection.
8 https://www.thinkuknow.co.uk/; https://www.gov.uk/guidance/prevent-duty-training.
9 https://www.internetmatters.org/schools-esafety/parent-online-support-pack-teachers/.

10 https://explore-education-statistics.service.gov.uk/find-statistics/special-educational-needs-in-england.
11 https://assets.publishing.service.gov.uk/government/uploads/system/uploads/attachment_data/file/1139561/SEND_and_alternative_provision_improvement_plan.pdf; https://www.theguardian.com/education/2023/mar/02/special-needs-services-children-england-plan; https://researchbriefings.files.parliament.uk/documents/SN07020/SN07020.pdf.
12 https://www.christinamitchell.co.uk/thrive-in-education.

Good reads

Cairns, K. & Cairns, B. (2016). *Attachment, Trauma and Resilience: Therapeutic Caring for Children*. Coram BAAF.
Forster, C.E.A. (2018). *You're Being Ridiculous! The Fun and Frenzy of Fostering*.
Moore, S.R. (2022). *Peaceful Discipline: Story Teaching, Brain Science & Better Behavior*.
The A&F Podcast @TheAandFPodcast.

7 Implied and specified tasks

Who tells us what we need to do and how?

When Vic joined Woodlands, a clear and honest account of the areas of significant need were outlined to us as class teachers and subject leads by her. We recognised as a team this would not be a 'fix overnight' job and that it was going to be a journey and evolution for the school.

– Jen.

Implied and specified tasks

I find this a scream, but we headteachers, as custodians of our nation's schools and educational establishments, are classed as role models for the communities we serve. Members of the public rightly have high expectations of us, given our influential position in relation to educational professionals, children and young people for whom we are responsible. I think this is right. I just wonder at the comparability between this expectation and the expectation of influential members of Parliament – I suspect this comparability lies in the Nolan Principles.[1] Food for thought.

Our leadership, therefore our ability to lead effectively, is classed as a significant factor in ensuring high-quality teaching and pupil attainment in our schools. Not only that, we are supposed to also provide a holistic, positive and enriching experience for pupils; nurture and keep them safe; prepare them for the next steps; and give them a foundation of character and social conscience. OK, so how does the existential translate to what we *actually* do, are meant to do and could physically do on a daily basis? To help us all know and understand, the government have helpfully created 'the headteachers' standards',[2] which lays out how we can meet the high expectations that everyone has of us; although, to be fair, they are non-statutory and don't really tell us anything.

DOI: 10.4324/9781003440000-8

Headteacher standards!

There are ten headteachers' standards, with the first six built on those enshrined within the teachers' standards, and the final four resolutely focussed on leadership responsibilities explicit for us headteachers. A handy list, no doubt, of what we are supposed to oversee, but still not really offering any ideas about the *how*.

1. School culture (teachers' standard 1)

2. Teaching (teachers' standards 2 and 4)

3. Curriculum and assessment (teachers' standards 3 and 6)

4. Behaviour (teachers' standard 7)

5. Additional and special educational needs (teachers' standard 5)

6. Professional development (teachers' standard 4)

7. Organisational management

8. School improvement

9. Working in partnership

10. Governance and accountability

So, who helps with the 'how'? First and foremost, I think, is positive mentoring from your headteacher when you are a deputy, but long before that when you are perhaps in another SLT role, or when you are a middle leader, or a teacher or student teacher. Alongside this, I think, sits professional accreditation (well, come on, I would say that; I love studying!) such as NPQH.[3] On that topic, if you are a headteacher and you are **not** coaching your leaders of the future (at every level) to understand the nature of their role and giving them opportunities to develop the requisite skills (including failing on occasion) and to challenge their thinking either through practice and reflection or professional study (preferably both), then something is amiss (see number 6 of the headteachers' standards!).

Broadly speaking about the headteachers standards, the explicit things I do and did at Woodlands and before are matched against them anyway and are contained in the chapters outlined here; the specified tasks are evident, but there are more. Many are implied and will be covered organically throughout the book: school culture and behaviour (Chapter 12), teaching and curriculum this chapter, assessment (Chapter 8), additional and special educational needs (Chapter 6), professional development (Chapter 10), organisational management (Chapter 11), school improvement (the whole book!), working in partnership (Chapter 6) and governance and accountability (Chapter 5).

Headteacher standards 2 and 3: teaching and curriculum

What did I do at Woodlands that made the difference? Amongst other general and systemic things, I specified that each subject must have coherence and that none were more important than the other for us to authentically offer a rich and varied curriculum for the pupils of Woodlands. In other words, I laid out the vision.

Whilst the initial focus was on maths and literacy, naturally, this would set the scene (prove the route for those military-minded bods) and shape how we would work systematically through each of the subjects to arrive at a place where all subject leads were confident, knowledgeable and empowered enough to speak about their subject, where planning was coherent and effective, made sense to all staff and pupils and was shared in an appropriate way with parents and external agencies. I set the goals. We would work as a team to ensure that assessments were realistic and provided us with useful data and usable information that would support the planning cycle. I reminded staff about how we would achieve them – as a team.

The headlines? OK, I will use maths as an example and share with you the headline information that Lottie, maths lead, and her oppo in Early Years Foundation Stage (EYFS), Annica, compiled for their subject overview this past year; it was useful as a handrail for Ofsted and helped them to feel strong when in their subject leader 'discussion' with the inspectors but is useful mainly to keep them current and to be able to share the journey of maths in our school with staff who become involved in the subject.

It took ages to do and was not all done at once; I am not going to lie. But it has proven invaluable and can be added to. This coming year, it will be Daisy who will take over from Lottie, and Annica will remain in the role so that there is always an experienced person leading who has a handle on the narrative behind the written content of what is contained in the following. This is to build capacity, to elevate Daisy's leadership experience in a core subject and also to bridge a leadership gap created by maternity leave. Daisy will be coached and mentored in her role as a temporary SLT member and also maths lead during the coming year, and this will strengthen both the staff as a collaborative and Daisy as an individual. Sitting behind the headlines that follow are a multitude of implied, explicit and repeated tasks that must be done to successfully accomplish what the team decided must be accomplished; you will see what I mean (but we would be here all day if I verbatim explained each one in detail).

There is one of these documents for each subject in our school, all of which have been crafted in the same way. Consistency.

Headlines are, in sections, as follows:

- Context

- Focus and Priorities

- Quality of Education:

- Intent and what the role of the subject leader might be in this

- Implementation and what the role of the subject leader might be in this

- Impact and what the role of the subject leader might be in this

■ Behaviour and Attitudes

■ Personal Development

■ EYFS

■ Leadership and Management

Context

Start simple: How long have you been leading this subject? What are your strengths in this area to lead?

I have been on a range of mathematics courses including three full day sessions on improving the teaching of mathematics with Cheshire East and subject leader development courses with maths specialists First4Maths. I have worked closely with Cheshire West and Chester (CWAC) and with SLEs, and developed my leadership skills through their support. I have also worked closely with Maths specialists from the Wirral and Cheshire Maths Hub to develop the mastery approach at Woodlands.

– Lottie

I have taught in EYFS for many years and I have a deep understanding how these young children learn. I have been moderated in all areas of learning with colleagues in the EYFS. Throughout my teaching I have supported Maths leads in the EYFS and throughout school. Last year I was responsible for the maths planning for the EYFS in the spring term. I am now keen to develop a deeper understanding of Maths throughout the key stages. I work closely with Lottie and she is helping with my understanding of the KS2 curriculum.

– Annica

Have you invested in resources this year; if so, what and why; if not, why not?

Has Ofsted produced a subject report or blog in your area? If yes, is this reflected in your action plan? The maths research review[4]

Have there been any national initiatives in your subject this year?

A recent influence for mathematics in education – not just in the last year – has been 'Mathematics Guidance: Key Stages 1 and 2' (non-statutory guidance for the National Curriculum (NC) in England, June 2020), which links to the Ready to Progress (RTP) criteria (as stated in the research review).

- The National Numeracy Strategy

- The Mathematics Teaching Exchange

- The Teaching for Mastery Programme (as related to the Mathematics Teaching Exchange) – National Centre of Excellence for Teaching Mathematics (NCETM)

What has happened since September 2018 when the current Headteacher took over, and specifically the 2019 Ofsted Report, in your subject?

- EYFS, Key Stage 1 (KS1) and Key Stage 2 (KS2) results published in July 2019. Significantly improved attainment across key stages (see CWAC) after one academic year.

- Worked closely with new SLEs to continue to embed White Rose Maths (WRM) at Woodlands and identify teachers/year groups in need of additional support. Rigorous monitoring schedule in place from April, summer term, 2019.

- Closures due to Covid-19 in the spring/summer of 2020 meant that the curriculum was not taught and monitored as rigorously (focus on key worker childcare). When schools returned, huge emphasis was placed on baseline: capturing the gaps and planning a recovery curriculum. A recovery curriculum was then established.

- Embedded updated WRM from Y1–Y6 2020–1. Lessons considered prior learning needed to achieve small steps in their current year. Teachers tracked skills back.

- Second school closures due to Covid-19. Maths taught in line with expectations per key stage (voiced over WRM materials, additional support and interventions still took place).

- First4Maths recovery documents supported teachers in identifying key NC objectives to be taught and priorities across the spring and summer terms. Ongoing use of this document has been adapted to meet the needs of the school and to address inclusion of RTP criteria.

- Two Ofsted monitoring visits (one virtual).

- School joined Developing Mastery with the Wirral and Cheshire Maths Hub (NCETM programme) August 2021.

- Ofsted inspection in January 2023.

Focus – subject priorities

How does your subject link to whole school priorities?

SDP: Many of the key areas of the SDP, such as 'quality of education', link to mathematics:

Intent – Ensure that the curriculum is coherently planned and sequenced towards cumulatively sufficient knowledge and skills for future learning. All areas of implementation in mathematics link to SDP.

Impact – Children will develop detailed knowledge and skills across the curriculum and, as a result, achieve well (both 'in-year' and also in 'end of key stage' tests).

Key Improvement Priority for all staff PM – Improve the progress of all children in reading, writing and numeracy across the school.

Our previous Section 5 Ofsted Report (May 2019) stated the following:

■ In mathematics, the quality of teaching is improving and is beginning to address the gaps in pupils' knowledge, skills and understanding. Effective training has ensured a consistent approach to teaching different methods of calculations.

■ Opportunities are increasingly provided for pupils to deepen their understanding through reasoning and problem-solving. Although pupils, particularly the most able pupils, tackle these effectively, teachers fail to draw out from pupils their methods or insist on appropriate mathematical vocabulary.

■ School performance information and work in pupils' books show that key stage 2 pupils' mathematics knowledge and understanding are improving, particularly their calculation skills. However, opportunities to deepen their understanding through reasoning and problem-solving are not consistent across year groups and classes.

These areas are all identified in the action plan with actions noted, and this is reviewed termly and annually.

What are the development priorities reflected in your action plan?

■ Raising the number of children working at the expected standard and above in mathematics in KS1 and KS2 to be at least in line with or better than the national average

■ Raising the percentage of children achieving at least national expectations for maths in EYFS (Early Learning Goals (ELG) for number and shape, space and measure)

■ Raising the number of children achieving the combined standard in reading, writing and maths for expected attainment and greater depth attainment in Y2 and Y6

■ Improving the quality of teaching of mathematics to raise attainment and accelerate progress across all cohorts/groups of learners

Drive to improve:

■ 'Maths talk' and children's use of mathematical vocabulary from EYFS – Y6

- Fluency and recall of number facts and multiplication tables

- Children's ability to reason and problem-solve effectively across year groups progressively

- Providing ample opportunity to develop reasoning and problem-solving

The aforementioned drives to improve were directly identified following the pandemic and school closures due to Covid-19.

Outline in Ofsted-friendly order: quality of education summary

Intent

How does the curriculum in your subject set out the knowledge and skills that pupils will gain at each stage?

In maths, small steps are strategically taught in a progressive order. Children learn about number and place value and then addition and subtraction, multiplication and divisions, fractions, etc. The fundamental knowledge and understanding of number and place value is applied from Term 1 onwards and repeated over time in a spiral form. In Y6, for example, application of knowledge of place value (Autumn 1) and multiplication and division (Autumn 2) is essential for work on fractions, decimals and multiplication (FDP) in the spring term. Teachers remind children how the skills link from previous units and year groups. We follow the EYFS framework and development matters.

How does the whole school approach inform your subject and the sequence of learning that supports the acquisition of knowledge that you want the children to know?

We teach maths across the school from EYFS to Y6 by following the small steps of progression as guided by the WRM scheme (being embedded in EYFS), an approach developed by the Maths Hub and the National Centre for Excellence in Teaching Mathematics. Fluency, reasoning and problem-solving are at the heart of the approach. It uses the Concrete Pictorial Abstract (CPA) approach to support children's learning and progression. A concrete approach refers to the physical resources that children can manipulate to support their learning; examples include clocks, place value counters and bead strings. A pictorial approach refers to the visual models that can be used to support the understanding of methods and concepts. Finally, the abstract approach is the written method that the progression of skills and knowledge works towards; an example of this is the written method of addition. By embedding this approach, we are allowing pupils to spend enough time to fully explore a topic and reinforcing it with practice before moving on to the next one. All ideas are built on previous knowledge, and pupils have ample opportunity to develop relationships between topics.

How is the curriculum planned and sequenced so that new knowledge and skills build on what has been taught before and towards its clearly defined end points? How do you enable children to learn more and remember more?

Across school, ALL subjects are planned and sequenced progressively. They build on key knowledge. In maths, knowledge is sequenced progressively, supported by WRM small steps, to ensure new skills are taught and mastered before moving on, and then skills are revisited through further units of work in a spiral. As mentioned, children require and discuss the prior knowledge which will be needed for new learning. Children are given opportunities to recap skills in time away from maths lessons, including morning tasks and cross-curricular work, as well as through whole school celebrations such as TTRockstars and Number Day. All of these additional opportunities to celebrate and practice mathematical skills, as well as the spiral approach, allow children to gain sticky knowledge and remember more.

Ofsted review reference – The initial focus of any sequence of learning should be that pupils are familiar with the facts and methods that will form the strategies taught and applied later in the topic sequence.

How do you ensure that the curriculum is ambitious for all pupils?

We provide opportunities to challenge and extend the understanding of all pupils through WRM resources in addition to I See Reasoning, Mathematical Challenges for the More Able, NCETM and NRICH. We teach towards a mastery approach so that all children have the opportunity to master the topic being taught in a stage-appropriate manner.

Where necessary, we will use WRM documents and DfE RTP Criteria to track back skills and still teach ambitiously towards these skills through our recovery curriculum, and children are challenged stage-appropriately.

How did you design the curriculum to meet the needs of your pupils? How do you enable pupils with EAL, SEND, vulnerable pupils and disadvantaged pupils to access the curriculum? How does the curriculum reflect the school's local context by addressing typical gaps in pupils' knowledge and skills?

Thematic and carefully planned curriculum for all pupils. Beginning with high-quality literacy texts and working in a thematic approach where possible – linking areas to develop sticky knowledge and a wider understanding. Cojo's character curriculum layers over and develops all children's character development in preparation for their future. The skills they develop are essential to all areas of learning: maths-rich environment from EYFS up, prioritisation of early number and mathematical knowledge, baseline early to identify specific areas of need in maths, interventions, tracking back within the progression of skills and gaps identified early and rigorous monitoring/pupil progress meetings to drive progress forwards.

Do you follow any commercial schemes? If so, which one, and how does it meet the needs of your pupils?

We teach maths across the school from EYFS to Y6 by following the small steps of progression as guided by the WRM scheme and White Rose premium (being embedded in EYFS), an approach developed by the Maths Hub and the National Centre for Excellence in Teaching Mathematics. Fluency, reasoning and problem-solving are at the heart of the approach. It uses the CPA approach to support children's learning and progression (as discussed earlier).

How does your subject promote reading?

Mathematical vocabulary is taught and discussed with children. It is modelled to children from all members of staff, and support materials such as the NCETM RTP presentations provide staff with the scaffolded questions and explicit knowledge which should be used.

How do you enable parents to support their children's learning?

What might the role of subject leader be in terms of intent?

- Having oversight of curriculum coverage and ensuring that the curriculum meets national requirements
- Ensuring that colleagues are aware of expectations
- Internal and external moderation practices
- Liaison with SLEs and SLT
- Planning for future curriculum development
- Follow-up and monitoring
- Ensuring that appropriate resources are in place to deliver an ambitious and academically challenging curriculum

Implementation

How is the curriculum in your subject taught and assessed in order to support pupils to build their knowledge and to apply that knowledge as skills?

What is the quality of learning in your subject, and how do you know? Where would you see the most effective teaching and learning? How is best practice shared across the school?

The quality of maths teaching is good across key stages, as evidenced in learning walks, formal observations and book scrutinies. A rigorous monitoring schedule is in place to assess the quality of teaching and learning through the aforementioned.

Moderation in-house and moderation within CWAC also help us monitor the quality of learning at Woodlands. Maths Hub subject specialists support the moderation of judgements of teaching and learning.

Effective teaching of maths can be seen across the key stages, and individual teachers have completed additional mathematics training, including mathematics specialist teacher programme (MAST). Good practice in maths has been identified by the SLE and members of the SLT as evidenced in feedback.

Staff meetings, moderation and briefings are used to share good practices of staff. Teachers observe best practices in school, especially early career teachers (ECTs).

What end points is the curriculum building towards, and how do you check that pupils are learning and remembering what they need to know in order to be able to reach those end points?

For all children to be confident mathematicians who are fluent in numbers and successful problem-solvers who are able to reason and apply mathematical concepts accurately, teachers must ensure full coverage of the NC objectives progressively through small steps, recapping key learning over time in order to ensure key knowledge is remembered. Teachers also understand that in the long term, beyond Y6, mathematics provides important tools for work in fields such as engineering, physics, architecture, medicine and business, and it also is an important tool for opening new doors to further study and employment.

How do you know what children have learned and remembered?

Regular assessment (both formative and summative), WRM end-of-unit assessments and ongoing evaluation against objectives using the First4Maths document. Regular and repeated fluency recaps (including flashback 4/fluent in 5) to recap prior knowledge and keep returning to it over time. As subject lead, I can monitor Insight sliders and end-of-unit/term assessments, follow up with pupil progress meetings involving further book looks and use the First4Maths document to ensure key objectives are repeated and reminded in different contexts.

How does assessment enable teachers to check learning in your subject?

Regular formative assessment within class and checking-in allows teachers to see if children are on track to meet small, progressive steps. End-of-unit and term assessments are also used for an overarching view of the methods and knowledge children have remembered over time. Analysis of assessments and formative assessments mean that planning is adapted to meet the needs of the children. Insight tracking of small steps/objectives also allows teachers to see gaps within knowledge and identify children off track.

How do you support children who are behind their peers to catch up?

Across the school, teachers 'baseline-assess' core subjects. An early baseline is used to assess which children may be behind their peers. Planning is adapted based on tracking back the progression of skills and also tracking back using RTP criteria to ensure prior knowledge is secure. Timely interventions and pre-teaching are used to intervene and secure objectives, especially RTP objectives.

How do you monitor the quality of teaching and learning?

A rigorous, systematic monitoring schedule is in place across all subjects. In maths, regular book looks, learning walks and lesson observations are used to monitor the quality of teaching and learning in line with the maths action plan and school SDP and SEF.

Across the whole school, we have a rigorous monitoring schedule to assess the quality of teaching and learning. In maths, we use the following:

Regular learning walks, formal observations and external support with observations, such as with SLE or Maths Hub support. SLT analyses summative assessment information (termly) and follows up with class teachers through pupil progress meetings. Pupils' work/book looks are scruitinised. Teachers' planning is monitored (including long-term subject coverage). All of the above leads to timely interventions and changes to CPD/support in place with the SLE/Maths Hubs.

What have you done to improve teaching in your subject?

- Specific training provided to all teachers, EYFS-Y6, to support priority improvements, such as improving problem-solving and reasoning. Staff training run by SLE x 2
- Training provided by First4Maths to support teachers new to Y2/Y6
- Training provided by First4Maths for the subject leader to improve subject knowledge and understanding of monitoring maths as a subject effectively times two (First4Maths)
- ECTs supported before the start of the school year times two maths workshops to support planning and reasoning, as well as problem-solving subject knowledge
- ECT support courses with professionals such as the First4Maths Team will continue to be booked where needed
- Subject leader delivered staff meetings on maths and improving planning and assessments, especially linked to the recovery curriculum

What training have you had in order to develop your subject knowledge?

- 'I have been on a range of mathematics courses including three full day sessions on improving the teaching of mathematics with Cheshire East and subject leader development courses with maths specialists First4Maths. I have worked closely with CWAC and with SLEs, and developed my leadership skills through their support. I am also working closely with Maths specialists from the Wirral and Cheshire Maths Hub to develop the mastery approach at Woodlands'.

– Lottie

■ 'I have attended a range of online courses on the new EYFS curriculum and I am now keen to attend some specific training on Maths in the EYFS. I will be working with Lottie on developing the links between EYFS and KS1 and 2'.

– Annica

How do you share this with colleagues?

Staff meetings, information sometimes fed back from me to all members of SLT to be shared in key stage briefings, workshops and informal meetings, one-on-one sessions. Email/Twitter sharing is good practice.

What CPD has been put in place?

As mentioned, learning walks, book looks, formal observations, planning monitoring and data analysis. Key year groups identified for support and targeted support given where appropriate, e.g., to ECTs or groups with a higher percentage of children off track to meet expected standard (EXS) or above.

What might the role of the subject leader be in terms of implementation?

■ Ensuring that teaching within the subject is effective and enables the acquisition of key knowledge and skills by building on prior learning sequenced

■ Leading CPD, providing ongoing guidance and support to colleagues

■ Developing assessment – how to check that pupils are learning and remembering the planned curriculum

■ Effective use of resources to impact outcomes (staff, resources, time)

■ Being an advocate for the subject. Championing the subject with colleagues, parents and pupils

Impact

What are the outcomes that pupils achieve as a result of the education they have received?

Confident mathematicians, fluent in number and able to reason mathematically and problem-solve, development of *children's appreciation of the beauty and power of mathematics and a sense of enjoyment and curiosity about the subject* (NC 2014) and ensure children understand the importance of maths in everyday life and the world around them, including the careers that revolve around mathematics (NC – critical to science, technology and engineering, and necessary for financial literacy and most forms of employment).

What do external and internal assessment information tell you about how effectively the curriculum is being implemented at Woodlands?

SATs results across the core subjects in KS1/KS2, external moderation, the new EYFS baseline, phonics screening and times tables check in Y4 are used to inform us of where the school is in relation to national and local schools. External moderation of maths and book scrutinies with external providers' quality assures our judgement of how the curriculum has been implemented.

Internal assessments on Insight, objective-based and end-of-unit-based, provide subject leaders with an overview of curriculum coverage and are monitored regularly to ensure CPD/staff support and interventions can be put in place.

Have you had to make any changes as a result of assessment data?

In maths, in line with the SDP, action plan and national initiatives, we have begun to embed the RTP criteria in maths.

Ofsted review link:

> Summative assessments of learning need to provide easily comparable information to all stakeholders, including parents and the pupils themselves, on a regular basis. Module exams provide short-term goals and a sense of achievement, but they can promote a 'just in time' approach to learning that means that knowledge is jettisoned soon after tests are taken. End-of-course examinations give greater assurance that the learning of content is long term. This suggests that a mixture of approaches is best: regular tests of content recently taught and learned and an objective, fair and accurate summative assessment at the end of the year or course.

How do *you* moderate?

What might the role of the subject leader be in terms of impact?

- Monitoring the effectiveness of teaching and the impact on learning. Checking that pupils are learning and remembering the planned curriculum. Ensuring that support is in place for pupils to catch up – monitoring the impact

- Evaluating and summarising all aspects of the subject to define next steps for improvement

- Feedback next steps

- Planning for next steps for staff, bespoke training or support where required

Outline in Ofsted-friendly order: behaviour and attitudes summary

How does the curriculum in your subject ensure pupils' motivation and embed positive attitudes to learning?

The curriculum in maths is supported by our character curriculum and Cojos' key character traits, especially teamwork, resilience and perseverance. The curriculum is systematically planned in small steps to allow children to learn declarative and procedural knowledge and there is time planned to revisit key knowledge. Children are then taught to apply these skills to reasoning and problem-solving (across a range of different contexts/question types).

Link to Ofsted review:

> Pupils are more likely to develop a positive attitude towards mathematics if they are successful in it, especially if they are aware of their success... Some pupils become anxious about mathematics. It is not the nature of the subject but failure to acquire knowledge that is at the root of the anxiety pathway. The origins of this anxiety may have even been present at the start of a pupil's academic journey. However, if teachers ensure that anxious pupils acquire core mathematical knowledge and start to experience success, those pupils will begin to associate the subject with enjoyment and motivation.

Outline in Ofsted-friendly order: personal development summary

Are there any opportunities for extra-curricular activities linked to your subject? If so, what is the range, quality and take-up?

Times tables clubs in Y3/Y4 (identified children invited). Maths boosters for Y6 focusing on reasoning and problem-solving (from Jan onwards) – previously very popular with 90%+ children attending. 'Times Tables Battles' across local schools and within school through TTRockstars. STEAM festival Y5/6.

As a subject leader, in your opinion, how does your subject contribute to pupils' personal development?

It helps develop their character traits such as resilience, teamwork and problem-solving, which link to Cojos. It also develops curiosity in maths and the wider world. Teachers promote this through maths.

How does your subject promote British values through the curriculum, assemblies, wider opportunities, visits, discussions and literature?

Promote democracy through mathematical debates and discussions. Listening to others and agreeing/disagreeing. Develop key character traits such as resilience and perseverance through problem-solving/reasoning and getting 'unstuck' in maths.

How does your subject develop pupils' character?

Up to the individual school.

How does your subject promote equality of opportunity and diversity?

We have developed, and continue to develop, a mastery approach to mathematics in which all children can achieve and will achieve their best. We aim to leave no child behind in maths and support those who are working below their peers to still be challenged in a stage-appropriate manner (following progression of skills).

How does your subject develop cultural capital?

Subject assemblies and a focus on key figures in mathematics. Introduce and remind children of inspirational figures who are/were the best in their field. The acquisition of number knowledge contributes to foundations for children to build on in later life and therefore supports the development of cultural capital.

How does the curriculum in your subject develop the knowledge and skills that pupils need in order to take advantage of opportunities, responsibilities and experiences of later life and so address social disadvantage?

Promoting the importance of 'why' in maths. Discussing how the knowledge we gain each year provides us with a deeper understanding of key concepts in maths.

Any evidence from pupil interviews?

Put your own in here.

Outline in Ofsted-friendly order: EYFS summary

How does your subject start in early years?

It starts from nursery and progresses into reception.

How does the school plan the curriculum linked to your subject? How have you helped to shape the EYFS curriculum?

EYFS is now following the same scheme as the rest of the school.[5]

How does the curriculum support pupils to develop their skills, knowledge and vocabulary?

The curriculum is progressive and follows the same CPA approach as the rest of the school. By embedding this approach, we are allowing pupils to spend enough time to fully explore a topic and then reinforcing it with practice before moving on to the next one. All ideas are built on previous knowledge, and pupils have ample opportunity to develop relationships between topics. The children will then develop a strong grounding in numbers, which is essential so that all children develop the necessary building blocks to excel mathematically.

How does the curriculum prepare pupils for Y1 and the NC?

The curriculum provides the building blocks for the children to have a deep understanding of numbers to ten and relationships between each number. It provides opportunities for the children to look for patterns between numbers and develop mathematical vocabulary, which will then be built upon in Y1 and the rest of the school.

How is your subject taught in EYFS?

Maths is taught through daily inputs, small-group, adult-led guided group work, enhancements, child-initiated activities and play inside and outside. Maths is also taught through other areas of the EYFS curriculum as links are made to different topics. This includes Pathways to Write Literacy units.

How do you, as a subject leader, know about progression in early years?

Annica – 'I have the privilege of teaching both Reception and Nursery children as well as planning the maths across EYFS. We work closely as a team to plot what needs to be covered and when. This enables me to check for progression and coverage of maths in EYFS. I share this routinely with Lottie'.

How do you, as a subject leader, know about progression across the age ranges?

Annica – 'I have attended staff meetings on Maths and I feel I have some knowledge of maths progression across the age ranges. However, I am keen to develop a deeper understanding of this progression. I will therefore access more training courses and carry out some learning walks throughout school to help with this. I will be working closely with teachers in other phases to further my knowledge of Maths'.

How do you ensure that children learn more and remember more?

The curriculum is well sequenced and covers numbers in depth, also through assessment checkpoints, including baseline assessment.

How do practitioners support children to catch up and keep up?

Using Tapestry to record observations and make notes about the children's progress enables staff to plan for different groups and to differentiate work, as well as for leaders to assign staff to booster groups to provide catch-up work.

How well are children doing in EYFS?

Outline in Ofsted-friendly order: leadership and management summary

How have you been developed as a subject leader? What CPD opportunities have you had in your current role?

I have been on a range of mathematics courses including three full day sessions on improving the teaching of mathematics with Cheshire East and subject leader development courses with maths specialists First4Maths. I have worked closely with CWAC and with SLEs, and developed my leadership skills through their support. I am also working closely with Maths specialists from the Wirral and Cheshire Maths Hub to develop the mastery approach at Woodlands.

– Lottie

How do you check the quality of education within your subject?

Working closely with the LA and with the Maths Hub to conduct learning reviews, book looks and observations. Gaining feedback from external providers and SLT.

How do you identify and implement improvements?

Data – which should be analysed and may be published, plus 'in-house', external reports and other contextual information, all contribute to the SDP, and from there, they inform PM from the headteacher down. Key priorities in mathematics identified through prior published reports and data are included in Ofsted section 5.

Can you outline a significant improvement on which you have led and its impact?

Embedding WRM and TTRS at Woodlands. Improved fluency and recall of TTRS, improved pupil outcomes.

How do you hold other staff to account? How are you held to account by the SLT and governors?

Rigorous monitoring of subjects through the strategies already mentioned. Support is put in place following consultation and coaching from the SLT where appropriate. Report to SLT through termly reports, PM reviews, formal and informal meetings and data sharing. Discuss maths at Woodlands regularly with the nominated governor who supports policies as well as with extra-curricular mathematics activities. Governors have an active and supporting role in shaping the curriculum and hold us to account when looking at the impact of the curriculum.

Is a policy in place?

Calculation policy and marking of maths policy in place. These were developed and refined with the support of SLT.

For each section, there were also 'next steps', as you can imagine, which complete the cycle of plan, do, review, plan…

Formula for systemic review

This chapter has given an overview of how I approached 'fixing' each of the curriculum tasks on the lists I generated (seen in Chapter 2), which ensured the overall improvement agenda was workable, cyclical and embedded, and begins to highlight for the reader the systems that facilitated the actions that needed to be taken for us to be successful. Although this will differ in each school, in Woodlands, subject and senior leaders established systems based on the needs of the pupils, which they assessed and planned for. They recorded it as an Ofsted-friendly document that would easily underpin any SEF judgements I made and support the governors' understanding of where we believed our school to be based on the evidence we had. This is different from doing things for Ofsted, as I am sure you will agree. And there was much more besides the systems, which you will see in the next section, but before then, a little reflection.

As with children in school, they rarely remember a maths lesson but will remember the extra-curricular and special events; staff are the same. During the last five years, with her brilliance in leading maths, the CPD that Lottie enjoyed that she felt has changed her as a practitioner or individual isn't the maths CPD she has participated in but something altogether different. We are not just here to create robots who teach our children, like robots, to gather and store information like computers.

> Inner-Armour training was very interesting to understand my own personality traits, how I may/may not respond to situations and events and the importance of having different perspectives/personalities within a team who see things differently. It also allowed me to evaluate how happy I was in different areas of my life and what needed to change in order to achieve a little more balance. North Star training was also very interesting and helped me to be more future-focused and the steps that I would need to take.
>
> – *Lottie.*

Takeaways

For each subject that needed review, the following was considered in our school – for consistency and maximal impact, and for ease when pulling them all together for an overall evaluation:

- Context
- Focus and Priorities
- Quality of Education:
    - Intent and what the role of the subject leader might be in this
    - Implementation and what the role of the subject leader might be in this
    - Impact and what the role of the subject leader might be in this
- Behaviour and Attitudes

- Personal Development

- EYFS

- Leadership and Management

Notes

1 https://www.gov.uk/government/publications/the-7-principles-of-public-life/the-7-principles-of-public-life--2.
2 https://www.gov.uk/government/publications/national-standards-of-excellence-for-headteachers/headteachers-standards-2020.
3 https://www.outstandingleaders.org/npqh.
4 https://www.gov.uk/government/publications/research-review-series-mathematics/research-review-series-mathematics.
5 https://assets.publishing.service.gov.uk/government/uploads/system/uploads/attachment_data/file/974907/EYFS_framework_-_March_2021.pdf.

Good reads

Blatchford, R. (2019). *The Primary Curriculum Leader's Handbook*. John Catt Educational LTD.
Glazzard, J. & Stones, S. (2021). *An Ambitious Primary School Curriculum*. Critical Publishing.
Kara, B. (2020). *A Little Guide for Teachers: Diversity in Schools*. Corwin UK.
Kenyon, G. (2019). *The Arts in Primary Education: Breathing Life, Colour and Culture into the Curriculum*. Bloomsbury.
Learning Matters. (2023). *The National Curriculum and the Teachers' Standards: Now Includes the CCF & the ECF (Ready to Teach)*. Learning Matters.
Ogier, S. (2022). *A Broad and Balanced Curriculum in Primary Schools: Educating the Whole Child (Exploring the Primary Curriculum)*. Learning Matters.
Sharma, L. (2020). *Curriculum to Classroom: A Handbook to Prompt Thinking Around Primary Curriculum Design and Delivery*. John Catt Educational LTD.
Waters, M. & Banks, C. (2022). *A Curious Curriculum: Teaching Foundation Subjects Well*. Crown House Publishing.

Revising the main effort
Taking stock and resetting the collective focus

I used the SDP and the SEF as well as the Ofsted report (2019) to prioritise areas of improvement for Maths and used guidance and CPD materials to support the implementation of these tasks. A mistake I have seen made in the past would be trying to make too many changes or improvements at once. This led to less improvement in some areas. From this, I now know a gradual process of change with clear vision, several key ingredients and monitoring are necessary. I have learnt that without a clear vision and key steps to get there being gradually implemented, the impact can be inconsistent or not as desired.

– Lottie

Revising the main effort – taking stock and creating opportunities

Much of school improvement, this book contends, is cyclical, and (at varying stages) therefore, elements of it are revisited to ensure that the strategies employed are proving successful. At these times, thinking about both the actions taken to date and the effects observed as a result is really valuable.

At Woodlands, we have utilised many strategies over the years: from compelling members of the LA to support us, to developing workforce capability and competence, from empowering staff and promoting confidence, authority, accountability and responsibility, to exploiting actionable intelligence and information about birth rates and SEND provision.

We have reassured all stakeholders in order to restore confidence and dispel fear, thus stabilising the staff and creating security that is sustainable by revisiting our systems and validating our views (internally and externally). This practice has also underpinned the creation of our school ethos.

All of these things we have done, but we have had to adapt and revisit some of our strategies, and this chapter will discuss examples of why and how we have done this.

DOI: 10.4324/9781003440000-9

Review one – post-Ofsted 2019

Very early on, following the original Ofsted inspection in April 2019, I realised that there would be no respite, no 'let up' in pace; we could not afford a moment to relax. I remember thinking, 'Yes, we might have retained the Requires Improvement, we might have received a 'Good' for strong leadership, and I might have received a letter from Amanda Spielman patting me on the back, but that really was irrelevant when I considered the work we still had to do'. All we had was the beginnings. Imagine starting a fire with just tinder and sticks; it takes a lot of effort expenditure and the right materials, and even then, it can take AGES and a lot of physical labour, and all you see to begin with is a tiny curl of smoke. We were at that tiny curl of smoke stage after two terms and with inspection one complete.

An 'RI' judgement from Ofsted with 'Good' for leadership was the very best outcome we could have hoped for – the absolute platinum standard; it was the first hurdle, and it bought us the time that we needed to focus on the deeper and more profound foundations of what school improvement was really about. Personally, I knew it was precarious after two terms, with the imminent departure of the funded non-class-based SLT and the financial backing of the LA, to think that we had turned the school around. If I had relaxed at that point, we would not have succeeded. To do so would've been more a decision based on ego than reality, so I remained pragmatic, and whilst everybody celebrated that we hadn't been forced into Inadequate (worse still, Special Measures and academy status) overnight. I was already focussed on the subsequent objective – the new Ofsted framework that came into practice in September of that year. Essentially, we had a term's reprieve before we were back in a window and under a new framework focussed on a broad curriculum; plus, we had only just put in a framework for maths and literacy that was bearing fruit, and I had to keep those plates spinning whilst also looking for the next threat.

We all knew that we had lots to do. I was excited, in a way, that the drive behind what we were going to do, which was in tune with what I wanted to create anyway, would also satisfy some new Ofsted expectations in terms of curriculum! YESSS! That summer, the entire term was about experimentation, about finding the joy of teaching for the staff and about injecting the joy of learning into everything that we did for the children. I was thrilled at the prospect and refused to see the scope of the issue as anything other than an opportunity coupled with a logistical issue that needed to be sorted out.

All the ways that we successfully experimented and refined our work were underpinned by one thing: collaboration. Whilst we remained in a vulnerable position, we still nevertheless wanted to collaborate with schools nearby. We were sadly tainted with the second RI judgement; there was nothing I could do about that other than accept it and ride the storm because what was on the outside certainly did not reflect the graft taking place on the inside.

The school remained very low in our area in terms of respect from the local community; everyone had heard of the demise of the school in terms of Ofsted rating, and nobody really wanted their children to join us. That was evident in the reception applications that spring and the number of disgruntled parents we won over who had received our school for their child on the basis that we were closer to them and their preferred school of choice was oversubscribed. Win them over we did though, one by one. It was galling, however, that the local newspaper would celebrate each year (as all local newspapers do) the pointless and futile 'league table', and we, of course, were at the bottom.

I knew this would change in time, but we all needed to have faith that good things would come to us, and when nothing is tangible, faith is everything. Staff began to have faith in me in the summer of 2019, despite me INSISTING we have Y6 moderation, perhaps because of it, but I believe it was as we solidified some of our practice. By then, we had a firm monitoring schedule in place to track the early impact of the implementation of our strategies in core subjects, supported by staff meetings which began to empower and inform, train and educate our staff. Staff worked as whole teams, there was no differentiation from TA to higher-level teaching assistant (HLTA), student teacher to teacher – everyone was trained and informed in a rigorously consistent way, as you saw evidenced in the previous chapter.

Post-Ofsted review – what next and why?

This was where we began to revise our main effort, which in September 2018 was originally to retain RI, to obtain a GOOD. To do this, we began to get creative. We worked on a project with Chester Zoo and a collaboration of schools in our area. This meant children could experiment and explore art, issues to do with the environment, issues to do with humanity and their own learning and barriers to success. For the majority of the children, almost their entire school lives, something had affected their learning and progress in a negative way, so whilst we were tackling behaviour and SEND and standards in externally assessed subjects, we also started to give them other tools and ways of working and thinking. It was a glorious term. I owed the Y6 children, particularly, the opportunity for joy and engagement. I let them plan and lead assemblies with me. I worked on a school magazine with some of them. I let them dream up charity events and made them happen. I talked to them about legacy and how they could pave the way for the following year groups. It was magic, and as I slowly watched the children and the environment come back to life, it was like seeing colour seep into a black-and-white image. Woodlands was definitely starting to look a lot more green than grey!

At this time, as the staff simply engaged with the whole school 'Zoo Project', I was doing my usual, scouring the outside world very closely for something to capture my imagination, something just to inspire my thinking, to ignite a spark in my mind. I did not know what I was looking for, simply 'inspiration'. I suppose, in retrospect, I was looking for something that would make our school unique. At this time, simultaneously having finished my doctorate, I became keen on pursuing a second career with the army reserves. This drew me to following military people on my social media feed; the media feed that I had only recently established the previous September. I found that one thing led to another, and I was following a whole range of military people, from generals to cadets, Royal Navy to American Air Force, who were beginning to make me think about leadership (one of my favourite topics), about leadership in the military, about the way that we work in and outside of the military and about the way my skills could be transferable.

From curriculum to character education – a new objective

I began to follow a company called Commando Joe's (CoJo's). I thought of this company and the work they did in schools, and I wondered if this was work that could support our own emerging ethos, our growing sense of individuality, despite the Ofsted grading. It *was* work that could support and underpin our ethos; I just didn't know it yet. I had no idea that a couple of years later, we would use it as a vehicle to bring our children back to school after a global pandemic had locked them down at home, and I didn't know that we would use it to engage with them across the airwaves before that, using our new school dog, Gus, as a topic. I certainly had no idea back then that one day, the children and staff at Woodlands would collaborate to write material for this national company that schools across the land would use, not once but twice!

At that time, during the summer term of 2019, I watched, I read, I researched and I quietly got on with the business of creating the best conditions possible for teachers. One of the things I did was to invite, at great cost and huge pressure on my disastrous budget (no offence, guys), Hywel Roberts and Deborah Kidd into school. It was one of the best things I have done in my entire leadership career. These two creative and wonderful human beings came into our school, and they modelled lessons with every single teacher (there were 21 classes at that time, three of which had job-share teachers); they modelled sessions with pupils about topics we suggested (based on what was in the national curriculum), and they made us all 'bothered'.

They talked to staff about 'bothered-ness' and about why we should be bothered; they talked about poverty, but not poverty in terms of lack of money, poverty in terms of lack of creativity and diversity of thought, lack of access to a really rich (authentically so) curriculum. It was wonderful stuff, like chicken soup for the tired teacher; they are, and always will be, I'm sure, the most humble, honest and genuinely good people in education, not to mention the most naturally engaging and talented. Their desire to see children and young people thrive, and think about their lives beyond the walls of the school, to seek challenge and to seek experience, is second to none. I was lucky enough that they had a couple of days free in their calendar that they could come and spend in my school because it is no mean feat, doing lessons for 21 classes in such an environment. TAs observed their work and participated in the learning, as well as teachers, supply teachers and student teachers, so the impact of that spend, although we had a deficit budget and it was quite a significant one, was hugely positive. We had to spend in order to facilitate the learning that took place amongst the teachers, to light a fire of passion in them that had been long put out.

The impact of their work became a series of 'values' that we all still subscribe to. We sat as a staff and we thought about what being bothered looked like to us. We asked ourselves what do we want to achieve? Even today, some five years on, the decisions that we made then still underpin our curriculum, and our ethos. The words that we chose to symbolise our work are not just words but create the golden thread which is seen throughout all the things that we learn and do, and one of those things that really made us think carefully about the what-next in terms of character education.

Take five?

So, whilst some people may have expected us to slow down, relax and calm down a little following that first inspection in 2019, the opposite was actually true (it was the same in spring 2023, by the way, but that is for a later chapter). I began 'old school' with a big sheet of temporary whiteboard on my wall, which was actually two big pieces of white plastic sheet. I started to map across the wall some of the key texts that we were using with our literacy curriculum. Those texts were engaging pupils and making them think about things that we felt quite passionate about; the company had embraced literature and learning and had chosen texts that could be used to start all kinds of enquiry. We looked at those texts, nevertheless, and wondered if they were right for us, if they were doing what we wanted them to do, if they were encouraging our children to learn and to want to know more. We thought about it. A LOT.

Some of the texts were changed based on how well they worked for us. In addition to that, we had to look at the following year because we planned (as I've said earlier) to have mixed-age-group classes. We had no choice, budget-wise. We had to go back to the literacy curriculum provider, the Literacy Company, to ask them if they could help us. Could they help us to make materials that we could use in mixed classes, which would be equally interesting, encouraging and engaging for our children, and help us build on the work we had done to date? They did. I think, again, what I said earlier is that if you choose the right people, the right products that are intuitive for your school, your setting, then they evolve in time with you, with your staff, with your school, with your children, and we are very blessed that is what happened for us.

We built our curriculum, in the end, around our literacy work. We knew that language was at the heart of everything, so we placed literacy at the heart of it all in terms of curriculum cohesion, but we didn't decide that until September 2019.

In September 2019, with my previous deputy head gone on secondment and my new deputy in place, I invited Mike Hamilton, the founder of Commando Joe's, to the school to talk to me about the programme and what it could offer.

I laughed with him in the way that I do (inappropriately), and I said I was already sold on his product. All he had to do was convince my much more discerning deputy head, and if he could convince her of the value of his programme for our children, then we would sign up there and then. I said to Sharon, my amazing deputy (talented, hardworking, dedicated, committed and funny), that she would be the person who would make the decision. I asked her to think carefully about what this man was offering, what his programme would offer and to listen to and challenge him. I told her nothing else. I didn't say that I was bought into it cognitively. I didn't say that I wanted to do it. I didn't say that I had researched it for months. I said this was an idea I was bringing to the table but that I wanted her to decide, so she must ask the questions; she must challenge him. And boy did she! However, by the end of that day, we had indeed committed to CoJo's in the same way that we committed to all things; we didn't buy it off the peg there and then and introduce it the following week. We certainly did not think about how it would be implemented before the end of the academic year. What we did was begin to create the conditions where it would be slowly introduced, built into (rather than bolted onto) a cohesive curriculum, and linked to all of the things we would teach from EYFS to Y6.

Ambitions of a challenging and cohesive curriculum: September 2019–September 2020

I began to piece this together on the whiteboard, on that piece of white sheeting on my wall. We looked at it, considered it, worked on it, adjusted it, and we debated if we should go values-driven, looking at character traits and bothered-ness; should we look at character development and then build literacy around that? Or, should we remain focussed on literacy and build a character programme around that? Sharon made the decision; she convinced me that we had a successful literacy programme that had borne fruit in the year of using it, tangible and credible results and all staff had bought in. She was right, and it was the way I wanted to go, but in 'red-teaming', she was able to verbalise our rationale, which meant the next step of sharing that rationale with all stakeholders was easy for us.

If you're not familiar with CoJo's, then do have a good look at it. I'm not saying it's for everyone, but it was certainly for us. We were able to sensibly map across some of the work we had done the previous year. I'd been doing the majority of it as we went, thinking about topics that we had resources for or that the pupils liked that fitted with new curriculum expectations (good old Gove). In fact, the character programme mapped quite well onto the whole school, as it was broken down into year group work. The Literacy Company, whose work we were using for literacy, funnily enough, was already mapped across so that history topics and geography topics made sense if we looked carefully at them, but it wasn't just as easy as talking about it superficially. We didn't say, 'Great, we're doing a topic on this era or this particular geographical aspect of the world. Let's just do some literacy that ties in, and we can say we have "done" it'.

I drafted a document. I made the staff critique it. I made them look at the year group. I made them look at how each 'topic' could be done and kept sending back one iteration after the next until I was happy it was challenging and detailed enough, and we began to plan for spring term 2020 with our new topics.

The questions were simple. The following is an example of the art and design technology (DT) template questions which every year group completed:

Topic and aims (taken from the NC documents for BOTH Art and DT):

artist/architect/designer:

Equipment and materials: (e.g., pencil, charcoal, paint, clay)

Technique: (e.g., designing, painting, sculpting, drawing)

Is this a design, make and review/ sketchbook activity?

If it is design, can they

- design purposeful, functional, appealing products for themselves and other users based on design criteria; and

- generate, develop, model and communicate their ideas through talking, drawing, templates, mock-ups and, where appropriate, information and communication technology?

If it is make, can they

- select from and use a range of tools and equipment to perform practical tasks (for example, cutting, shaping, joining and finishing) and

- select from and use a wide range of materials and components, including construction materials, textiles and ingredients, according to their characteristics?

If it is evaluate, can they:

- explore and evaluate a range of existing products and

- evaluate their ideas and products against design criteria?

Do children

- build structures, exploring how they can be made stronger, stiffer and more stable; and

- explore and use mechanisms (for example, levers, sliders, wheels and axles) in their products?

Cooking and nutrition

- use the basic principles of a healthy and varied diet to prepare dishes and

- understand where food comes from.

Language: e.g., colour, pattern, texture, line, shape, form, space, stronger, stiffer, stable, mechanisms, levers, sliders, wheels, axles

Context: e.g., local community, industry, garden, home, school, playground

Planning for the term ahead meant that we could review, discuss, refine and challenge. I asked one of the more experienced staff to research knowledge organisers as part of their PM (and mine), as this was the hot topic of the day and an education buzzword. Like any fashion trend, I was cautious. Could we use them? I didn't know, and as we had become accustomed to, that September, he researched and brought a whole range to a staff meeting, which we pulled to pieces and made our own with the best bits for us, and then agreed to trial and come together and review the next half term. I delegated this task to him and empowered him to come and talk to me about it, work on it and share it with colleagues.

Alongside this, the curriculum planning took more than a term. The bouncing back of drafts and professional challenge I was issuing for each year group was a process, and one we shared. As we went to the new year, the spring term in January 2020, we were in a good place. We had the start of a cohesive curriculum, the makings of a robust way of planning for each 'unit of work', for want of a better expression; we were laser focussed on standards, vocabulary, progression; we were building up stamina and endurance; we were getting match ready; we were all buzzing with excitement about our newfound *esprit de corps*!

Only, you recall, in January 2020, the whole world was metaphorically going up in flames. I was a little bit behind the curve on this because I don't watch much TV, as you can imagine; if you read my last book, you know that something has to give in my busy life, and it's TV. So, whilst I was focussed on the job at hand, which was to continue to map out the curriculum with a comprehensive series of staff meetings that we had established and with the rigorous monitoring schedule we were implementing, the world outside our little island was battling Covid-19, and it was steadily getting closer.

The children were really enjoying what we were doing. We were experimenting. We were trialling new products, new strategies, new resources across the board in art, DT, languages, music, science. We looked at new providers; we looked at new schemes. We really did have a good look around and trialled everything that was on offer. We knew our literacy and numeracy systems were working. They were showing me tangible evidence. We knew everything was working; our plans were coming to fruition, and we knew that the next step for us was to really tighten up our planning, make it watertight, including e-safety, computing, 'No Outsiders' and CoJo's[1] so that by the end of that academic year, everything would be in place to launch our 'ambitious' curriculum in the September of 2020. All staff were trained and fighting fit, informed, consistent, strong.

The sound of screeching brakes – or was it?

As they say in the military, no plan survives first contact. Our exciting and super-ambitious plans were laid out before us; we had purpose, direction, energy and commitment, and we knew that by the summer of 2020, we would be successful in achieving our objectives. Sadly, this was not to be. Covid-19 closed our schools in March 2020, and – although in the background – the teachers, many of whom worked from home, were coming into school on a rota basis and continued to plan; continued to prepare everything for the next term, the next academic year; and continued to do online training and meetings, we were not galvanised towards the same goal.

Review two – Covid-19 pandemic

We were fragmented. For the first time, we were working against our naturally evolving team ethos, working in the bunkers of our homes, working away from one another; after having built into a crescendo of such a marvellous team, with such a fantastic camaraderie, we found ourselves disconnected, dismantled and distanced from one another, which was a huge challenge.

I'll talk later, in Chapter 12, about the impact of Covid and building a culture, but for now, suffice it to say that although we continued staff training, professional development, planning and preparation, we did not work collaboratively in the same sense – not many people could at this strange time in history. Life was paused. We focussed, as the rest of the world did, on staying safe, keeping healthy, minimising transmission risk and following the rules (well, everyone except the *obvious*, that is). In school, to begin with, we focussed on offering childcare, essentially, on making sure that the children of our key workers, those who were keeping the healthcare and economic wheels of industry in our country in motion, were in our school and were as safe as they could be. We washed our hands. We kept our distance. We wore face masks. We sat 2 m apart. We didn't socialise. My son did not do his General Certificate of Secondary Education (GCSEs); he did not have a 'prom' or a leaving event. It was just, well, over.

Yet, we had to make some preparations in the summer of 2020 – for us, this meant evaluating need, and we had to recruit both a new site maintenance officer, as well as cleaners, TAs and teachers. I decided to be radical; we had no children in school and therefore couldn't ask teachers to teach and observe them interact – so I asked them to teach the recruitment panel something, a skill or something different. We employed someone who taught us how to decorate a cake (I promise it had nothing to do with expecting them to bring cakes in, although this was an implied expectation), someone who taught us running techniques (again, this wasn't the only reason they were employed) and someone who did a super maths problem that made me smile.

We came back to school in September 2020. We had to re-establish the staff expectations of school culture – our team ethos. Yet, we were still unable to work together, still unable to be in the staff room at the same time, still unable to meet together to train. Because our school was so big, and we wanted to minimise the chances of us having to close 'bubbles' (as they were called then), we only worked in year groups. This 'siloed effect' did nothing to help us in our efforts to improve, but nevertheless, we continued – as so many did – we talked from home on ZOOM or TEAMS, and we tried to minimise the need to close and send children and staff home. We were lucky that term; we only closed Y2 (three classes), but that Christmas, the entire EYFS department (plus me, as I had been over in EYFS for a single day to help prepare the environment for the new year) and every child had to isolate over the holiday. I was away from my family over Christmas, I felt alone and isolated, and it was difficult. My heart was broken. It was painful for everyone. Parents were angry; children didn't have a clue what was going on; we tried to keep it all calm and still had Ofsted expectations placed on us.

> I realised the scale of the challenge as soon as I began teaching at Woodlands, in September 2020. I saw the drive and ambition behind everything we were doing at school. As it was my first term as an NQT it was challenging to prioritise tasks initially. However, as this was my first experience of teaching, I had nothing else to compare it to.
>
> – *Emma*

We spent a lot of time and a lot of energy managing those expectations, the expectations of parents, the safety of everyone in our community and the learning of our children. Each September, I write the SDP and SEF based on the collective understanding of all stakeholders about the direction of the school, set by both internal data gathered before the summer and also our PM targets set before the summer. There are no surprises, and as you have seen, the work we do is deconstructed into Ofsted-friendly sections so it is easily understood by a range of stakeholders (including Ofsted) at a glance and with no extra work. On the basis of the new guidance, our SEF and SDP had to change to reflect the huge influence that Covid-19 had on both our children's learning progress and development and Ofsted external expectations.

That meant we repeated what we had done two years before. That September, with the new guidance hot off the press, we paused curriculum training for staff that term and switched fire to research – with our IT expert – which system we could most easily and effectively adapt to be able to teach remotely and interact safely, as I predicted we might well need it when we smashed into another lockdown. We did General Data Protection Regulation (GDPR) checks and informed parents (another hidden pitfall). And we established a home learning policy – challenged as we were by the ASIA, whom we had to convince that we were not slacking (rightly so) and that there was, indeed, 'urgency', even if she didn't see that as being evident on September 3, 2020.

No SATs had taken place that summer, so we had no published data to base comparisons on; the term before had no progress data; we last saw **all** children in school in March 2020. SATs were no great loss to us. They are a total nonsense, anyway. The main point for us was that the children in our school were fed, kept safe and fully safeguarded as we drove out to houses and talked to children from the end of their pathways, the end of their drives, the end of their streets. Staff recorded a video message for the children each week, and I recorded one for each of them also. We checked on parents; we delivered food parcels. We worked with social services (as under pressure as they were), and we did our best. But in terms of planning our curriculum, addressing Ofsted findings from April 2019, and driving our school improvement agenda? The school development plan, essentially, was on hold. The Covid-19 recovery plan was the main effort.

From September 2020, we continued to work towards our ambitious curriculum; we continued to try to teach it – at times, remotely. Teachers began to prepare lessons both for home learning for children who were isolating with Covid and also for teaching inside of school, so the entire plan shifted. We had to review our main effort in light of obvious contextual national/global issues. Because we had learned to work effectively as a team, and as a result, this was easier than it sounds, thankfully, as the pressure was intense.

Our team ethic is what has saved us, I think, throughout it all.

> Unfortunately, since joining Woodlands, I experienced the death of my Mum and Dad, some extended family difficulties, C-19 occurred and I have had a few health problems. I've never experienced things like this before and before this had barely had a day off work. Despite these difficulties, I've felt very supported at school by an incredible team of people.
>
> *– Alice*

Ofsted monitoring – keep on trucking!

Hilariously, we had TWO Ofsted monitoring visits during this time.

TWO.

The first was a remote one, in which they looked at all of our online learning, planning, feedback, engagement, the offer, safeguarding – everything. The report was innocuous given the four days of pre-inspection, and inspection activity.[2]

> You, other leaders and teachers have spent your time and energy wisely since the previous inspection. Your careful consideration of what pupils should learn means that you have established a well-planned and structured curriculum. This has stood everyone in good stead for the current testing times. You have deftly overcome the challenges caused by the third national lockdown. As a result, all pupils continue to enjoy a relevant and purposeful education, whether they learn in school or at home. In September 2020, you forged ahead with the implementation of the new curriculum. However, your plans to elevate teachers' subject knowledge in order to teach the more ambitious curriculum content did not happen. Due to the pandemic, teachers' training took a different tack. This has paid dividends for the current situation. All staff and pupils are well versed in the systems for remote education. This means that pupils have not lost learning time. Pupils continue to study the same range of subjects that they would in usual circumstances. This is the case whether pupils learn

at school or at home. Pupils are mostly following their typical curriculum in English and mathematics. This is not so for some other subjects that require specialist resources, such as art and science. Subject leaders have adapted the curriculum appropriately, moving topics around to ensure that pupils continue to learn.

The second was an in-person socially distanced one, in which they looked at all of our online learning, planning, feedback, engagement, the offer, safeguarding – everything, a mere eight weeks later.[3]

> One of the first improvements you undertook was developing the role of subject leaders. They are now playing a more influential role in developing the curriculum. You and other senior leaders have supported their development well. This has enabled them to understand the strengths and areas for development in their subjects. They evaluate the effectiveness of any initiatives precisely and accurately. This has made a positive contribution to the improvements in the curriculum, especially in English and mathematics. Subject leaders receive training and opportunities to research their curriculum areas. This is helping to develop their confidence and skills. Their work to improve the quality of education pupils receive is bearing fruit. Within this improving curriculum, there are many opportunities for pupils to practise what they already know before they learn new things.

We couldn't have done any more. Literally.

We were cross at the time because, although we had to tell parents that we were having monitoring visits, and they were rooting for us in the main, there was no way of changing the outcome of our grading. We were stuck with RI. We still awaited the big push for the Section 5 inspection. The reports were irritating because OF COURSE pupils hadn't been able to get stuck into DT. They were stuck at home like the rest of the world! I let it go. I had bigger fish to fry, as they say round our way, and wanted to focus on what we had told them we were focussing on, and they had then used in their reported 'further actions'.

Review three – from RI, via a pandemic, to good: September 2023

We naturally review our main effort each academic year and there is now a very established way that we do so. My PM is set in July based on a full evaluation of the year (which is also in the summer FGB headteacher report). My PM targets influence those of staff, as do their individual roles in school and the overall SDP. We know where our children are internally, so we can plan against the following years and what we want to focus on, the specific progress initiatives that we want to see. This coming year, 2023–4, it's writing for us. In terms of BIG GOALS, the first one, obviously, in September 2018 was the looming Ofsted. The second one was the curriculum imperative in April 2019, ready for the implementation of the new Ofsted inspection schedule. Following that was the online learning imperative of the pandemic. The most recent one is of course Ofsted actions from the January inspection of 2023 and also some exciting things I will share later (because let's not forget, we did have a positive outcome of the inspection in January 2023[4], and this opened lots of doors!).

Takeaways

- Revising the main effort should happen on the basis of any fluctuations in funding, finances, staffing or any kind of national agenda, influence or global threat. (For us, of course, we had all of the above!).

- Revising the main effort should happen with the input of all stakeholders in a systematic way – SEF/SDP is useful for reflecting this, and the 'Headteacher Termly Report for Govs' is useful for reviewing it.

- Revising the main effort could happen on the basis of any opportunities that may present: academisation, growth in provision, etc.

Notes

1 https://commandojoes.co.uk/; https://no-outsiders.com/.
2 https://files.ofsted.gov.uk/v1/file/50161001.
3 https://files.ofsted.gov.uk/v1/file/50164752.
4 https://files.ofsted.gov.uk/v1/file/50210703.

Good reads

Bradbury, A. & Swailes, R. (Eds.). (2022). *Early Childhood Theories Today*. Learning Matters.

Cree, J. & Robb, M. (2021). *The Essential Guide to Forest School and Nature Pedagogy*. Routledge.

Fabrega, A.L. (2023). *The Learning Game: Teaching Kids to Think for Themselves, Embrace Challenge, and Love Learning*. Harriman House.

Kidd, D. (2020). *A Curriculum of Hope: As Rich in Humanity as in Knowledge*. Independent Thinking Press.

Lemov, D. (2021). *Teach Like a Champion 3.0: 63 Techniques that Put Students on the Path to College*. Jossey-Bass.

Morrison McGill, R. (2023). *The Teacher Toolkit Guide to Questioning*. Bloomsbury Education.

Myatt, M. & Tomsett, J. (2021). *Huh: Curriculum Conversations between Subject and Senior Leaders*. John Catt Educational LTD.

Roberts, H. & Gilbert, I. (2023). *Botheredness: Stories, Stance and Pedagogy*. Independent Thinking Press.

Wyatt, P.A. (2022). *How to Lead for Daring New Leaders: The No-Nonsense Guide to Develop Basic Leadership Skills. Discover Your Power to Be in Charge*. Eagle Ridge Books.

9 Choosing the most effective strategy

Right people, resources, outcome!

If I was to move to a different school and encounter the same type of issues, I would repeat in that school what was successful in Woodlands. Teamwork and communication with all staff are key. It has been pivotal to our school to come together and work as a team to make the improvements necessary. I would ensure that all staff – like our staff – know the why and the how of the journey ahead. I have learnt from working at Woodlands the strength that comes from working in a team that are all striving for the same goal. Each change that was implemented by Vic has been explained, shared and communicated, from changing the school's key values, to adapting the behaviour policy and overhauling the curriculum.

– Lottie

Choosing the most effective strategy to have the best effect!

Using the information collected through comprehensive and systematic intelligence gathering covered in previous chapters, finding the right solutions for the school and implementing them effectively to drive it forward has been my bedrock. How the systemic management of change takes place is vital for the school culture as much as school improvement and the two go hand in hand. There is no formula for this – which aspect you choose is a personal thing.

The reality about deciding what the correct strategies or products, staffing structure or allocation of funding is that in any school, it will be totally different. There will obviously be elements of similarity, but the combinations and the recipe will be entirely unique. There is no one-size-fits-all, and this is a concept that has eluded successive governments for almost as long as I have been alive.

I think, and I said in *Leading with Love*, that we can all bake a cake. We all have a favourite cake, even me, and mine is actually Bakewell Tart. I looked at Mary Berry's recipe for Bakewell Tart;[1] it was almost perfect, but actually, there was too

DOI: 10.4324/9781003440000-10

much butter for me in the pastry. DON'T TELL HER!!! It was kind of greasy at the bottom (and it wasn't just my poor skills), so I simply reduced the amount of butter in the pastry slightly, and I decided I wanted a bit more almond in the filling, so the recipe is almost the same, all the same ingredients and same cook and so on, but I tested and adjusted it to suit me, to my own taste. Leadership is kind of like that and so is school improvement.

Get with the programme!

So, back to reality, in the last chapter, I spoke about my desire to find something that made Woodlands unique. I wanted something that gave it an identity, something that was special. As you know, Mike convinced Sharon and the rest is history – one of the things that is unique about our school is our commitment to character education, and it is based on Cojos. But to prove the point, I didn't use Cojos in my last school, and that was just as much of a success as Woodlands is.

In my previous school, in an almost ignored triangle of industrial Cheshire, I was looking for something to address issues to do with acceptance, tolerance and diversity, as well as how children interacted with one another and the lack of respect that I saw between them when I arrived. I was searching my brain, and the internet, for inspiration, and I remembered one day when I was in the bath that when I was in teacher training (many years before), I did a training programme called Philosophy for Children (P4C).[2] When I looked into P4C as a headteacher, I realised it could be really beneficial in my school. I went through the same process as I did in Woodlands, focussed money and time and effort into establishing it, threading it through the SDP and staff PM, and this meant I ensured that every single staff member was trained in it and able to use it. I'm not sure what it's like there now, of course, because staff have come and gone, and more importantly, I've not been headteacher there for five years, and it's none of my business. When I was there, we used it as a vehicle to teach geography, history, religious education (RE) and spiritual, moral, social and cultural (SMSC) development.

I did there exactly what I have done at Woodlands. I began by mapping out the curriculum that our children were already doing, which in our team, we were happy with. As I said, what we wanted to do was develop an understanding of diversity, inclusion, 'British values' and global issues, and I wanted to start to develop a formal SMSC programme in our school. We didn't have one at the time; it was ad hoc and based more on previous government agendas. I couldn't buy one off the shelf at that time, so I crafted one using P4C as a vehicle, and that's what I used to describe it.

It was a vehicle to teach geography topics and history topics, and to help children battle with some of the morality and social issues that that were going on in our world: everything from hunger to deforestation, plastic pollution in the oceans to war and conflict and homelessness to poverty. I mapped out the programme of study for each year group, created folders and sourced and compiled resources for all the staff who taught it. For each year group, including an overview of what they would do (which matched what they were already doing), I created lesson plans, question starters, question suggestions (you can take the teacher out of the classroom...). The resources that are often used for P4C are photographs or a piece of writing that stimulates the children into generating their own questions, which the group then votes on which question they are going to debate, the outcome of which can be some very profound work that can be built upon in the rest of the learning that's going on in a cohesive way.

It taught children to discuss things they had perhaps not thought of before, to take notice of our world, the world outside of where they lived, and the big issues that globally we all faced. It taught them to be respectful of one another's opinions, their cultural differences and so on, and for me, that was really important in a school where there was anywhere from 20% to 40% of Gypsy, Romany and Traveller families (GRT). That divide between the village community and the GRT community was sometimes quite tangible and quite toxic, and one way of trying to get away from that was to start with educating the children to think differently and get them working effectively together, reducing racism, increasing tolerance and understanding, learning together and being increasingly respectful of one another's different cultures and different ideas.

It really benefited that school and helped language development for pupils, as much as it had a beneficial impact on behaviour and on how they learned to communicate with each other. Rather than children behaving in mean and disrespectful ways, they learned how to use and say phrases that empowered them without undermining others. I think this is about life skills more than primary school skills, and our children needed to hear it and learn it in school to be able to model it outside for their adults and take it with them into their own adult lives. For example, 'I understand what you are saying and where you're coming from with that; however, I disagree with you because my family believes ...', and even having that kind of language, that ability to respectfully disagree, really helped us with a lot of our behaviour issues. It didn't help me mend the wider community, but it helped inside the fences of the school.

Seeing the wood for the trees

Having the right strategies, choosing the right programmes, finding the right focus in your school will be different for everyone – and that can be part of the challenge of headship in any case, particularly when you are taking over a school that's in a difficult situation. When you're looking around for inspiration from other people and what they are doing that is perhaps inspiring and really appeals to you, there is A LOT of stuff out there, but not all of it will be right for your school.

I talked earlier about maths, for example, and Maths no Problem (Singapore maths), although I would have loved for it to be different, was not the answer in Woodlands Primary School when I took over.[3] It had to be something different, a different approach that was more manageable for us, and sometimes deciding what is not right or right for the school can be unpopular. Sometimes it will involve you, as I said in the previous chapter, revisiting your main effort. What it is you really want to achieve. What is the main goal that everybody is working towards? If the programmes you are using are just not working, then they need to go.

Do the research!

Tactical pause here; no need to 'take a knee', but do stop for a sec. I'm not suggesting that people drop things after five minutes or a week, but I think serious consideration is to be given to the research phase of any kind of new system or programme implementation, the cost-benefit analysis, staff preparedness/skill to embrace a new system/programme, implementation of the training, the follow-up and then the assessment of the success of that programme. Then, and only then, if it is not successful, it is time to cut your losses and look for something different. And yes, I think that that takes a little bit of bravery and an awful lot of awareness!

For me, coming into Woodlands, there were no programmes! I had carte blanche. I was able to put troops to task and as part of staff PM ask them to do the research into what was out there, to look around other schools, media outlets and innovations, and to then make our decisions based on what we knew of our school (which was, and remains, key), and what we thought would work, and put the two things together. Admittedly, I was lucky that I had some people working with me, who remained with me (and who still remain with me now), who are committed to the future of the school, who had seen it before I got there and so had that corporate knowledge, and they helped me to decide what was best for our school. I know every headteacher will not have that, but I do think it's extremely useful, and I think once you have hit on the right strategy or programme you just know it. As with most things, if it's right, and everybody's bought into it, then it just flows, and in actual fact, it doesn't feel like effort or work at all; in many ways, it just feels like everybody's just flowing in the same direction. 'Flow' some may call it.[4]

One of the things that I spoke about in Chapter 6 was PP. I already mentioned that I took it over in the first year I was at Woodlands, set it up and modelled how we would do things, and then in the second year, whilst I worked on the same format with the wider curriculum, I handed PP over to my deputy, Sharon. Now, Sharon has got a million skills, she has got a real ability and interest in systems, and her mind works in such a way that she loves tracking, data and analysis, and this was just up her street, so much so that she planned to use this focus to work on her NPQH project. In the same way that the previous deputy had worked on a tracking system, implementing it and presenting it to the governors as her focus, Sharon planned to do the same for PP. Genius. Except along came Covid, and she switched fire to writing, which was our school focus last year (and will be again this year).

This is definitely a method of working that I would recommend and have done in many aspects of my career (including when leading the coaching module for the leadership MA at Chester University). If any of the staff want to do post-graduate study, get them to use whatever they do in their day job to create the data. They will then research around the topic, become more informed, have their thinking challenged and be better in their day job as a result, and therefore the school team will be better informed, stronger, more improvement focussed, etc. They will also minimise the strain on themselves! It is a tough gig committing to extra personal study when working full time, and one set of data can often be used to satisfy lots of different outcomes. It really does make sense.

> In terms of key people who helped me prioritise tasks, and tools that helped me, Vic has an amazing talent of being able to see when you need a challenge and to invest in your career. For me personally, she has helped me to regain my confidence and find what I love about my profession – nurturing and supporting others. She knows exactly what to do to help you to enhance your teaching and professional development, even if it not something you can see in yourself at the time. Vic and our SLT are key people who help me to prioritise any tasks. For science, I found the PLAN assessment website and Developing Experts website excellent to support with assessment, insight statements, planning and overviews. I also found the primarily science training outstanding as a subject leader to support with working scientifically and deep dives.[5]
>
> – *Roisin*

Anyway, that was a quick segue; what I wanted to say next is that only 50% of any new programme or system, even if it is the absolutely PERFECT one for the school, is down to making an informed choice about the programme itself. The other 50% (and yes, I am generalising; I am not splitting hairs over whether it is a 70/30 division or whatever) is down to human beings, the staff who implement the programme and the leadership team who oversee the implementation.

Right people – right strategy – right outcome

I think that it is the human that you give any task to and their existing skills (the ones that you can see and the ones that are latent within them that just need you to coach them to the fore) that make a difference in school improvement – or that has been my experience, I should say! For me, the calculation of an individual and their skills, plus an effective programme or strategy, plus the right environment and support, equals the difference between success and failure.

Even then, it's not just the skills that the person you have empowered with a task innately has or has developed over time, or that they may not have seen in themselves but you've seen a little spark of that just needs to be encouraged. It's also about the framework – the structure that you put around them.

I think that if people have a framework with which to support themselves as they grow, to help them as they climb and to scaffold their successes, then they will climb, grow and be successful! Think about it; we are all human. We do exactly this for children. We do it in terms of learning a new maths concept or learning how to use a particular convention in literacy, so why should we not do it for our staff when they are learning to become better versions of themselves, better leaders or better people to drive their subject or project in school? We are not born with the skills we need to be organised or forward-thinking or able to run several complex projects simultaneously. We might be born with an innate talent, passion or drive; perhaps, we develop it as a result of our childhoods and how we are shaped and moulded by them, but I don't care who you are, there are certain times in life when even those attributes won't help and you can falter, stall and stop without systems and support.

I have said in public, and certainly in my leadership book, things that have been reiterated in this book both from my experiences and from the staff whose quotes I've littered throughout. You will see that there are times when people have to dig deep to find the energy to continue. Often, they do so when they have looked left and right at the members of their team and not wanted to let them down. No different from what any soldier I have ever spoken to has said to me. If you have a strong team ethic, then it becomes the team effort that drives people forward.

Don't 'carry on regardless'

I know once you've got systems and (I am sure) scaffolding in terms of policies, routine discussion, training, monitoring and an open-door policy, if staff are concerned or want to run something past a more experienced member of the team (therefore receive team support), then there is only success waiting for you.

I also think it's okay to stop and actively consider, 'Am I approaching this in the right way?' I think it's not just about the strategies or the programmes or projects that you purchase; it's not about just the staff that you put in place to run those projects or their skills, either those they have or those they develop running those projects. It's also VERY MUCH about *your* way of working, your influence as head.

I said earlier on that I was working 20 hours a day at the very start of the school improvement journey and that this was unsustainable. I'm a person who has a lot of energy and who is able to compartmentalise and look after my own health, but actually, at the end of that first Ofsted, after two terms of working at that pace, it was obvious it couldn't carry on. Equally, there have been times since when I have paused to consider if I am approaching something in the correct way. Now, for example, in the summer of 2023, when I consider the way that I've been working for the last term, is one of those times. It has proven unsustainable, and, in all honesty, I might be sitting here writing a book to share our school experiences, and hopefully, it will help you if you are reading it, but actually, even that has proven to be quite the challenge given how tired I'd become towards the end of last term.

I won't go as far as to say I am burnt out, but another week of the pace of work we were working at (see Chapter 16 for the reasons), and I might have been!

If I could offer advice, it would be to keep reviewing whether your approach is right, whether it's helping you achieve your focus – if it isn't then, really, don't carry on regardless. The approach to achieving a goal for me is a mixture of ingredients: the right person, in the right place, doing the right job, with the right equipment, support, training and team, and in the right time scale. The right person in the right job is vital, but it is worth noting the outcome when the balance is off.

> When I realised the scale of what needed to be done, it negatively impacted my work-life balance, as I would stay at work most days till 6 pm, work into the evening, spend hours 'CPOMs-ing' as a result of the legacy of poor behaviour and also work at weekends, too. I crashed my car in the carpark of the gym I went to one night after work as I was so mentally exhausted that I wasn't concentrating and didn't see the 'no entry' sign that I ran over. (No one was hurt and the car lived to tell another tale). I have not returned to any gym since.
>
> – *Emily*

Marathon, not a sprint

I think the best way to summarise this chapter on having the right people in the right job, doing the right thing, with the right strategies, in the right timeframe is that really school improvement has to be seen as a marathon, not a sprint. I talked earlier in the book about the different kinds of leadership. The most effective kind of leadership that has some longevity, some kind of long-lasting impact, has nothing to do with working until you burn yourself or any of your staff out. It has not much to do with Ofsted. I think, therefore, it is a marathon, not a sprint, and we can all take ownership of what that looks like for us and our schools.

I do try to be a good role model to staff, but there are times when the balance is gone, and I am at risk of burnout. I can remove tasks from staff to give them a break; there is capacity now in school where I can ask someone else to do their job for a fixed period whilst they manage something else or complete something, or deal with home issues, for example. But the big difference as headteacher is that I have to keep going and keep driving for everybody else, and at those times when I am beyond tired, but still need to be behind the team and planning ahead for the school and responding to complaints and fighting for outcomes for vulnerable pupils, I have to rely on my core team to give me energy. We are not robots. It is possible for some staff to do some of the tasks that I usually do, but there are certain things that headteachers cannot delegate, and they have to be done by the headteacher, so when I am worn out, I try and focus on those tasks and allow my team to do the rest. Only do what only you can do.

I liken it to your body as a system. If you're cold, your body system has to keep your core warm, protect that core temperature – keep it stable – or you die. I think it's the same thing in school. There are things on the periphery that you can either stop doing or delegate out to other people, but at the heart of it, you've got to keep that system going, the core of the school has got to be kept going, and you are the only person to do that, and continue to drive that forward, which means you've got to take time to look after yourself. I know it sounds very cliché, and it's very 'of the moment' to reference the concept of 'teacher well-being' and 'headteacher well-being' – and as a result, some people might be dismissive and disregard it as just a tired expression – but it is genuinely true that without it, schools do not function well. You know it is.

On a personal level, and this isn't a pity party, but you need to know it, I've been driving home from the gym this last couple of weeks (the first couple of weeks of the summer break 2023), and I felt quite emotional, I think I even cried, and I think it's because I'm beginning to relax, to decompress, after last term. As I said earlier in this chapter, there are times when I've found myself in a position where I have worn myself out, and this is one of those times. I have to remember that in order to be my best self for everyone else, I have to make sure I've got the energy necessary, which involves me taking care of myself, and that is as important as everything else, if not more so.

That's not to say that the strategy I have had has not been right, but it is an acknowledgement that, at times, the balance is DEFINITELY off. I would say continuing to train your mind and your body is really important, particularly when things are tough. It's certainly what got me, as a person, through Covid. I think it got several of my staff team through Covid. I didn't just ensure that the staff had continued professional training online when they were not in school during the lockdowns, I also made sure that they had access for a number of months to online workouts. Many may not have the money to pay for themselves to do online gym sessions, so I ensured that everyone did have access. Important note here: when I say 'staff', of course, I'm **always** speaking about everybody in school, from the cleaners right the way through to the admin team, and I think it's important that I offered my whole staff that well-being when they were off because many of them struggled. I knew they were struggling, and I couldn't do anything because we were all so disparate and distanced from one another, but I could offer the physical training as much as I could the psychological training (that I know I have shared some staff comment about).

I have just recalled some funny comments on 'Twitter' about that offer at the time, about whether I was **expecting** staff to do workouts (!) or if it would be part of their performance management (!). The answer to those questions was, of course, absolutely not. It was an **offer**, part of a suite of offers, to help keep my staff mentally and physically healthy, their minds and bodies connected during Covid and beyond. It kept them all going, I think, having a range of things to choose from offered something for everyone. The psychological support I brought in when we were back in school was part of this, and we devoted whole training days to it because I felt it was so important.

I think also that continuation to prepare for and work on school improvement throughout Covid, despite any lockdowns and mess arounds, despite the vitriol in the press and the anxiety, just to keep people focussed on the systems and the structures, not all the white noise around that was swirling around about 'lost generations', and so on, was invaluable, so I am happy with our approach and strategies, but I am equally happy that we did and do continue to review them. After all, most stuff is something that we can't influence or affect; what we *can* influence is how we respond and, as such, what goes on in our school, and in order to do that, we must influence what goes on for us as humans. That is why headteachers are so very important.

Takeaways

- Successful school leadership, be that in a school in crisis or one riding the wave of national success, is about routines, systems and structure.

- Try to be a good role model to staff; try to protect the balance and prevent the risk of burnout.

- School improvement is like making a cake! (Actually, wait one, I could be onto something here! My nan used to say that you can't make a cake without breaking a few eggs. Maybe school improvement IS about breaking a few eggs as well, I need to think that through a bit more. Maybe if you're reading this, you should X me now – Twitter is dead, long live the X – and #schoolimprovementislikeacake – not that catchy, though what about #breakanegg? That's it! #breakanegg!!!!)

Notes

1 https://www.bbc.co.uk/food/recipes/marys_bakewell_tart_12584.
2 https://p4c.com/.
3 https://mathsnoproblem.com/en/approach/what-is-singapore-maths.
4 Peifer C, Wolters G, Harmat L, Heutte J, Tan J, Freire T, Tavares D, Fonte C, Orsted-Andersen F, van den Hout J, Šimleša M, Pola L, Ceja L, and Triberti S (2022) 'A scoping review of flow research' *Frontiers in Psychology* (13) https://doi.org/10.3389/fpsyg.2022.815665.
5 https://www.planassessment.com/.

Good reads

Clutterbuck, D. (2020). *Coaching the Team at Work 2: The Definitive Guide to Team Coaching*. Nicholas Brealey International.
Csikszentmihalyi, M. (2002). *Flow: The Psychology of Happiness*. Rider.

Gaut, B. & Gaut, M. (2011). *Philosophy for Young Children: A Practical Guide.* Routledge.

Morgan, A. (2022). *Coaching International Teams: Improving Communication, Inclusion and Productivity.* Econcise.

Pedrick, C. (2020). *Simplifying Coaching: How to Have More Transformational Conversations by Doing Less.* Open University Press.

Sanchez, K.G. (2022). *Leadership for the New Female Manager: The New Manager's Guide to Mastering Leadership Skills: 21 Powerful Strategies for Coaching High-Performance.* Virago Publishing.

Zhuo, J. (2019). *The Making of a Manager: What to Do When Everyone Looks to You.* Virgin Books.

The messy business of human resources
Managing staff, the basics

The biggest mistake of my career was not having self-confidence. What helped me was stepping back and seeing the bigger picture. Most importantly having a great team to work with. I had felt like I had let the team down and Vic helped me to bring things into perspective. She made me realise that If I can't help myself, I can't help others. This was the first time in my career that I felt there was a leader that showed compassion for their team. I always remember the day when I was in the office in floods of tears and she asked me what my biggest fear was. I replied, 'losing this career because it is not just a job but a passion'. It was that day that I started to get on the road to recovery and I am still here doing what I love.

– Arzoo

The messy business of human resources

If Chapter 1 was the chapter that shone a light on the ugly side of education influenced by politics, then Chapter 10 could be classed as the chapter that shines a light on the ugly side of school improvement influenced by HR. Don't fret, my HR friends. HR advisors are wonderful, but the generic staffing issues that we deal with are summarised in verbal shorthand as 'HR' (in the same way that in the army, they are 'G1'). Every school has them, some more than others, and schools in crisis more so than any school I have come across. I am sitting here with palpitations even thinking back to this aspect of school improvement, but in true 'me' style, I have to share with you what it felt like so you know what to expect and also so that you can survive, as your staff can, and thrive.

For Richard, a superstar and temporary LA-funded member of the SLT I inherited, HR issues were the most stressful part of his role in school, and I can fully appreciate why:

DOI: 10.4324/9781003440000-11

Working through performance-related issues were the most stressful points for me in the school improvement journey. I didn't always feel like I had the capacity to support colleagues fully. I regularly felt caught between supporting the staff professionally and personally, and monitoring the quality of their work (and reporting this).

There are some instances where prioritising has to take place in order to achieve the desired outcome and goals, be that HR or support focus, physical environment focus or financial focus. In the last chapter, I talked about right people, right job, right resources.

Competing priorities

There have been times (and will inevitably be more times) in holistic school improvement where there are competing priorities that cause anxiety. In the case of Woodlands and many other schools at this time, for lots of legacy reasons (Covid-19 and austerity notwithstanding), at the macro-level, there was a huge competition between focusing on standards and also finances, and which would be addressed first. When asked directly, the director of education in 2019 said he wanted me to focus on both. I will say, and there are many in this position today, this was difficult! There was the constant competition of my values and beliefs versus what I knew I must do to protect the school, staff and community from Ofsted outcomes that were negative. There were times when I had to increase pressure on myself and others to ensure that this protection was bulletproof, and this has not always been easy. When I know that I have to dial up pressure, I try to do it in a progressive way, like training for a big event. There is no way that you can go 0–60 as they say: put people in boiling hot water (unlike an egg), blast them at boiling point for a period of time and expect good outcomes (I love a boiled egg but not a boiled team member!). You have to start cold or lukewarm and slowly increase the intensity to minimise injury and ensure that everyone reaches the game-day matchfit and ready.

There have also been times when staff have had competing priorities, and these have had a huge impact on their ability (whether temporary or permanent) to do the job they are employed to do; this is the hardest thing of all to manage, I think. One example is Arzoo, employed by me as EYFS lead in the summer of 2020 as we came out of lockdown one. Little did we know that a perfect storm of many family bereavements, illness, the dramatic and indescribable impact of Covid on the EYFS team, increasing her hours to start with us so she was full-time and moving from Wales to the United Kingdom would render this role impossible for Arzoo to manage within 18 months. Conscious that I did not want to see her destroy herself or her team, I ensured she had a support plan and the help of Sharon, and I enlisted the guidance of several high-profile EYFS practitioners, our previous deputy head who was running a large nursery and pre-school and the LA EYFS team. To no avail. It was not the right space, time or place for Arzoo, and whilst she stayed with us, and has since 'found herself' again (and does a truly AMAZING job with Y1 and Forest Schools, winning awards of all kinds), it was tricky to manage at the time, pre-Ofsted and mid/post-Covid, and simultaneously ensure that she felt nurtured and cared for. But manage it we did.

> When I started at Woodlands, I was extremely confident that I had the capabilities to take EYFS through their journey; fuelled by the confidence of the SLT. However, I went through a blip, both emotionally and medically, and lost all my self-confidence and cocooned myself away. I feel that I just completely lost everything that I had wanted and worked so hard to get in an instant of losing my self-confidence.
>
> *– Arzoo*

So how have we done it all? I will let Annica outline what this meant for Woodlands.

> On the first INSET day, Vic explained the scale of the job we had in front of us. At that point I fully appreciated the scale of the work that needed to be done in our particular area, and what made the penny drop was when Vic talked to those of us who were on Upper Pay Scale about the amount of work that needed doing. I was always confident that I could deliver what was needed as a class teacher. I chose to step down from the Upper Pay Scale as I was conscious about keeping my work life balance and being able to be there for my family, This felt like a HUGE relief. My main priority was to focus on being an outstanding teacher and concentrate on my subject leader responsibilities within the EYFS, not several different subject areas across the whole school.
>
> *– Annica*

Setting the scene

This makes it sound awful; maybe it was. I don't know, but I was setting out the expectations for everyone, at every level of school, from TA to myself and how we would need to work as a team.

I explained that, as part of the PM cycle, I would go through everyone's job description with them before setting up PM objectives related to teaching and learning and an aspect of school improvement that would be their responsibility (some people had already said they weren't even sure they could locate one and their staff files were at that time incomplete). I explained that I needed help, genuinely, and that the help from the SLT would be supplemented by those most experienced staff, who must have demonstrated that their impact was pretty hefty in the past, that they were highly competent in all elements of the relevant teacher standards, and that their achievements and contributions to the school had been, and were still, substantial and sustained. Many of those staff had multiple subjects to coordinate.

I was reaching out to ask for them to help me coach the less experienced and temporary staff, as we needed to work on school improvement – and fast.

What happened was that some staff on the UPS asked to give it up. I took advice from HR and asked if they were able to as I had never heard of this before, and the answer was that although it was unusual, if it came from the staff member, then yes. I was SHOCKED, but this was the nature of the school at the time. The impact on Annica was evident; she welcomed it: the lack of pressure it meant, the ability to focus on her teaching it offered. She had no expectations on her of anything other than her own class teaching. THIS IS NOT RIGHT FOR EVERYONE, but it was right for those few staff in Woodlands, all of whom just wanted to find stability, focus on the job of teaching and helping pupils learn and doing it well (which I can speak from personal experience and say they all have done over the last five years, and are super happy, evidently).

Naturally, it made me realise that the capacity I thought I had in terms of experience and leadership outside of the externally funded and temporary SLT wasn't quite there. So, it was back to the drawing board. If you are new to leadership, you cannot ask people to take on more responsibility than their job description, pay grade or experience dictates; if ever you are not sure, then speak to your HR advisors. This involved actively seeking out those who were interested and showed an aptitude and then training them on the job, alongside creating opportunities for them to do professional qualifications. Lottie had been teaching for three years when I got there. She was not on UPS.

> As Headteacher, Vic has always supported us with prioritising tasks, starting with sharing the SEF and SDP at the beginning of the year. Vic has also invested in us as people, including me as a leader. As a result of this investment, I have been able to undertake an NPQSL. The modules of my NPQSL and additional research have supported me with prioritising key tasks. Lots of these have come from the EEF such as 'PUTTING EVIDENCE TO WORK: A SCHOOL'S GUIDE TO IMPLEMENTATION' as well as their research into assessment and feedback. Their guides are fantastic to support figuring out what needs to be changed, what the active ingredients are, and what timeframe these changes could be implemented, based on the priorities in my action plan (which come directly from the SEF/SDP).
>
> – *Lottie*

Staffing structure

I think the issue of performance-related pay (see Chapter 1) is one that does not compute with education, and yet it is expected to. I am not a headteacher in an academy or anything to do with a MAT, so I have no idea if it is different, but I think the whole pay conversation is just a proper nightmare. This situation made me focus on the staffing structure that first term as a priority because how could

I set objectives without understanding roles/job descriptions and therefore expectations on each person? We therefore needed to look at the staffing structure, the contracts, the job descriptions and pay grades and review these to make sure they were all consistent.

It quickly became apparent that the staffing structure had been affected by a number of things but most notably by so many staff leaving. So, we began from scratch in terms of firstly understanding and then reviewing roles against need and job descriptions, including why we had some staff on permanent and some on temporary contracts, some on full-time hours and some on a combination of part-time for one contract and part-time for another and so on. It was quite complicated.

Understandably, staff were quite unnerved by the process of reviewing working practice, and although we had our one-to-one conversations, I could not give them any solutions to some of the complexity – there were no quick answers. If you have done this before as a headteacher, then you too will know that it is never easy; you are potentially threatening a person's income and their standard of living, and then layer over this either perceived or real threat the fact that in our society most 'reviews' are conducted to save money and make cuts, and you can see why staff would be nervous! It happened to me in my first ever job when the school was being closed down by the LA, and we were all due to be redeployed, so I completely understood.

I knew, having been a headteacher and done a TA review at my previous school for something else, and in the school before that as a deputy, that any job description review or staffing review would need to involve HR. Most pressing for me at that time, and in terms of prioritising, were the teachers – the recruitment of permanent staff, retention and active support, quickly followed by TAs and then support staff.

Building for the future

BUT WAIT! As you will remember from previous chapters, there were also the grave concerns around the following year. I knew the pupil numbers had decreased in the school due to the uncertainties, and I knew that I needed to look at some kind of radical changes to do with mixed-age classes, but I wasn't ready to share these because, in those early days, I was not yet the substantive headteacher and had bigger fish to fry, the imminent Ofsted for one, and – of course – the pupils who needed to be taught and become high-school prepared! In addition, my ongoing discussions with the LA were added to this cocktail with respect to the dilapidated and dangerous mobile classroom that was on site, which housed the only accessible toilet.

Although this physical environment consideration became quite challenging because I was coming into the conversation very late on, I knew we could not afford to have the building either fixed or removed, and we needed an accessible loo. Actually, in the end, as energy sapping as it was, it became a lever for us to get support from the LA to, in the first instance, remove the mobile classroom and, in the second instance, install a new accessible toilet. The governors fully supported me, and we invested heavily into that programme because we wanted to future-proof the school, and we knew that part of that involved having a proper medical room, which also housed the accessible toilet and unisex staff toilets (which are almost hotel standard)!

So, as crazy as it sounds, I knew that the mobile classroom was going, as I did not have the need for the two rooms in it. I knew that I was asking the LA to support us in removing the mobile, and as a result, they had to look at our staffing and our pupil numbers to see whether they were prepared to support us in part-funding the work on the mobile classroom. It was also important that they also saw the positive direction of travel for our school. They were not prepared to support renovating or replacing two classrooms when we had lost two classes worth of children and therefore did not need it. They were not necessary, so removing the mobile became the only option. In removing it, they needed to replace the accessible toilet, and this became an academic decision – with us leading the narrative – and included the refurbishment that we wanted and the design specification that future-proofed the school for inclusivity.

Staff were unaware of the wider implications of all of this. They didn't need to know; they needed to focus on the job in hand, teaching children to the best of their ability. I knew though. I knew that I needed to increase pupil numbers, which meant getting better data, retaining the best staff, training them and enthusing them to stay with me and work hard with me, which would increase income and then allow us to spend on the building, resources, staff, the environment and so on and so on – the relentlessness of it. Therefore, I **had** to ensure I prioritised the teachers, ensuring that the permanent teachers had the correct job descriptions that matched what they were doing and that they were paid commensurate with their roles and responsibilities.

For example, anybody who was doing a leadership role on a short task, a TLR and one of those examples is the person who was in post very early on, before my arrival, to lead maths. His contract was temporary. I knew that he would not stay in the school (and I supported him in gaining employment the following year; he has since become extremely successful). In the meantime, I needed to develop someone else's skills in maths, hence Lottie's role, with at least one person to work on the maths that we needed to build into the future, and therefore, that person needed to have the correct training, and subsequently the correct pay for the project that they were going to work on, which meant a clear staffing structure, with rationale, presented to the governors alongside the financial recovery plan.

I needed to look at the configuration of the leadership team and I knew that the LA, as soon as the Ofsted inspection had happened, provided it was as successful as I hoped, would pull out much of the funding (which did happen). I was eventually left with a leadership team that was quite thin on the ground for what needed to continue to build success, and this was part of our financial recovery, so I had a deputy (non-class-based) and four TLRs in phases to try to distribute some of that leadership requirement. Those people all needed their contracts setting up, and they needed real clarity about the expectations upon them, and they all needed to understand the way their impact would be measured so that they would not be set up to fail. This involved building in coaching time and leadership meetings, as well as covering these during the day so that there would be minimal impact on the pupils' learning and their workload.

Having established who the permanent teachers would be and the leadership structure, pupil numbers and classes, we then looked at the temporary teachers. Some of them had come to us from supply agencies, and if we wanted to keep them, we had to pay a 'finder's-fee'. There were some teachers on temporary part-time contracts whom we wanted to offer a full-time permanent contract to as they had proved themselves in the two terms leading up to Ofsted that they were very adept. I wanted to make sure that they stayed with us, we had invested heavily in their training and their development, and they had in turn heavily invested back into our school.

I also wanted to start to build the structure of subject leadership, so I asked all teachers if there was anybody who was interested in leading a subject and suggested that people talk to me during their PM meetings about wanting to take on those additional subject leadership responsibilities, conscious at the time that the main effort had to be on the quality of teaching. I did not want to overburden anybody in that year with anything extra other than simply focusing on their job, which was to learn their craft (or relearn their craft), and just become really, really good classroom practitioners who would ensure the children were making progress and achieving.

HR is also you as a 'human resource'!

This sounds easier than perhaps it was and quite easy to say in a book in a few words, for this is what we did. **But**, it involved many, many one-to-one meetings, discussions with finance, the leadership team at the time, the governors, the staff themselves. The staff had already seen the way I worked with the SENDCos, so they knew that I was interested in facilitation, in making things work for the individuals, as well as the school, that I was interested in fairness and in ensuring that we got maximal commitment from our staff because of the amount of work that we needed to do to drive the standards up and move forward in our school.

However, with the fledgling relationship that I was building as the now substantive head, I still had to build trust between the staff and me, and this was not easy.

The worst of times and the best of times

You know that you are going to have lots of conversations with people that will change their lives, perhaps for the better, but in this case, in the short term at least, perhaps not. During management conversations about performance, you will certainly change their working life, perhaps change their role, and as a result change their cash-flow/income and therefore family dynamic, and that is a real responsibility. It will weigh heavily on your mind if you're any kind of human being because nobody wants to think that they are hurting someone; nobody wants to think they are having a negative impact on someone else's life.

However, when I was in those dark moments, in that first term at Woodlands and similarly during my first couple of terms as head at my previous school, when I was wrestling in my mind about what I should do for the best, working on my conscience about some staff members, here's what I did. I put, **at the heart of every decision I made**, the pupils in that school. At Woodlands, I thought of the Y6 pupils and wanted the best for them; I thought about the pupils who were in the infants and the years ahead where we could shape their education if we got it right, and I made my decisions.

Making tough decisions is always tough

I suppose in my mind, I could argue that I feel I made those decisions 'courageously', but actually, it wasn't really courage. It was simply a sense of moral purpose. I won't discuss prickly issues like 'support plans' or 'capability' or 'absence management' here, as they would take up a whole book on their own simply in terms of policy. But make no bones about it: these are all contentious issues that you may or may not come across when leading a school.

What got me through those months, if I'm honest, is a sense of duty to the children, a sense of purpose towards protecting the school and the main effort. Around me, scaffolding my growth in the HR arena and supporting me when I was crushed by the weight of it all, was the guidance of people in HR who really were very supportive.

As for the governors? It is impossible to say how supportive the governors were at that time, and indeed are. Whilst they may not have known the HR law, as I did not, they may not have known how things would pan out, as I did not, they did stand shoulder-to-shoulder with me, and they did help me to go through (step-by-step), the processes that we needed to implement. This is so important for a headteacher to be able to work with governors with transparency and enjoy positive challenges and debate about decisions that can feel overwhelming.

I had a great deal of support at this time from a lot of people, but all of those things, all in the same mix, at the same time, sometimes felt insurmountable. Some nights, I would lie there, or some mornings at 0500; in the gym, I would stand there and just think, 'This is not possible', yet I knew that with tenacity and with all of those experts working with me on what needed to be done, eventually, we would find a way through. And we did by the end of that first year, as I said before, although it was difficult.

I wasn't on my own:

> I would say, when I realised the scale of what needed to be done, I initially felt like it might be impossible, and I felt fearful that I would let myself, the children and the school down. Since the first term I have worked at Woodlands, I would say Ofsted and the pressures coming with improving the Ofsted grading have negatively affected my well-being and work-life balance. I have experienced tell-tale signs of teacher burn-out. Personally, I take things to heart and I strive to be the best I can be. I can also be quite controlling over planning. All of these things combined have meant I have spent many weeknights/weekends/half terms working, and this has caused disagreements or upset with my family members and partner.
>
> *– Lottie*

At the end of that first year, we had survived an Ofsted inspection, we had a staffing structure in place and we had staff PM in place which was linked to school improvement and outlined in the SEF and SDP, which was linked to the period in their careers that they were in and with the skills they had shown they possessed, underpinned by a Pay Policy that had been reviewed by governors. Subject leadership for the following year was informed by staff passions they had shared themselves, with a review of the TA roles imminent.

We had begun to make new staffing appointments based on parity and fairness. All of the contracts were very explicit; recruitment was safe and in line with national expectations. Job descriptions were clear at appointment, and for those employed, they were clearer after PM meetings. Everybody began to have complete clarity in what they were expected to do, which meant that holding people to account against those expectations became much easier.

Staff saw the amount of work we were putting in, and they began to see the output of that work. The successes were coming in thick and fast, and we were building on the positive experiences that we had. I spoke in my last book, *Leading with Love*, and this one, about a situation that I had with the Y6 team, who were scandalised that first summer that I wasn't prepared to let that year's group leave without being moderated. Moderation in our LA is voluntary if you are not selected for it. We weren't selected that year, and I opted in. The results were so dramatically good that year that had we not done moderation, it is highly unlikely that anybody would have believed the successes that those teachers had made with those children. What this meant was that the teachers were able to cite the proven track record in subsequent job applications that they made; they were able to speak with authenticity in job interviews that they had and talk about what they had done to affect that wonderful progress and that tangible impact on children's lives.

Equally, it meant that I could authentically share with my colleagues, with the LA, and with parents that, without a shadow of a doubt, we had indeed achieved those results with those children, which was a very empowering thing for the staff and the school, and validated the work we had put in. All the staff could see that the decisions I was making, be they hard or easy to swallow, were all made with the pupils and then staff at the heart.

That is not to say that it wasn't exhausting and extremely upsetting at times. It was.

If ever there was an endorsement for how I work, it is the following:

> I am almost at the end of a Level 5 Apprenticeship by the NCE which has literally changed my life, both professionally and personally. It has allowed me to reflect on who I am, how I come across and what makes me tick. Then, by knowing myself, I have developed better emotional intelligence to know other people better and adapt my behaviour to meet their needs. I am no longer the pacesetter who thinks she knows best, but rather a more open-minded practitioner who asks first, listens more and actively seeks new and creative ways of working, often allowing other people to develop their leadership capacity by allowing them to lead the way.
>
> – Emily

Takeaways

- Managing HR can be messy.

- Always seek advice: legal, HR, union.

- Have clarity; use job descriptions and standards to support expectations.

- Make decisions based on legislation, a clear and transparent rationale and organisational need.

- Never meet anyone alone.

- Make notes in a meeting and follow up in writing.

- Always have the children at the heart.

- Make tough decisions and communicate them with compassion and respect.

Good reads

Armstrong, S. & Mitchell, B. (2019). *The Essential HR Handbook – Tenth Anniversary Edition: A Quick and Handy Resource for Any Manager or HR Professional.* Career Press.
Tomsett, J. & Uttley, J. (2020). *Putting Staff First: A Blueprint for Revitalising Our Schools: A Blueprint for a Revitalised Profession.* John Catt Educational LTD.

Coordinating the moving parts
Project management for improvement

I did not feel very confident in my own personal ability as this had plummeted before Vic's arrival. It changed very quickly as I got to know Vic, saw, understood and lived her vision for the school, when she spent 1:1 time supporting and coaching me and the positive and empowering impact she had on the school instantly. Initially, I had no confidence in myself in my teaching or ability to lead a subject well. I very quickly realised that I had the full support from the senior leadership team and had a HT who was approachable and wanted the best for the school and every single person who works there.

– Roisin

Coordinating the moving parts

I feel certain that, had either of the two executive heads who were at the school before me stayed, then they would have been equally as successful as I have been, given we had the same set of raw materials, but I was the one lucky enough to apply for and get the substantive role. As leaders, we have to start (and, more importantly, maintain) plate spinning whilst also maintaining morale and momentum, energy and drive, simultaneously keeping an eye on the deadlines and timeframes, the objectives and the cash flow. We develop and possess so many transferable skills because of these constant demands, and yet none of us really thinks we do![1]

This chapter will exemplify how we have managed to maintain the plate spinning at Woodlands, from which plate to start with, how to empower others to keep plates spinning whilst you start on others and how you pick up the pieces of broken plate when it goes wrong – which it is likely to at some point! These are all useful things to consider and reflect upon if you are new to leadership or considering it (particularly in challenging schools/schools facing challenges where there are so many plates that need to be picked up and spun).

DOI: 10.4324/9781003440000-12

When we become teachers, none of us imagine that, in fact, we are becoming high-functioning project managers who shoulder the responsibility of knowing that success or failure of so many outcomes, not least for their class of children, lies with them. For school leaders, this responsibility is multiplied and also combined with a responsibility for the teachers and all of the other staff, the fabric of the building and the future – that's why staying focussed and organised is critical.[2]

The ability to keep members of the team on task, to handle the inevitable issues that will develop and to keep moving the variety of projects forward so that the objectives are achieved on time takes much more than simple luck and skill. What does it take?

Firstly, as outlined in Chapters 2 and 4, it is vital to understand the situation fully, which will then help define the scope and create a detailed and dynamic SDP. That plan may be made up of several action plans underpinning it. At Woodlands, I do the overall SDP based on our curriculum focus and on the Ofsted criteria each year; this then feeds into the SEF and my termly report to governors. I don't do it **FOR** Ofsted; I do it for the key stakeholders in my school. I use the Ofsted headings to scaffold the understanding of the governors and wider staff so that they can easily see where I take my priorities from and how I am assessing our grading. It makes it more streamlined, and if I need a format anyway, why wouldn't I choose one that is intuitive and makes sense to **everyone** who may see it? I do the 'headline' and strategic side of the planning. Sitting behind the SDP is the array of subject leader action plans. To be clear, I might do a Leadership Action Plan and a Pupil Outcomes Action Plan in the SDP, for example, but behind that, the maths lead would outline in her action plan how she proposes to improve maths outcomes across the school. This happens for all subjects and ensures that everything is in one place. I don't share this 80-odd page document with Ofsted. I share the first few pages: the overall priorities and the action plans directly associated with the Ofsted areas for inspection. The subject leaders share their individual ones with attached governors, LA representatives and Ofsted when they come in.

Define what the successful 'end state' looks like

Deciding on achievable and measurable end goals was the first step towards successfully navigating that first year and has been a proven strategy each year of my career in headship. From there, I like to draw out what my team **won't** be doing, weeding out the extraneous and superfluous activities that add no value to anyone. This is as important as carefully explaining what they **will** be doing that year as a team and is based on the routine reviews that we do of impact. Sharing the priorities and being clear and transparent so that every stakeholder knows what we are all working towards helps me to communicate the most important aspects of the main effort that year and gives people an understanding of their part in that. This is always my first task, and you have read now several quotes from staff about it, it happens in September when we all meet together.

From the big-picture stuff that gets shared with everyone comes the detailed stuff that is shared with groups or individuals, for example, setting the budget. Because the budget is key to establishing spending limits and then, through regular check-ins, knowing where we are up to in terms of our limits so that we don't overspend, it is vital to understand finances VERY early on. Now, once you have been in a school for a year, you have an excellent handle on things, but when you first arrive, it is a different story.

The ideal scenario (and I will talk more about finances in Chapter 13) is that you set a budget the year before, which means you can afford a teacher for each class, afford to give all staff a pay rise (whether you do or don't based on their PM isn't important, what is important is that you *plan* to be able to do so), you can afford to have TAs to support vulnerable children (I refrained from saying enough TAs because there never will be) you can afford to train staff, conduct essential maintenance on your building and so on. You set a budget and then try to work within it the following year.

Right people, right responsibilities

Not everyone is involved in this; it will differ, and even as an experienced head, for me, it has differed depending on the school, the personalities of those involved and the situation. Now, for us, Sue, the bursar; one of our governors; and I set the budget with the LA advisor, and we then take it to FGB. The governor does a RoV to outline what took place in our finance meeting, and the numerous considerations we made before setting it, and with a few questions from FGB, it is signed off. It is now that simple. Teachers, TAs, etc., do not get involved in budget setting; this is a specific discussion.

Equally, neither the bursar nor the TAs get involved in action planning for subjects, the teaching staff do this, and it is as important as the budget setting. I quality assure the action plans, but they are initially done by the individual. An action plan for each subject, written in detail, helps break down what can otherwise feel like an overwhelming task, especially for those new to both school and subject leadership. That is why I decided early on that in such a large school, we needed to develop templates (for working practice as well as storing information) and to work in teams. Whether you are the maths lead, as Lottie was the last four years, and you are moving to lead on writing next year, the written template and the processes are the same now. There is a two-/three-person team when a teacher who is fresh out of their ECT years takes on a subject; usually, the person who is handing over will work alongside them to ensure they know what they are doing. Roisin worked with Emma for a year as Emma emerged from her ECT year and took on science, even though Roisin was leading on Initial Teacher Training (ITT) and ECT mentoring. Nobody is ever alone doing what could feel like an enormous job. This also means that should anyone be absent, there is no single point of failure.

Before those of you working in smaller schools slam the book closed in disgust, in my last school, I had a maths lead who was also a Y6 teacher, KS2 lead and my assistant head, and a phonics and literacy lead who was also a Y2 teacher, KS1 lead, my assistant head, a SENDCo and a science and an RE lead. I lead on humanities, SMSC and safeguarding. It is tougher in smaller schools, as you lack the people to share the load with; this is why I advocate collaboration and why I offer support to many schools up and down the country who contact me. Where we can help our colleagues, we should because the smaller the school, the bigger the individual load carried by each member of the team and the more hats they must wear.

The framework is key!

Anyway, inherent in constructing an action plan, whether that is my strategic one or the next layer down of operational subject leadership, is to clearly lay out the timelines/cost/review cycle as well as the objectives. Knowing when everything has to be done helps everyone stay organised and keep a grip on the resource management responsibilities, be that human resources in terms of booster teaching or financial resources if you are ordering equipment the term before it is needed.

For me, at the strategic level, I also have to assign roles and responsibilities, in other words, delegate! Again, once you have been in a school for a year, you know which of the current staff you can rely upon to work independently and who may need support at various stages along the way. You know if you are assigning a task to someone who has never had that level of responsibility before because you know your team. I use the PM sessions just before the summer, when we are washing up the year and congratulating staff on achievements, to make suggestions about the year ahead, where their careers could go and what they could explore and become a part of. The outcome of these conversations helps me when I am assigning roles and responsibilities the next year as I try to tie in organisational needs with personal preferences of the staff member and the skills they possess. It is vital for each team member to know what they are participating in, why they are doing it, and what they specifically are responsible for delivering. It is also useful for me to establish with them at this point who they're collaborating with, which reduces anxiety and increases confidence.

Check-ins, but not at the airport!

Again, an action plan allows you to set milestones which encourage you to measure the progress in a given area, a 'check-in' if you like. For us, I ask for the milestones in subjects to be reviewed on a termly basis through a 'Subject Leader Report' – sounds grand, but it is a three-column table in a Word document that tells me what they have done, the impact of it and where the evidence can be located. It is useful to keep everyone focussed and me informed. At the end of the year, the three terms of reviews are in one document and are shared in a booklet for the governors demonstrating progress to action plan with little to no extra work.

I have a schedule of formal 'check-ins' of various types to ensure everyone is doing what they should be, what they planned to and that nothing is hindering them from making progress. Those meetings range from weekly SLT sessions, which have altered in time of the day, length and regularity over the years as we test and adjust to find the perfect way of doing it for us, to twice-yearly PM meetings with staff to check in and celebrate their successes. They involve the whole staff as appropriate; for example, at the end of last term, I had three pieces of vital intelligence to share with them all, and I wanted them to hear the same message from me personally, so I called them all together to share that message and wish them a good summer. Or they involve groups of staff; for example, when I needed to share information about TA reviews, I only spoke to the TAs. This means efficiency and effective use of time for all concerned. Equally, being clear with individuals about time-sensitive information that you need, giving them a specific date deadline in their diaries and having both of you check in via email in the intervening time is also vital. Not all things need to be done in person.

As I said in Chapter 8, reviewing and, where necessary, reprioritising tasks towards achieving the main effort is essential periodically. If the weekly meeting schedule is happening and everyone knows their roles and responsibilities, then this review doesn't have to be a huge task – it can be as simple as discussing why something is not progressing as planned and finding solutions to this to enable it to happen. Having that time set aside to look at the different aspects of a huge plan regularly offers the opportunity to see what has been done, what still needs to be actioned, and who might need a status update or a revised timeline. Of course, it also gives me a chance to congratulate and thank people where appropriate.

When we meet, we always bring diaries and plan backwards from key dates; a small example might be the date we want the annual reports to go out to parents. Work back to give staff a week to PDF and set up emails for them to go out. Work back and that is my deadline to have them all read, commented on and signed and back to staff. Work backwards and my deputy has proofread them all before they come to me and so on.

On the topic of annual reports, and I suppose in many ways in light of both how we revolutionised how the governors work and how we shared and stored information some years ago, we did decide to take advantage of different communication methods, and now we do use 'Google' to enable us to work on a document from remote locations. I know there will be those of you reading this who are far more tech savvy than me and will have much better systems, but for us, the dynamics of our staff and the need we have currently, it suits us fine! Not only do we edit documents, but staff also book-in PM slots with me around their timetables using this method; there are a lot of staff, and it is a quick way, rather than emailing all of them, to coordinate. Let's be honest: if there aren't easy ways for **everyone** to communicate, collaboration and progress can be adversely affected.

As I said earlier when talking about the curriculum, I use a visual method to organise my complex working-thought processes, which means I can clarify my thinking, but more importantly, other people can see all the moving parts as one whole. If I am in the 'storming' phase, and it is all over the wall, it gives staff the opportunity to discuss, question and begin to understand (equally, it can give everyone a bad headache and eye strain!). Most staff will only focus on their part of the school improvement plan; if they don't sometimes see how their part influences and affects the other moving parts, then other things can become challenging. It was no different for me when I set out on the Woodlands School Improvement Project!

Hyperfocus

We can talk all day long about the hypothetical, but one of the most complicated parts of taking on a school in a crisis is that it's almost like a concentrated version of normal headship. The question is – what IS normal? Normal headship involves managing and coordinating several moving parts so that the whole keeps moving forward in the same direction. 'Simples', as they say.

Earlier in the book, I mentioned the different teams that you as headteacher are part of, must manage and must get going when you take on that new school. One of those teams is of course the Administration Team, another one is the Site Maintenance Team, you have the mid-days (the lunchtime guys), you have the TAs, the teachers, the governors and any extra people who work in your school – for example, coaches or after-school club providers and so on.

Now, the thing is, when you are in a school in crisis, you have all of those things, but you also have to quality assure the work and input of every single person and every activity they are doing, and keep a close eye on the cost of each activity, which can be quite a challenge. That challenge can be particularly acute in a school the size of Woodlands when all of the systems either do not exist or need a review. For me, one of the challenges when I got to Woodlands was looking at all the moving parts and working out how they could synchronise and work together as opposed to becoming barriers, and for that job, luckily, my mind was perfect. I will take you down a little rabbit warren now so you can see how convoluted it can sound and indeed be!

I needed to know if we could afford to invest in staff training to improve the ability to teach effectively and influence outcomes for pupils who would be learning more. For that, I needed to bring together the finance team and the leadership team as we prioritised what kind of training we wanted or needed, who needed the training and why, how much it would cost, whether it was effective and how we would know we got 'bang for our buck'. For that, we needed to understand the staff's needs and abilities, where they were in time and space and where we were meeting them in terms of this improvement journey. For that, I had to speak to them or observe them, or both, whilst also looking at data.

To do this for the whole school, I needed the eyes and ears of my trusted leadership team and gave each person a role. I said earlier on, in my 'state of the nation address', I told everybody that they would be allocated a senior leader, and they were. For example, Richard became basically the KS2 senior leader. He attended all of the Y3 and Y4 PPA time and all of the Y5 and Y6 PPA time. He made sure that the team was planning appropriately, that they were focussed on progression, on differentiation (that's not a good word anymore, let's say, that the teaching was tailored to meet the needs of the children) and, most importantly, that there was follow-up. If teachers planned to teach something, and they did and it didn't work, Richard facilitated conversations about why it didn't work. If something has been taught and the children didn't understand it, Richard facilitated conversations about what teachers could do differently to help the children understand what it is they have decided that the children needed to learn and so on. That had to be done consistently, repeatedly, robustly. We had three classes in every year group at that time, and I needed to make sure that, at every level, this same process was happening.

In addition, it was also about deployment of TAs, so for that, I had my SENDCo, Alice, who worked together with me and with each leader, like Richard. We also had Isobel in the EYFS, Sharon in KS1 and my deputy head at the time Kathryn; thankfully, we therefore had capacity in the first year to look at everything, to iron everything out.

So, teachers were teaching, and children were supported. We then looked at progress data, and part of that was using the new tracking system and making sure the way we got the data to input into the tracking system was moderated. Following some training, we used the monitoring schedule to look at books and see if it was making an impact, we observed lessons to see if the strategies we had agreed we would use were in place, we supported planning to try to ensure that the strategies were at least planned for, and if they were not, we questioned why not. We had to source and implement assessment materials to make sure we could assess gaps in learning not just in a group or a class but a whole phase or year group.

Now you see some of the considerations, simply to see if the money was worth spending on some staff training!

> As an inspirational leader, Vic helped me to develop my role rapidly and ensured I prioritised the right things at the right time! The coaching and mentoring from Vic was invaluable, as was what I learnt on the NPQH. Access to Neil Jurd's leadership work and also attending conferences and accessing online training/podcast also supported how to prioritise tasks!
>
> – *Sharon, Deputy Head*

Prioritising

The main point about that is that to accomplish this task, to see if we were spending appropriately in all aspects (I am only using staff training as an example) when we had a limited budget, we regularly met as a leadership team. We talked about commonalities: what are common threads across the school? What do I need for the whole staff teacher training, and what do we need for bespoke training for one or two members of staff?

From there, we worked out a training plan. We knew we needed to address all of the staff in terms of their teaching; they had been so de-skilled for years and were downbeat about the nature of the environment, so I wanted to light a fire in them as a whole to ignite their passion for teaching. We had whole staff training for that, from Hywel Roberts and Deborah Kidd. We needed it. It then helped me understand some issues about staff performance that we discussed in Chapter 10. Were staff not able to teach because they had not been trained and supported? Once the training and support were there, were they still not able to teach? Was this environment the right one for them? What were their barriers to success?

We needed some staff trained in subject leadership of computing, for example, something that was a little bit more bespoke. We weren't at the point where we could roll out whole staff training on that; we just needed the subject coordinator to begin to wrap her head around what was expected of her in the coming year, to start her research on what she knew, what she knew she didn't know – you know the drill.

We needed to train staff in 'safer recruitment'. I was the only person trained, and we needed more staff on the leadership team who were trained to make sure that when we were recruiting, we were really 'belt and braces' robust, not least as I knew our recruitment processes would be checked by Ofsted.

Effective delegation

There were lots of mini projects all going on at one time which involved teams of people, appropriately selected to look at things, who were all feeding back to me as a central hub and a decision maker. They were becoming empowered, but they were hesitant at first, their confidence grew in time, but it was not quick. This involved changing the culture; it involved a monumental shift in understanding who was responsible for what, who was being delegated which powers and to what extent those powers were delegated to those individuals. An obvious example is, no I couldn't spend £50,000 on a project without asking the governors. The Administration Team couldn't spend more than £2000 without checking with me. It took Sharon and I, or Sue and Sharon, to sign off on a cheque. There were subtle decisions also – to what extent was I willing to delegate and how controlling was I as a leader – were questions I was answering in practice.

Whilst we were trying to look at and embed all those processes, and we'll talk more about finances in Chapter 13, we had to consider (in light of our new way of working) everything else. It was an ugly world at times. I did not have the answers people wanted when they wanted them. I needed time and faith.

Personality management!

We had lots of different staff personalities to contend with. I know I have already shared Emily's views about how much she struggled with looking at the enormity of what needed to be done, and at that time, she was a year two teacher. I gave her constructive feedback when she originally applied for the EYFS lead role, which she took on and blazed a trail with! I could see that she was keen and had a huge desire to want to lead and do the right thing, but she needed to work on her leadership capabilities. Incidentally, she has done *really* well in this, and I have coached her through all aspects of both the academic and real-life side of leadership, which she is a natural at. When someone has a passion for something, if you can harness that passion and train them, then it's absolutely a winning combination. Emily is fabulous!

We needed to develop all of the staff in a variety of ways; part of that is through effective PM, which stops careers from stalling and stagnating, alongside preventing loss of enthusiasm. An example of how we managed staff development is Daisy, who was a newly qualified teacher at that time. She was very keen and subsequently became the PE and the Cojo lead at the same time as doing an MA in sports and PE. Another example is that one of our TAs spent five years doing a degree and is keen to do a qualification in teaching with us (which she will, finishing within the next year, on an apprenticeship basis). The deputy head at the time was so good, so talented that she desperately needed to do NPQH and then find herself a job in a different environment as a headteacher and use all the skills that she learned and developed in that new environment – which she did!!! We had another TA who was already on the way to being qualified in a degree, alongside doing her job, and she also became a qualified ELSA for us; she, too, is wonderful.

External visitors

Of course, we were also trying to manage the raft of external people coming in and the weekly practical and tangible significant demands of that: emotional demands of Ofsted dropping by any minute, the general demands of the accountability system, feeding back to governors regularly, managing the requirements of the substantial complex leadership and finance issues.

Physical environment

We also had to think about the physical environment in the early days. The list of moving parts was and is long. Back then, we had a wide range of HR issues, staff training, the physical environment, pupil outcomes, behaviour, policies, finance, governance, teaching, learning, Ofsted. In terms of development, we needed to upgrade the entire school environment; the IT infrastructure wasn't there; the internet infrastructure wasn't there; the site wasn't conducive to good learning.

We needed to think about all of those things very early on and try to work out how we could afford to do the things we wanted to do.

Really, all I can say is, managing all of that without a diary, without prioritising and blocking out time, without working from home occasionally on a key document (and expecting staff to do the same), without putting in follow-up dates, without making lists, without being strict with myself and others on deadlines and, finally, working with my team, curating our relationships, in particular within my leadership team, would have been physically impossible to do.

Takeaways

- The role of the headteacher is to keep members of the team on task, effectively handle the inevitable issues that develop and keep momentum in the variety of projects always on the go so the school objectives are achieved on time. This takes much more than simple luck and skill.

- You need as much information as possible and an action plan to work through priority tasks.

- Diarise and block time, and give (and stick to) appropriate deadlines.

- Work from home periodically to complete essential tasks uninterrupted.

- There will be lots of projects all going on at the same time which involve teams of people, appropriately selected, who will need to feed back to you as a central hub and a decision maker.

- Everyone must understand who is responsible for what, who is being delegated which powers and to what extent those powers are delegated to those individuals.

- Culture establishment is a unique conundrum for each school and each headteacher.

Notes

1 https://www.twinkl.co.uk/blog/top-ten-transferable-skills-youve-gained-from-teaching.
2 https://redbooth.com/hub/10-ways-project-managers-stay-organized/.

Good reads

Morrison McGill, R. (2015). *Teacher Toolkit: Helping You Survive Your First Five Years*. Bloomsbury.

Rycroft-Smith, L. & Dutaut, J.L. (2017). *Flip the System UK: A Teachers' Manifesto: A Teachers' Manifesto*. Routledge.

Woodley, H. & Morrison McGill, R. (2015). *Toxic Schools: How to Avoid Them and How to Leave Them*. John Catt Educational LTD.

12 Building culture
How, what and why

We are a school where every child matters. Our school has a shared vision of improving outcomes for pupils and ensuring pupils leave Woodlands prepared for the next stage in their learning lives – ready to function and thrive in the future. To achieve these things, we always work as a team – never needing to make decisions or face challenges alone. We always communicate and make decisions together.

– Lottie

Building culture, whilst eating strategy for breakfast

For some, including Tom Bennett,[1] culture is about pupil behaviour, which he specifies in his review 'Creating a Culture: How School Leaders Can Optimise Behaviour'[2]:

The way students behave in school is strongly correlated with their eventual outcomes. When behaviour in general improves throughout a school the impact is:

- students achieve more academically and socially

- time is reclaimed for better and more learning

- staff satisfaction improves, retention is higher, recruitment is less problematic.

Standards of behaviour remain a significant challenge for many schools. There are many things that schools can do to improve, and leadership is key to this. Teachers alone, no matter how skilled, cannot intervene with the same impact as a school leader can.

I wonder if it is more complex than this. Some of you might subscribe to the opposite notion that it is the adults who create the weather. As Paul Dix said, 'When The Adults Change, Everything Changes'.[3]

How you build culture, both explicitly by what you say and how you behave on a daily basis (each interaction, decision, review, idea) but moreover the consistency you apply to this over time, for me, is what matters and will be explored in

DOI: 10.4324/9781003440000-13

this chapter, which should be a short one, really (because there is nothing prescriptive that I can say that we did), although it isn't! It feels like everything we did is what created the culture I enjoy, which, as you can see, the staff also enjoy!

Leaders can sometimes be unaware of the small things they can say or do that undermine, or conversely build, their main effort or key message, their co-creation of organisational culture. Habits can be difficult to change, and routines take a whilst to establish. Staff may not inherently know what to do or say to create an improved school culture. If you were to simply tell them what they must do, many will get it wrong in the early days, and it is all subjective anyway: it is the skill of the leader to encourage staff to get back on track whilst rewarding them for trying and to not seem patronising; that is key. For us, it was built in many ways: from staff meetings to the staff handbook, how we created and implemented policies to modelling conversations and coaching people about how to manage parents, pupils and workload.

> There is a clear vision, not just in relation to the curriculum for children (character building, developing lifelong skills) but in relation to ensuring children leave Woodlands as the best versions of themselves and are able to contribute to society and the community they live in. There is a big focus on a team approach and supporting one another as members of staff.
>
> – *Alice*

This chapter will cover some of the significant moments when this has been modelled – from 'managing' staff to managing support from the LA for specific subjects, from managing governor issues to sharing information with parents, and there will be a number of anecdotes that will support you as leaders when thinking about culture creation.

You don't get a second chance at a first impression

First and foremost, as my grandad used to say, 'You don't get a second chance at a first impression'. And he was right. When chief of the Australian Army Lieutenant-General David Morrison delivered a leadership speech, recognised as one of the greatest leadership speeches in recent years, it resonated for three main reasons: it reiterated his inclusive stance for the entire organisation and thus made *every* member responsible for leadership at some level; it was clear and unequivocal; the tone in which he delivered the message was congruent with the content of the message and made it even more powerful to hear.[4]

Now, I wasn't aware of his speech when I took over at Woodlands, but I was aware of communicating clearly and effectively the task that we were facing, explicitly saying we needed to work as a team, ensuring everyone knew that meant inclusively – the **whole** team – and explicitly asking for help from the team to protect the future of our organisation. I think that the quotes of the staff you have read so far illustrate that the message was pretty hard-hitting and pretty overt, so I obviously made the correct first impression, but as I have also said, anyone can stand at the front of the assembled troops and make a speech, what matters is in the follow-up.

> The culture of our school is a team that works hard and is united together to achieve the organisation's shared vision of supporting the academic, social, emotional, mental, personal and physical development of pupils. It is underpinned by everyone's desire to be their best selves and continuous drive to seek new opportunities and improvements. It is underpinned by teamwork, love for one another and determination for our school and its stakeholders to achieve better outcomes.
>
> – *Emily*

What does a school with a positive culture look like?

I think that successful schools have something intangible, a '*je ne sais quoi*', something you just can't put your finger on, but that embodies the following kind of ideals, especially amongst the staff: shared, co-created core values underpinning all decisions; shared belief in making a difference for the community, parents and pupils; genuine care about and compassion for one another, which empowers the collective to do and be the best; strong team ethic, striving for constructive feedback and working on areas of weakness; strong commitment to innovation and creativity.

> If I walked into Woodlands without knowing the school, the school culture would be evident. It is about community and working as a whole to support our children and families in the best way possible. We are hardworking but also fun loving. We adore the children that we teach and want the very best for each and every individual. What underpins this community spirit is how we pick each other up, how we support each other on a daily basis and how we have the highest of expectations for our children. If the culture of our school was less about team and community, I believe staff would give less of themselves to their work and standards would slip. It is important for people who are working so hard to feel valued. When people don't feel valued is when the negatives come: less effort at work, guilty feelings affecting personal wellbeing, mental and physical health.
>
> – *Mel G*

No 'i' in team!

I think when it is distilled, what we are talking about is the generation and maintenance of teamwork! Naturally, this is underpinned by a sense of organisational order created by effective, well-known and well-understood systems. From that comes tangible productivity, delivering against shared goals that are known and understood by all. So, it is relationships which underpin teamwork, and which are created through communication and collaboration, that create culture for me.

That is the kind of culture I want to create because it is what I believe in; it is what I think creates the right conditions for staff to feel calm and regulated, and when the staff are able to self-regulate, then they are brilliantly able to help children do the same. Only then can you begin to tackle behaviour of pupils.

I should caveat the aforementioned with the following obvious statement: problems still exist even in schools where there is wonderful culture; of course they do. Schools are filled with humans and are inherently places of learning about ALL aspects of life. Learning can be a messy business, especially when young people are learning about things like boundaries and respect, but there's always a strong core thread of optimism amongst the staff, despite the issues being managed, in a school that has a positive culture.

For us, at Woodlands, we needed to really work out what our core values were, what characteristics they were based on and what our main effort was. We did that in the first year as we worked through issues, experimented with things, discussed things and engaged in whole staff training. Any barriers that were there between staff and any mistrust between staff and myself had dissipated by the end of the first year, so our core values emerged. I think it is easy to see that misunderstandings and a lack of interest can result when staff are not clear about, or have no congruence with, the vision or values they are working towards.

When the adults changed

When we mapped Cojos character trait development into our curriculum, we were able to build our values into the things we taught the children and therefore overtly include them into the values and vision of our school – but to do this properly took us two years. Nobody likes this, not even me. I used to think that just by pure force of nature and personality, you could instil your values into the entire team very quickly – sadly, you can't (and I can have a forceful character!). You can force people to do as you say, for a short period of time, if that is really how you like to do things, but for people to *want* to do things the way you do them because they see the value in that approach and the force multiplication it offers, well, that's a whole different story.

Our character education and our values are subtly within things like the personalised floor mats that are at each entrance of our school, as well as overtly in displays around the school for all children and visitors to see daily. They underpin the SMSC curriculum and are inherent in assemblies and charity endeavours, as well as curriculum initiatives where we can also support the pastoral development of both younger and older pupils as they are either mentored or mentees. Enlisting older pupils to mentor younger ones can be an effective method of building friendships, supporting transition, increasing inclusion and developing language whilst empowering young people to do the right thing.

> A school full of very caring, dedicated teachers and support staff who work extremely hard to provide the best learning experience possible for each and every child. We are a school where everyone looks out for each other and we always work as a team.
>
> *– Annica*

We regularly and publicly recognise staff and pupil achievements and positive behaviour in a host of ways, from postcards sent home to parents, to 'Hot Choc Friday', to headteacher stickers, to certificate assemblies. When we acknowledge our pupils for their accomplishments in front of their peers, we focus on rewarding the right behaviour, rewarding pupils for being seen to uphold the school values. It also helps them make the cognitive link between effort and achievement, boosts their motivation to do more of the same, and thus supports the systemic behavioural changes you sometimes need – I know we did! Naturally, this is tempered by understanding our individual children and whether they would appreciate a public display of celebration! It was the talented Sharon who drafted the reworked Behaviour for Learning Policy once we had removed the complicated tilts and other bits and bobs of the previous iteration which was so complex that even I could not master it (I know, unsurprising, I am totally lacking in common sense!) Mel G is working on the latest iteration (no complacency!) which will be implemented in January 2024.

> My hardest years as a teacher have been when there was a 'blame' culture and leadership were ready to pull you up on the slightest thing in a negative way. I firmly believe if you support your staff and listen to them (no matter what grade they are) they will work hard and will want to because they care. If you feel supported, trusted, and valued in a sometimes-difficult job, it goes along way.
>
> *– Gill*

It is slightly different when I recognise staff for their achievements and accomplishments, sometimes this is done in my blog to parents, and sometimes a written letter to them or their family, sometimes a WhatsApp or a call, sometimes an email to all staff to celebrate something, sometimes a card and a gift, sometimes it is a nomination for an award (as I did for Alice, she was successful in gaining the National SENDCo of the Year Award, Silver – did I mention that already?) and sometimes it is a coffee-run when I know we are all tired and need a treat. But it is just as important to recognise and appreciate staff as it is pupils. To remain committed to their often thankless and unrewarding job when they are navigating the school improvement agenda in a school in a category, staff need the support and encouragement of you as leaders but also community members and governors. I am able to set the tone by actively listening and paying attention to what is going on in the lives of the staff and showing support when issues arise but also sharing their successes with our governors who have often written to staff to congratulate them.

> I feel that the school culture is all about the team as one, there's consistency and fairness. Credit is given to all not just one. There is a huge team effort present.

> *– Arzoo*

When is zero-tolerance OK?

I do have a zero-tolerance attitude. My zero-tolerance approach is for abuse of staff and pupils by staff, pupils and parents. The safer everyone feels at your school, psychologically especially, the more relaxed and productive the atmosphere and culture will be.

To make that happen at Woodlands, I needed to establish clear behaviour guidelines for all. I called the police to deal with aggressive parents; I called the parents to help us deal with aggressive pupils; I put support in place for pupils with additional needs and asked for help from a range of agencies to enable those pupils to remain in school, but once the threshold had been passed, and safety of pupils and adults had been compromised, I had to formally send children home through the suspension and exclusion pathway, I also had to revoke the licence of parents to be on school grounds.

I never shouted or raised my voice; I was just clear and gave choices and boundaries. The children and parents all know the expectation of behaviour and attitude in our school. I model it: staff emulate me, pupils emulate staff. We ask questions and discuss issues that arise, we also share that information with parents in the hope that they will support us. Sometimes they don't, but mostly, they do, as they see what we are trying to achieve. When they don't, I refer them to our governors, and sometimes they bypass governors and complain to Ofsted and even – on two occasions – to the DfE (which I will talk about a bit more in Chapter 15). When poor behaviour is not directly addressed, pupils and parents may think it is acceptable. Addressing the problem head-on will show it is a key value and respecting self and others is one of ours.

This is one of the most fundamental ways in which I demonstrated my own leadership narrative in the early months during my first few terms at Woodlands. Not only did I show care and compassion for staff with myriad issues, but I also showed compassion to staff who were angry and hurt, worried and stressed out. I showed compassion to parents who were angry and hurt. I made sure that whilst we had an open-door policy for parents to come and tell us how they felt about their children, I was clear that whilst they could share their feelings, they certainly couldn't shout at us or be aggressive towards us. When I stepped in to protect individual teachers from personal, verbal and physical attacks, those teachers knew and understood that they would be protected by me.

It is a moral obligation for the leadership of any school to protect the pupils *and* the staff, not just pupils. If you look after the staff, they will look after the pupils, and for me, that is how our culture was built. **It was built on consistency and follow-through**. To create a positive school culture, fair and equitable rules must be observed by everyone, there has to be fairness and parity. If anyone perceives that the policies are not fairly upheld, the school culture suffers, and respect for you as the leader will dwindle.

I will say that engaging parents and enlisting their support was crucial, but the strategies I used were exactly the same as with everyone else.

> As our leader, I think Vic has given all staff the motivation to be innovative, lead and feel confident about knowing what is expected by subject leaders. Advice and coaching given prior to any visits by Ofsted have really been helpful and made speaking to inspectors much easier. The whole of SLT have been supportive and I feel I can go and seek support or advice from every member of the SLT team. I have also done a lot of research both on the internet and Twitter and kept up to date with current trends and practices. I am constantly reflecting and trying to better myself with the aim of giving the children the best possible chance to succeed and enjoy learning.
>
> *– Pete*

Model the expectations you have of others

I would say that in order to build culture, you need to model the behaviour that you want to see and model the expectations that you want to see achieved. The standard that you walk past is the standard that you will accept, someone said – and they were right. Those behaviour standards that you have as a head, those expectations, have got to be communicated and achieved by working collaboratively. That way, they can be amplified throughout your school and out into the community.

I didn't just look for individuals who had done a really good job; I didn't look to celebrate one or two people who were doing great things. I looked to support everybody to rise up to be as great as the people who were clearly doing really well. I expected them to reach behind them and help raise up other people; that way, we made sure we celebrated everybody.

In our school, everybody gets involved; no job is too big or too small for people to get involved in. As head, I'm not too good to do jobs like unblocking toilets, chopping back hedges or blowing leaves in the winter. I don't see myself as being above any of those jobs, too important, and therefore I wouldn't see any member of staff as being too good, or not good enough, to do any job in our school. That is why the core SLT is a mixture of teachers, admin experts and pastoral experts. This is why, when we devised the dreaded 'barrier duty' timetable, we had me and the caretaker on one barrier and the SENDCo and bursar on the other, or the learning support mentor (LSM) and the deputy on another or any mixture thereof![5] The sense of equality and inclusion that this promotes is now tangible, but perhaps it wasn't initially.

How I support and celebrate our staff, both internally and externally, is really important. I want them to know they are valued by me, and I want the world to know that they are valued by me because they are truly wonderful human beings. I am sure that similar fabulous people exist in all schools, but these guys are mine to care for and nurture.

Our work is often celebrated and promoted through articles in the local newspaper. We work closely with our PTA, which is obviously a part of our parent support network, as is the Parent Forum, which, once a term, meets with the deputy head to talk about school initiatives and their feelings about various different things, giving us that parental perspective that we may not get in a written questionnaire or an online survey. I have used my blog to build bridges and communicate, which I now have paused on a temporary basis. I use Twitter (now called X) and LinkedIn to celebrate what goes on in our school and to share a little bit about my character and my belief system. This means that people can stalk me on the internet and see that I am, in person, exactly as I am in our school and in my personal life, which brings me really to the final point.

The Covid conundrum

Everybody has said that Covid was a nightmare for education, and for many, many people, it was that and more. For us as a school, we were blessed we did not lose anyone to the virus. Whilst it undoubtedly prevented us from doing the work we wanted to do, delayed us and presented us with huge challenges, it actually presented us with opportunities. For Sharon, who is my amazing deputy head, it gave her a chance to really showcase some of her organisational skills. She has such attention to detail, such good organisational ability and a grasp on lots of different moving parts, so for her, completing endless rotas and attending numerous meetings, updating remote learning policy iteration after iteration, re-writing the Covid-19 policy for the website, risk assessments and the high stakes decision-making that she did, which she shared with SLT, was dazzling at a time when the world felt like a dark and scary place. Covid, and managing the impact of that pandemic on our school, just gave her a chance to shine.

In fact, we coined for her the title of our very own 'Covid Queen'. Having spent years in the shadow of others, and lacking confidence in her own ability, it gave her a real sense of purpose and real ownership of everything that was Covid. She focussed on something in our school that was absolutely critical; whilst I pushed forward with the important curriculum development and all other aspects of school improvement, she was able to really lead on my behalf on the acute pandemic-created problems. This was true delegation and true evidence of our school culture of teamwork at its finest.

I do not need to be all things to all people. I have a large, talented and diverse staff. Their talents, blended with my own, mean collectively, we can be all things to all people: we are stronger together. For one person to think that they can do that, and do it well, is perhaps a little arrogant and perhaps a little ill-informed because none of us are that good.

I was really pleased for staff, such as Emily, that Covid had allowed them a chance to reset and gave them the chance to come back to school with renewed purpose. Emily is one of our exceptional young leaders and we were at risk of losing her due to the complex situation the school was in. I think she will not be on her own feeling this. There will be many staff in our school who, after almost two years of relentlessly hard work with me, were able to press pause and evaluate what they were doing, and why. *'Covid gave me the mental break I needed and re-energised me to tackle the changes more positively and confidently when we returned'* (Emily).

For me, I think Covid was awful, but it also gave us opportunities as a staff, in a dreadful global and national situation, to be creative and to do so in a period where we were not expecting Ofsted any day. We're going to look to the positives we took from that time, rather than take the narrative of lost generations and failed children. We simply will continue to work with our children in the best way possible and look back on some of the positives that Covid has left us with, including just knowing all of our wonderful Sharon's amazing skills!

Just quickly, on the subject of staff showing their skills and Covid, I would be remiss not to share with you the amazing work of Alice at this time – it's a few bullet points, but just look at how amazing she was (and of course IS)!

OFSTED information on SEND remote learning

How do we support and develop the behaviour expected of pupils at Woodlands Primary School?

- Annually reviewed behaviour policy

- Analyse patterns/triggers

- Positive adult role models

- Cojos curriculum introduced and underpins behaviour expectations and values

- Consistent strategies and approaches used

- Reward system (postcards home)

- Social stories (particularly for children with ASD)

- Next Steps (CAMHs) cards used to identify areas of strength and difficulty

- Individualised behaviour management strategies when needed are effective (reasonable adjustments and adaptations to learning environment)

- Whole school 'Attachment and Trauma' training July 2020 in order to support children who may display these difficulties

- SENDCo and learning mentor attended 'Our Ways of Working'/'Trauma Informed Practice' in the autumn term of 2020 and used resources shared with the Pastoral Team

- Mental Health Support Team (MHST) meetings, referrals discussed and assessment carried out

- Where 'new' difficult behaviours are presenting (during lockdown), these are discussed with TA, teacher and Pastoral Team. ELSA pack created and shared with parents. Good communication with parents to support

- Where there are exceptions to effective behaviour, these are children with complex needs. SENDCo/Pastoral Team involvement to identify reasons for these difficulties with clear plan of support. Leading to multi-agency approach to address difficulties and put appropriate support in place in a timely manner

How has the role of the TA been developed since September?

- Deployed appropriately for 1:1 support. Prior to September, each key adult sent a personalised video message to the child they would be working with so they could introduce themselves. All SEND information shared with TA.

- TA appraisals carried out to review previous targets and set new ones, taking into account changes in the school environment and role.

- Remote ELSA due to shielding.

- TAs supporting in bubbles continued with interventions/support within bubbles.

How are we ensuring that SEND pupils are engaging in online learning? What feedback are we providing to them?

- Work packs provided to run alongside Google Classroom.

- Differentiated tasks set to meet outcomes in SEND paperwork/EHCP.

- Reasonable adjustments and adaptations made to activities to match needs. Set by 1:1 key adults.

- TAs, teachers and Pastoral Team are in contact with children and parents (Google Classroom, emails, phone calls).

- TAs and teachers responding to work put on Google Classroom (live comments and next steps when responding to work).

- Pastoral Team sent evidence of work completed via email.

How are we ensuring our pre-SEND pupils continue to be supported through a graduated approach in lockdown and when providing online learning?

■ Continued liaison with outside agencies involved with children; Speech and Language Therapy and Mental Health Support Team (SALT) referrals if children are attending school, visitors continuing to come to school (MHST)

■ Monitoring of Early Alert children, if new difficulties arise, address with appropriate support (ELSA, SENDCo, adaptations to curriculum) and monitor by communicating with parents/carers

■ Gaps identified (if work not set or completed, this is followed up by a member of SLT) and interventions put in place or additional/personalised work set

■ SALT resources sent home to continue to be used as were being delivered in school

How are we ensuring that work is differentiated and pitched at the correct ability for SEND pupils?

■ By knowing our children and their needs well

■ TA, teachers and Pastoral Team are aware of what needs to be done to meet their needs

■ Adaptations made to learning activities to ensure SEND children can access them

■ Tasks match outcomes in SEND paperwork (following outside agency recommendations)

■ Specific tasks set: fine motor skills, handwriting, personalised maths, phonics videos, individualised PowerPoint presentations set by the key adult who usually supports them in school. TA in touch with child and family on Google Classroom, email and phone call

■ Access to physical resources (sent home for children at home)

■ Those in school have access to familiar key adult support and adaptations to the curriculum

How are we differentiating the foundation curriculum for SEND pupils to ensure that it is accessible?

■ Scaffolding – writing templates, drama techniques

■ Adult support (scribing)

■ Creative and crafty ideas

■ Small groups in quiet rooms

- Pre-teaching vocabulary

- Visual aids/real-life experiences

- Use of information technology (IT) to support (videos)

- Short burst activities with frequent brain break/bounce break with key adult

- Presentations rather than writing (voice recording)

- 1:1 adult support (for children with 1:1) for those in school

- Outside and practical where possible – geography, art, PE

- Mixed ability groups where appropriate

- Discussion work – sharing ideas/presenting ideas

What remote support are we providing for SEND families to access online learning?

- Personalised work packs

- Laptops

- Differentiated tasks (set on Google Classroom and separately)

- Access to aids: writing slopes, coloured paper/books, footrests, fiddle toys/ chair bands

- Access to physical resources

What is the role of the TA in supporting online learning, learning in a bubble and what training have they been provided with?

- Training/webinars attended during the summer term in preparation for current/new role

- Whole school 'Attachment and Trauma' training

- Training to use Google Classroom early in the autumn term

- TAs commenting on children's work on Google Classroom and offering feedback/marking

- Key adult support in bubble with the child they would be working with

- Continued interventions/support

How are we ensuring that pupils who require additional support from external agencies are still receiving this during lockdown? Have any agencies disengaged with us during this time?

- Varied since March lockdown, September and January lockdowns

- Initially, community paediatricians were not holding any appointments following referrals

- SALT were unable to visit school – some parents did not wish for their child to access virtual SALT sessions

- Education Access Team (EAT) were unable to visit initially but needed to carry out sessions from September 2020

- Educational Psychology Team unable to offer planning meetings and consultations; weekly helpline was offered instead, which we have accessed for advice and guidance. Educational Psychology Team carried out online meetings in relation to EHC assessments

- Children attending school still supported/visited by SALT, counsellor, MHST, EAT and Educational Psychology Team (since autumn term 2020) with appropriate Risk Assessments in place

- Reasonable endeavours completed for children with EHCPs to ensure outcomes are continued to be met for those children attending school and at home

What support is in place to support social-emotional mental health (SEMH) pupils?

- Whole school 'Attachment and Trauma' training

- Our Ways of Working/Trauma Informed Practice resources shared

- Half termly pastoral meetings to review support and plan for new children to receive pastoral support (ELSA, wishes and feelings, learning mentor)

- Pastoral Team offering ELSA resource packs tailored to individual need

- Pastoral Team offering support to parents/carers to address any well-being difficulties

- Children's Mental Health Week (Express Yourself) activities planned for this week

- Well-being/mindfulness resources used throughout the week/term to address general SEMH needs

- Screen-free afternoon planned to enable children to get outside and be active

How are we supporting SEND pupils who are identified as having safeguarding concerns around them?

- Rigorous and high-quality record-keeping and systematic approach is evident in child concern cases through CPOMs

- Continued high-quality record-keeping; any communication with parents/carers, outside agency logged on CPOMs and actions/recommendations shared with relevant teachers/TAs and SLT

- SENDCo/DSL and deputy designated safeguarding lead (DSL) attending online Team Around the Family (TAF), child in need (CiN), Child Protection meetings/conferences and personal protection plan (PEP) meetings

- SENDCo/DSL and deputy SL carried out home visits

- Continued safeguarding supervision half termly with Safeguarding Children in Education (SCiE) Team and local primary schools

- SLT and Pastoral Team checking in with vulnerable families weekly (email, phone call, face-to-face, distanced when dropping children off who are attending school)

- Liaison with social worker, family intervention worker (FiW) and TAF Leads

- Liaison with TAF advisor (TAF assessment underway)

- Phone call to Integrated Access and Referral Team (iART) when required

What support is being provided by the LA?

- SENDCo been in contact with the local MP to gain support

- Meetings with SEN advisor to seek clarification and advice following rejection of top-up funding request (autumn term 2020); however, the SEN Team has not been as accessible as prior to the March lockdown

- EAT support from the outreach officer following referrals

- Continued SENDCo cluster meetings to share good practice and keep up to date with SEND policy and procedure

Initially I was ignorant to how much work needed to be done and the timescale it would take to completely overhaul the operational running of an organisation and change the culture of a more supportive and positive place to work. After the penny dropped, I doubted my ability as the class' behaviour was negatively impacting my wellbeing. I could see each part we reviewed improved teaching and learning, but it felt slow and like we had a mountain of things to tackle before we could move out of the fast lane. Covid gave me the mental break I needed and re-energised me to tackle the changes more positively and confidently when we returned.

– Emily

Takeaways

- You don't get a second chance at a first impression (you can have that one on my grandad, Ron!)

- Anyone can stand at the front of the assembled troops and make a speech; what matters is in the follow-up – never say things you don't mean.

- Model the behaviour that you want to see, and model the expectations that you want to see achieved.

- The generation and maintenance of teamwork is key.

- Naturally, this is underpinned by a sense of organisational order created by effective, well-known and understood systems.

- From that comes tangible productivity, delivering against shared goals that are known and understood by all.

- So, it is relationships, which underpin teamwork and which are created through communication and collaboration, that enable school improvement.

Notes

1 https://www.theguardian.com/education/2020/aug/08/englands-school-behaviour-tsar-letting-children-off-again-and-again-is-like-a-snooze-alarm#:~:text=Interview-,England's%20school%20behaviour%20tsar%3A%20'Letting%20children%20off%20again%20and%20again,is%20like%20a%20snooze%20alarm'&text=Reputations%20can%20be%20made,government's%20behaviour%20tsar%20in%20England.
2 https://assets.publishing.service.gov.uk/government/uploads/system/uploads/attachment_data/file/602487/Tom_Bennett_Independent_Review_of_Behaviour_in_Schools.pdf.
3 https://assets.publishing.service.gov.uk/government/uploads/system/uploads/attachment_data/file/602487/Tom_Bennett_Independent_Review_of_Behaviour_in_Schools.pdf.
4 https://www.youtube.com/watch?v=s_TfZdIhIgg.
5 http://schoolstreets.org.uk/.

Good reads

Lemov, D., Lewis, H., Williams, D., & Frazier, D. (2022). *Reconnect: Building School Culture for Meaning, Purpose, and Belonging*. Jossey-Bass.

Sharma, L. (2023). *Building Culture: A Handbook to Harnessing Human Nature to Create Strong School Teams*. John Catt Educational LTD.

Sinek, S. (2017). *Leaders Eat Last: Why Some Teams Pull Together and Others Don't*. Penguin.

Whitaker, T. (2020). *What Great Principals Do Differently: Twenty Things That Matter Most*. Eye on Education.

13 Financial considerations

The full Monty

The most stressful point for me in the 5-year school improvement journey was a combination – all of the changes and uncertainty induced huge anxiety, plus taking on a new role. Having an extremely supportive Headteacher and wonderful colleagues was a massive help: we were 'all in the same boat'. The Headteacher initially supported, guided and mentored us/me through many processes: getting systems/websites in place – e.g. INSIGHT and CPOMs and this was extremely helpful. Drawing on support from other schools/colleagues who had been through similar was also massively advantageous. But some of it was genuinely getting stuck in and giving it a go. I think if someone has faith in you and shows appreciation for what you are doing, it helps a lot.

– Sue

Financial considerations

As a headteacher, you must be assured, as must your governors and the LA by extension (if you are a maintained school), that the systems, including the broad areas identified next, are all in order:

- Robustness: train governors so that they are proactively involved in review and know how to challenge, also that this is routinely shown in the minutes of any meetings

- Segregation of duties: ensure it is not opaque

- School fund!

- Purchasing and procurement: including pre-approval, reconciliation of statements, information and details to support the items purchased, etc.

- Overtime claims and expenses

DOI: 10.4324/9781003440000-14

■ Contracts: including quote and tender processes to ensure that they provide value for money

Financial audits, for those unfamiliar, can have four different outcomes: usually a sliding scale of 1–4, where 4 is best. If this section does not send a shiver down your spine, then it should because the implications of getting it wrong are scary – do not fear, however; it should be a team effort, and understanding the whole financial picture will help you avoid the pitfalls. So, the wording of the **worst** outcome which you may encounter (for information and to ensure you know and understand the importance of your and the governors' role in financial management) is as follows:

Urgent system revision required (one or more of the following)

■ Key controls are absent or rarely applied

■ Evidence of (or the potential for) significant financial/other losses

■ Key management information does not exist

■ System/process objectives are not being met, or are being met at a significant and unnecessary cost or use of resources

Impact: A very high probability of loss, fraud, impropriety, waste, damage to reputation and/or failure to deliver organisational objectives.

Debt: the penny drop

If you have inherited a school in debt, and you will recall from my conversations with colleagues summarised in Chapter 3 that this is not an unusual situation, then take heart. Many who take on a school in difficulty know school systems need addressing in many areas, and financial practice will likely be one of those areas; even if you are not aware of it at the interview/appointment stage, you might become aware as you gain intelligence about each element of your school through audit/review. However, this section should help you feel able to address those systems by supporting key school staff to address the issues raised in any school audits, particularly financial ones.

I am sure that there are many who encountered debt in their school who shudder to remember how they felt when they realised the degree of debt that their school was in. In the current climate, there will be thousands of heads who feel *viscerally* the strain of debt management caused by so many contributory factors of which we are aware. There will be some of you in this position now who are going to work each day trying to decide what the future will hold and how to manage, knowing that you have to find a way to recover your budget and to establish all of the requisite financial management systems, having never done it before and not quite sure how to approach this, whilst also managing the curriculum and myriad component parts.

As I said previously, I had inherited a 'PA', although she did not perform as a PA for me at all; instead, during the first term I was there as substantive headteacher, she worked alongside me and others to begin to establish the website and different aspects of school that we needed to ensure that we were compliant for Ofsted purposes. She was naturally my 'go-to' person. Sue Moss, the one and only. Although she was keen to work with me and felt pleased that I had faith in her, I think it is fair to say that she felt the same degree of anxiety as I did (if not more so) about establishing the financial systems because neither of us knew what we were doing, to begin with. On this, there should never be a single point of failure in any system, let alone the financial one, and I would advocate that there is always more than one person trained in basic system management if this is at all possible in your school.

As you can imagine, once the cat is out of the bag in terms of debt, no amount of platitudes and explanations, reassurances or supportive chats can possibly help prevent the wider sense of fear that can spread throughout the staff body, mainly in relation to jobs no doubt being in jeopardy if the school has no money. This can all happen very quickly; the fear and panic can spread rapidly, and as headteacher, you will need answers and a governor-backed plan and then, as ever, to communicate that plan to staff in an acceptable and timely way with the guidance of HR.

The Audit Team, which works for an LA, will be able to help a maintained school to gain support from the LA Finance Team. If you don't have one, your LA can allocate a budget officer who can guide you through the budget situation and subsequently help you to set a Budget Recovery Plan (over a period of a number of weeks) ready to submit to your governors in a FGB meeting, and also to the LA (who naturally will have a very keen interest in you not having a deficit budget). You do not need to recover the debt on your own or think you have nobody to turn to, although it may feel like it. Being honest, once 'the buck stops with you' and you are the substantive head of a school, lots of things can make you feel anxious or overwhelmed. And you will have peaks and troughs. But you rise up.

Any kind of debt, even the threat of it when you look at your three-year projections, can make heads feel a bit fed up, and I am no different from the hundreds of heads I see routinely posting on social media about their school budgets and the impact of real-time cuts in central funding that we receive, amongst other localised, contextual, issues that individual schools face.

I could not let the early financial setbacks stop us or impede our school improvement momentum. Everyone was looking to me to set the tone, and you will all recall that my take on leadership and establishment of organisational culture is that you and it are defined decision by decision. So, that is what we did, made incremental improvements, decision by decision.

> Initially, with regards to my new role, as Bursar, I was not confident at all that I could meet the expectations. The role was completely new to me, the budget/financial systems needed work, every team in school required a restructure, from leadership and governance, to support staff. I had no

handover or official training for the role. The job seemed MASSIVE and unachievable! This changed fairly rapidly once Vic outlined our plan. Her enthusiasm, passion, fighting spirit, support, genuine love for the school and staff and her personal belief in me and us and what we could achieve, and how, was infectious.

– Sue

Alongside setting, and adhering to, a budget, you as a headteacher will have to understand whatever system your school uses to pay people, to procure services and buy things, take receipt of money and report and record all of the transactions you make. Back then, we used 'Oracle'; we now use 'Best4Business'. When I say understand the system, though, I don't just mean the interface. I mean to the micro-level: if you permit ordering online, if you only order through registered companies for the LA, if you use a credit card, if you are prepared to take cash from parents for services and meals, how you take cash to the bank, who you bank with, who signs cheques and a hundred other things. We had to look at everything. Every. Single. Thing. Finances were no different.

Manual of internal financial procedures

'The bible' for finances in state maintained schools, as it happens (something that I did not know at that time), is a document called the 'Manual of Internal Financial Procedures' (MIFP). That document sets out how you run all of your finances – all aspects of financial management within your school. As such, it will be different for every school. The way we now organise it means that it has appendices, so it is linked to various policies in your school which will be annually updated (unlike some of the other sections, these will be reviewed but not necessarily changed).

We have found that it is better not to have those policies embedded within the document but – rather – supplementary to it. If it is embedded, it's less likely to be updated regularly, or at all, which could result in it being less relevant to what is happening in the school. Naturally, we began with a review of that manual. This proved to be extremely helpful, and we used that manual, and each reviewed section, as a handrail to guide us through each aspect of what we did and to put in place the foundations of what we now do.

That document, and the contents page that follows, is a comprehensive and wide-ranging document but a good starting point for anyone who inherits an issue with finances.

A. **Governance**

B. **Financial Planning**

C. **Budget Monitoring**

D. **Purchasing**

E. **Income**

F. **Banking**

G. **Payroll**

H. **Data Security**

I. **Tax**

J. **Voluntary Funds**

K. **Assets**

L. **Insurance**

M. **Appendices**

To recap, when people talk to me about finances in a school, I know that this is a nebulous topic. Are they asking about budget setting and management? Are they asking about benchmarking? Are they referring to financial management and auditing? Are they talking to me about procurement and best-value purchasing? Are they asking about income generation and banking? Is the conversation about the school fund? Are they referring to the SFVS? As you can see, the list goes on. Finances are only one of the points of failure for new and experienced headteachers because there are many aspects to finances that must be understood, and without good advice, excellent practices and a system of checks and balances, you can easily fall foul of the world of money in your school whilst focussing on the things you are actually trained to do – as in, teach!

MAT or not?

My good pal, who shall remain anonymous, and MAT leadership member, tells me what I already know, that too many people over complicate finance and it is as simple as this – what comes in must be as much if not more than what goes out. What comes in is almost entirely down to number of pupils, so you must do everything possible to fill to capacity in every year group. You can market until you are blue in the face, but the single biggest pull will be your parent body. They will tell everyone far and wide whether their children are safe, happy and have good experiences at your school. Money out is 80% staff, 15% utilities, etc. (which you can do almost nothing about), so you actually only have about 5% to choose what else to do with. So, if you need to spend less, it almost always means spending less on staffing. If you are spending more than 80% on staff, you are probably heading for trouble.

With regard to MAT finances or finances in a MAT, there is, again, very little difference, other than that much of it is centralised, and there are trust central finance staff members to take some of the burden off heads and away from schools. In our MAT, the general rule is this: anything that has to do with ordering, etc., sits in the schools, but anything that actually hits the bank account (procurement, payments, BACS runs, etc.) is all handled by the Central Finance Team. Heads get a huge amount of support for the setting of their budgets from the CFO. Budgets are agreed on by the board and monitored by local governing bodies.

Finally, for small primaries, there is financial security. If you have an annual income of a few hundred thousand as a school, there is some security in suddenly being part of a company that has an annual income of tens of millions and cannot and will not let you go under.

Food for thought, no?

From manuals to manual labour

Having established *The Financial Bible*, '**The Manual**', we then had to make sure it was in place, and we were meticulously and mercilessly scrutinised by the LA to ensure that we were adhering to the practice we were exemplifying in that manual. How did I do it? Manual labour is how, hard graft, blood sweat and many tears!

Finance by numbers

The first thing I did was ask for governor training in fraud and finances from the LA, and this took place one Thursday night in January 2019 in the junior IT room, as a matter of urgency. Funny, I now see emails from this team on the topic of fraud prevention and smile at myself, five years seem a long time ago! Moreover, Sue attends update meetings and fraud training with new governors, who all feel very relieved when they look at the faces of other poor souls who are shocked to discover what they *should* be doing, safe in the knowledge that we have been doing it for years.

As painful as it was, what we went through now means that we can all sleep at night without any worry, knowing that what we do is not just fit for purpose but is best practice. As you should already know, selfishly keeping our knowledge and expertise to ourselves is not a way of working that I know, so we share our skills (and at times, Sue has probably wanted to throttle me – metaphorically speaking – for offering her services to less experienced colleagues to help them out of the same pickle we were in with our practice!). Sue herself acknowledges this journey:

> A necessary and complete overhaul of leadership and governance, has, following a very challenging journey, resulted in the necessary and now recognised school improvement. The support, both professionally and personally, from Headteacher and wider SLT and Governors, in my ability to do my job gave me the confidence to see it through.

The SFVS form at the time stated that governing bodies of maintained schools had a formal responsibility for the financial management of their schools, and some of our governors had not been aware of that expectation so explicitly. Equally, the headteacher and governors should be aware of *all* key financial processes within the school, even if they are not operationally in control of them, and these should be outlined and explained within the MIFP. Between the two key documents, the SFVS and the MIFP, that our governors had previously not been fully conversant with or understood the importance of (but after training had a total handle on), we were ready. We were able to establish the financial culture at Woodlands – 'how we do it around here'. As I said earlier, the first aspect had to be the systems, the first aspect of *any* school improvement focus has to be to look at the policy and the systems and how they are all arrived at.

Sue and I did not just update and review these two documents on our own. We reviewed everything contained within both financial audits, the SFVS and the MIFP, and set out an extensive action plan that we shared with governors. Then we got on with it.

Sue and I did the groundwork and the 'understand' piece of how it *could* and *would* work in our school, with two sites, the number of pupils and staff and so on. We then scheduled time with the governors to meet and review progress towards our objectives and shared this at various points with our governors, who wrote RoVs that were shared with the entire FGB so that they knew and understood what we were doing (and how, more importantly).

We bought in an eternal clerking service, which I had used in my previous school and which (after doing some research) other schools used and found extremely effective, and therefore, we minuted discussions effectively in our governing body meetings because by now we had a clerk who guided us very effectively through what we had to do, including offering some suggested questions to be asked in meetings.

Once policies had been reviewed and ratified by governors, we ensured that we religiously and rigorously adhered to those policies.

We became a cashless school. We transferred all of our money management to an online system which benefitted parents (after a period of adjustment) because they could pay for services online. It meant that we could, at a glance, see who had and had not paid for various things, including school meals, school trips and so on. It minimised the time spent queueing at the bank to pay in cash, which also enabled us to minimise the risk associated with an individual carrying such cash and – indeed – storing it in the school office minimised the opportunity for inadvertent mismanagement of funds or a risk of a break-in at school. It also supported us when it came to the annual school fund audit, which we reinstated, and so on.

Whilst we had a period of approximately six months of hard work, challenging conversations, and further financial anxiety, in the end, we did set a deficit budget and recovery plan which we were able to adhere to, and within two years, we had indeed recovered our budget. This was through incremental, yet painful, decision-making, consolidation of classes, support from the LA for academic improvement (in the form of subject specialists who would come and support without our paying for it) and income generation from taking on student teachers, review of contracts, challenging contractors about price and drawing on the help of colleagues and networks to find deals. I suppose it was a form of what I now know to be called 'incremental budgeting'. Again, the idea of incremental improvements is something I learned from British cycling, from Dave Brailsford and his strategy of 'the aggregation of marginal gains'. Brailsford said, 'The whole principle came from the idea that if you broke down everything you could think of that goes into riding a bike, and then improve it by 1 percent, you will get a significant increase when you put them all together'.[1]

As per our MIFP, we got quotes for everything that we spent money on in school, so we compared what the quote was offering us with best value. We looked at how much it would cost for maintenance or renewal, whether there was a discount and so on, and this was a time-consuming part of our financial management, but it was and is vital both if you are in a deficit position and in order to prevent yourself going into one.

How do you become money 'savvy' – not all financial management is about cutting costs

We looked to create income for things such as student teachers, but this had implications for what I was asking already pressured teachers to do and their workload, not to mention training; we looked at outreach work and using our large school for hosting training; again, the infrastructure needed to be improved and that meant IT capability and internet; I knew we had the capability to train others once we had raised the standard within school, but I also knew that I could not offer that on a paid basis until Ofsted had been and gone, as I needed staff in school. Some staff left, and inevitably, we chose not to replace them, which helped our budget forecasting position but not necessarily our offer in school. We also reviewed job descriptions and roles: we knew that we had to pay some people more because they were doing a more challenging role, and we knew some people had been appointed on contracts that were not fit for purpose. For example, Sue, who had by now taken over the finances in the school, as a bursar, had to be paid in accordance with her new job description and the new responsibilities she was shouldering.

Financial savvy is about looking at fair and equitable ways of working and establishing really clear and transparent expectations of staff in terms of job roles and job descriptions. I know I have said this before in this book. It is about appointing the right people to do the right jobs. It is about training and investment in people who will stay and produce excellent outcomes for children – this in turn saves you training new staff because the ones you have invested in leave for new pastures, feeling undervalued and overworked.

At the same time, we looked at the external provider for the nursery and pre-school on site, and we agreed with them that they would offer provision for 2-year-olds, and we would offer provision for 3-year-olds because it was financially non-viable for us both to be offering both of those options at the time. Those of you who do have a nursery and preschool will know that the funding that comes to you from the government does not cover staffing costs in terms of ratio expectations, so whenever you are operating a nursery or a preschool as a school, very often you are operating at a significant loss. The gain for you is further down the line when you have already built relationships with the families of those young people who will then go on to become members of your school at statutory school age, so we had to both look at the short-term financial impact and also the longer-term financial gains through pupil numbers.

It was having that long-term view that really did help us because whilst we wanted to try to recover the budget deficit quickly, we also needed to 'speculate in order to accumulate', and that does take, as I said earlier, some courage, some long-term thinking and the backing (absolutely) of the governors, as well as the LA or, in the case of an academy chain, the board of directors.

Long term, we needed pupils. Anyone in a leadership role in a school knows that a large pupil exodus as a result of a double RI, or the school around the corner being graded Outstanding, or a combination or anything similar, could be the potential death knell to a school's financial health. We knew that positive promotion, 'wow' school building improvement and publicity, improved outcomes for children (which are thrown crudely into league tables) living our values, and, finally, the 'Good' from Ofsted would all help us to attract pupils, which is what we all need as headteachers, for our finances. Nothing else, just pupils. This is the deepest part of the school accountability agenda that I fundamentally disagree with, by the way.

The impact of publicly shaming schools through Ofsted and league tables means that competition for pupils becomes inevitable. The 'per pupil' funding formula means that a school in a category from Ofsted is less able to invest in its buildings and staff, pupils and infrastructure, as it has fewer pupils when parents take them to schools not in a category (even though these inspections are fluid and a school that is one day Outstanding could be RI the next!) boosting their bank balances. This is the root of off-rolling, of schools not wishing to accept and support those with SEND, and the total imbalance in what we all do to support one another as headteachers. But that's all outlined in Chapter 1.

What I would say, having looked at the MIFP now several times, is that it's important to review all components of it annually so that it is absolutely reflective of what you do. It is the thing that will ensure that you maintain integrity, that your school future will be protected and that should you need to, you can ensure that all of the money that you are entrusted to take care of as a custodian is able to be tracked.

I know we have been making money through small things over the years; for example, I would perhaps be asked to do a leadership talk, or a coaching talk or do some SIP work for another school. The money that I would make, I would then be able to spend, exactly like I would my own money, a hundred pounds here or there on books, or soft furnishings or an app or a programme. However, this isn't going to have a big impact on your finances or future, it is a drop in the ocean. I didn't want to go back into debt at school once we had recovered it, so I chose to make money and then look at spending money. It's a very simple equation. Regularly meeting with the LA budget advisor helps us to continually reassess and make real-time changes and decisions on affordability, which keeps us safe.

To talk about big money changes and future-proofing the school, I had to look to the pupil numbers. In the summer of 2023, which is when I'm writing this book, we know that we will have only two classes joining us in September in reception. The reasons for this are slightly complex: there is a low birth rate trend in our small area of Ellesmere Port, and this began last year and will continue for another four years. In addition, our 'Good' judgement from Ofsted came four weeks after the deadline for applying for reception places for parents in our area. When they applied, we still (on paper) were a 'double RI school'. Also, there are seven schools in our area, including faith schools and a school with an Outstanding judgement it received in 2015, which may all draw parents to apply to them before applying to us. We had to do something BIG to begin to protect the future, but nothing could happen until and unless Ofsted came and visited us and gave us a 'Good'.

Shortly after our Ofsted inspection raised our profile to a 'Good' school in January 2023, we were briefed by the LA about the birth rate. I knew it had dropped the previous year, but I thought this was a one-off. I could see they were predicting it would drop in 2023, and I knew our inspection report would come out too late. I knew we had gone from three classes per year, a three-form-entry school, down to two and a half, and this year, we were just short of two classes. This was a huge concern for such a big school, one that we've invested significant money in, and naturally tracking the birth rate through for the next five years, which is what I was busy looking at, continued shrinkage in our school would have been catastrophic – remember, bums on seats equals cash in the bank, staff in jobs and so on.

Unfortunately, as I have said, the way schools are funded means that without pupils, you have no way of surviving into the future and certainly no way of investing in the framework and fabric of your school. Therefore, for me, finances hold many different layers, many different constraints and issues and many future problems. There is always an 'immediate', as I said. I'm always looking at immediate, short-term, medium-term and long-term implications of anything to do with my school and (whilst doing this) setting the conditions for future successes. For me, once the threat of the deficit was rectified and a plan was put into place to ensure we came out of debt, there evolved a more long-term view and now, after five years, we are in a position with our 'Good' Ofsted grade to start to think about future-proofing our finances and building on the framework I established with the team.

That framework is underpinned by investing in the school, as well as cutting costs. Ensuring that we have invested, and continue to invest, in our school means that we become a more attractive prospect to parents who are looking around.

Previously, this meant that prospective parents take in not just the Ofsted report, which was clearly a snapshot of what goes on (and has a good chunk of political influence in there to boot), but also when they come to our school for a visit, they see what is on offer for their child: the good relationships between adults and students, the good relationships between adults and other adults in school and how we interact with visitors and one another.

For me, the whole package, taken as a holistic view, is about the best use of money and the best practice of investing in staff, making sure they are trained to the highest degree, which will have an impact on children; making sure the environment is the best it can be, which will have an impact on children, and reaping the benefits when they are realised both in your internal progress and also in terms of standardised national testing. It is also so that we all have a really lovely place to work because we are in school (both children and adults) an awful lot of our time, and school should be (and is) a lovely place to spend a lot of our time and a lot of our life! It should be safe and secure, enriching and inspiring, and that is the kind of school that we are now in the luxurious position of having, but it has taken five long, hard years of commitment and dedication and real-time investment in looking at all financial practices and best value.

The Romans called a period of five years a 'lustrum', and what a lustrum it has been!

> We now have a culture of support and genuine care for each other. We have a culture where everyone wants everyone to be and do their best. We have a culture that invests in individual people and their ambitions and goals. What underpins this? It has to come from the top, from the Headteacher, senior leaders, from having faith in people, encouraging staff and children to know that nothing is impossible. You want everyone to buy into and be invested in what you are trying to achieve. You want people to do what they do because they want to do it.
>
> *– Sue*

Takeaways

- The headteacher should be aware of all key financial processes within the school.

- The governors should be aware of all key financial processes within the school, even if they are not operationally in control of them.

- There are audits available that are thorough and can give you an excellent baseline understanding of your financial practice from which you can plan for improvement.

- These financial processes should be outlined and explained within the MIFP and SFVS and their appendices.

- Between the two key documents, the SFVS and the MIFP, all financial processes should be reviewed annually and understood by all stakeholders.

- Finances could be the biggest headache a headteacher faces; knowledge is key.

- If you encounter debt or go into debt, try not to despair – there are people who can, should and will assist.

- Financial recovery is about investing in the school as well as cutting costs, but it is always based on pupils.

Note

1 https://www.bbc.co.uk/sport/olympics/19174302.

Good reads

Cordiner, J. (2020). *Productivity for School Business Professionals: 4 (School Financial Success Guides)*. School Financial Success Publications.

Cordiner, J. & Flint, N. (2018a). *School Budget Mastery: The Basics and beyond: 1 (School Financial Success Guides)*. School Financial Success Publications.

Cordiner, J. & Flint, N. (2018b). *Forecasting Mainstream School Funding: 5 (School Financial Success Guides)*. School Financial Success Publications.

Cordiner, J. & Flint, N. (2018c). *Leading a School Budget Review: Volume 2 (School Financial Success Guides)*. School Financial Success Publications.

Cordiner, J. & Flint, N. (2019). *Forecasting Your School's Funding: A Practical Toolkit for a Realistic Multi-year Budget: 3 (School Financial Success Guides)*. School Financial Success Publications.

Khan, H. & Campbell, C. (2021). *Financial Intelligence for School Business Leaders*. Independently Published.

Mason, R. (2016). *Finance for Non-Financial Managers in a Week: Understand Finance in Seven Simple Steps*. Teach Yourself.

Helpful links

Julie Cordiner. X: @juliecordiner
Facebook page: https://www.facebook.com/SchoolFinancialSuccess

14 Academic considerations
Systematic, routine, research-based

One stressful point earlier in the improvement journey was SATs and external moderation in 2019 as a relatively inexperienced teacher who was very aware of pressure and expectations of getting the Y6 cohort to a certain level and showing significant progress. Our most recent Ofsted felt very stressful, being aware of how hard we have all worked as a team. As I was now in a leadership role compared to 2019, I felt the heightened level of responsibility and worried about letting the team down. I overcame all of the above with the support of the year group team and other members of the SLT. I felt prepared for all of the above through clear discussions, understanding the school's development plan and areas of improvement, and from being able to access training/CPD to prepare (subject leader courses, moderation training etc). We have never been left to worry/stress on our own, and there has always been someone to talk to.

– Lottie

Academic considerations

Having considered the finances in the previous chapter, of course, we have to consider the academics! To be clear, whilst trying to muddle our way through the financial documentation, practice, policy and planning; establishing routines and a system so that everybody was clear on how we do things; and ensuring that there was transparency and the systems were effective and easy to manage for all of the Administration Team, we had to do a similar thing for the academic side of school.

I am not losing the plot, by the way, but for at least the third time, I can summarise the dichotomy this presented with a snippet of conversation I had in an SLT meeting with the director of education when he visited school during that first year. Firstly, he said in the meeting, with absolute unfettered exuberance, that he had told a conference packed with my colleagues that he wanted to take my blood and clone me for what I was doing at Woodlands (I have never been to another

DOI: 10.4324/9781003440000-15

conference as I was, and remain, mortified). Secondly, I said to him that I could prioritise either the finances or the academics in the short term – I asked him which he wanted me to focus on. He replied with a laugh, 'Both'.

Assessment and moderation

I think it's important to talk about things like assessment and moderation when talking about academics, which are the kind of 'checks and balances' needed for teachers and headteachers in order to inform policy change and practice improvement from the academic perspective, even though they can be almost, well, *dirty words*. It isn't the practice that is bad but rather how it is *weaponised* that is fundamentally wrong.

For me, again, just to reassure you that I am in full possession of my faculties, one of the early indicators to all of the staff about how we were going to do things around here was Y6 when, in my first year, the 2018–19 year, when we had *SO* many other workstreams and issues to resolve, I requested moderation…

We had to think carefully about how we both managed our expectations of those Y6 children and supported them to make rapid progress, alongside also understanding whether our strategies had worked and which of them we could translate to both other years and future work. Many of the teachers were new to the school. Again, as I said previously, we had a large sector of the staff cohort who were not permanent teachers. They had either been recently employed or were on a supply contract from an agency. This meant that in Y6, we had: somebody who had been teaching for three years in the school (in Y3), somebody who was newly qualified, and somebody who had been asked to look at maths on a temporary TLR contract for one year. I had appointed none of them and had no idea of their calibre, ability, skill set or disposition. What none of them had any experience with was Y6, a school in challenging circumstances, working as a large team, moderation across that team or challenge and rigour to the degree that we had to employ in that school during that first year. In this respect, they were all on a level playing field.

Having established the reading and writing strategies that we planned to use very early on, we then needed to work out a way of measuring how much progress we were making across the school internally and making sure that we were applying that approach in a consistent fashion. This would then inform the tracking system and subsequently inform the necessary conversations with parents, pupils, other staff, leaders, governors aaaaaand last but not least, Ofsted.

In my previous school, I had established a very simple but very robust monitoring schedule, the basis of which became the monitoring schedule that we use at Woodlands. That monitoring schedule is based very simply on the focus for the year in terms of the SDP (which actually then feeds into each staff member's PM objectives and in essence directs the way that we all work in order to ensure that we make progress in the area of focus).

In the 2018 to 2019 school year, we had to focus on writing as a priority. Having looked at, and assessed, the Y6 students in September 2018 using methods brought with me from my previous school (nothing special: past SATs paper questions and NFER, for example), I knew that there was significant work to do to ensure they started secondary school prepared and academically ready.

Although we don't operate in a blame culture, let's be honest, without immediate intervention and robust support to ensure the Y6 pupils were ready for secondary school that academic year, this would have rendered us ineffective in the eyes of Ofsted, and to be honest, it would have cast doubts on my ability to lead the school to improvement. To that end, a robust monitoring schedule was established at Woodlands in exactly the same way as it had been established at my previous school.

Monitoring schedule

Each week, senior leaders focused on one aspect of school improvement. The monitoring schedule was shared with all staff so that it was completely transparent. Everybody knew what was coming, when and why. There were no nasty shocks or surprises. We all knew the reason why we were visiting certain elements of monitoring on that schedule, and everybody knew that they were working towards those small checkpoints, which were organised on a termly basis. The SLT processes also ensured that as an SLT we worked together.

During that time, the governors were becoming equally well informed, as the outcomes of the monitoring schedule were shared as part of the termly headteacher's statutory report. The impact of the monitoring schedule, again, meant that we had a very firm handrail which guided our practice and steered our conversations with all staff about school improvement. It influenced when the LA support staff came to look at various subject areas so that we did not repeat or overdo some of the monitoring in the same area and overlook other areas. It enabled us to ensure balance.

As previously mentioned, a senior leader was attached to each key phase in school and sat with the teachers and the teaching assistants in the weekly PPA sessions. This was to plan the work for the following week, assess the quality of the work completed the week before and compare the work in the books in all three classes so that staff could see and understand at the point of planning what the children were producing and how it could be improved incrementally. The input at the planning stage supported teachers adhering to the pedagogy and the framework that we were using; this ensured that we were all very clear on the expectations, which meant that when we followed up the following week in the monitoring session as SLT, we knew what we should be looking for and it tied up any potentially loose ends. It also meant that we were very focused and very cohesive, tightly drawn together on exactly what we were doing and why.

Monitoring the plan rather than the people

Step one in the cycle was the framework or the overview. For writing, this also tied into the reading framework. We therefore ensured that pupils had access to cohesive and relevant content and material underpinned by good strategies. We bought in the consultants for the products we were using to train staff in order to be able to use that material to then implement it successfully. We made sure that senior leaders were in the training and subsequently planned writing activities with teachers that teachers could then discuss afterwards and ensure they understood the progressive nature of what they were teaching: building challenge and rigour for the children, building consolidation in their understanding and ensuring that any gaps in the prior knowledge were addressed through really focused quality-first teaching that was going on in their classrooms. They had never had such intensive support. The next stage was the teachers actually putting the planning into place and discussing it with one another on a daily and weekly basis. Staff ensured that they were at least in line with one another on a daily basis, and if things were not working, they were able to discuss and adapt for the following day.

At certain points through the term, the work was then cross-referenced vertically, as well as horizontally, and included the teachers. We made sure that we looked at moderation both across the three classes in the year group and across the key stage. For example, the three Y6 classes would be moderated at first, and then we would look at how that corresponded to the content and quality of the work produced in the three Y5 classes, and after how it corresponded to Y4 and Y3 to ensure that what we were looking at, from a strategic level, was progressive building blocks in terms of children's knowledge and understanding. We would then match it to what was happening across the whole school, reception and emergent writing and reading all the way to Y6. Involving the teachers in this was vital and also time-consuming. Sometimes senior leaders taught classes so we could work with teachers – an image paints a thousand words, after all, and the point was for the monitoring to have impact! It was so time-consuming and laborious that it needed impact in order for it to be worthwhile effort expenditure.

Where the progress or clarity was not evident, we would then intervene as a leadership team, and that intervention became part of the planning process. The senior leader would go into the planning time and explain to the teachers where this was going wrong because all the senior leaders were involved and invested. We had collectively worked out the barriers and what could and should be done to build and improve, and this was put into action.

The monitoring schedule allowed us to routinely, at least every other week, if not weekly, ensure that any gaps in either teacher knowledge and ability or pupil knowledge and ability were addressed so that, at the point of learning, almost, we were able to go back, revisit, rectify and re-teach where necessary. The outcome of that practice, and the impact on children, was that I knew we were making a lot of progress.

Alongside our own monitoring and the training of staff internally by this process, we had a lot of people in from the LA who were double-checking our monitoring and conducting their own for the purposes of the School Improvement Team. They were involved at every level within school: finance, maths, phonics, early years, literacy and so on. When those initial indicators were looking so positive across the board, it was both gratifying and affirming, but it was also scary. I was conscious that I could not allow any speculation about the quality of what the children were producing to detract from our school improvement progress overall, both in the public domain and in terms of the LA's confidence in me as a leader, not to mention in our school's ability to continue to progress.

I knew that proving our integrity and the accuracy of our marking and moderation in writing would have an impact on the ASIA and on what she discussed with Ofsted when they came in, and demonstrating 'capacity for improvement' was vital for us to be able to show to Ofsted that we were on a trajectory of success and thus retain the RI judgement.

That year we were not selected for LA moderation at Y6 or at Y2!

I elected, however, to have moderation at Y6.

This caused a lot of issues, primarily in terms of the Y6 staff at the time but also in terms of how that rippled out through the rest of the staff about why I was contradicting myself (for example, having said to staff I would minimise workload, why was I suddenly asking for moderation, which would dramatically increase workload?) The Y6 staff were very anxious about the impact of preparation of the materials; you have to rank the books in the year group – for us, at that time, this was 90 children, and in order to rank them, you have to understand exactly where each pupil was. It was a very challenging time.

Nevertheless, I knew that it was the right thing to do and I had the courage of my convictions. I did explain to staff the reason why it was important, but this fell, at that time, upon deaf ears. We had successfully survived Ofsted, and they had all observed that we were definitely on the right track and that we had capacity to improve, so despite gaining a second RI, they knew I was a good leader (not to mention the leadership judgement and my receiving a letter from Amanda Spielman), yet the staff were still extremely cross with me when in the June of that year, we had our moderation in Y6.

The outcome of that moderation was that it successfully corroborated what we had thought: it validated externally and internally our standards and our understanding of where we were. It reinforced, across the SLT, that our practice was robust and effective, that what they had learned alongside each other, with and from me, was useful and valuable information in terms of school improvement because those systems have since been implemented across the board, not just in writing. It enabled staff members, as I said previously, to legitimately and authentically make reference to the work they had been a part of in any future applications, and they were able to reinforce their application with this information at interview and offer examples.

The process was positively beneficial for everybody, if overshadowed initially with dissent, but the main people who benefitted, of course, were the children who left for high school with a very clear understanding of their abilities, 80% of whom were able to access the curriculum with no further input (and increase of 50% on the previous year). I do not agree with SATs in the way that they are currently configured, simply because I do not see that they add any value to the pupils. I do believe, however, that in doing our monitoring the way we did, the way that it enhanced what we knew and understood about our pupils, we were able not just to ensure they made progress during the school year but also that they moved up to high school with a really positive transition conversation taking place between the Y7 tutors and our Y6 staff about what those children needed once they had arrived, in other words, what we had not quite been able to help them gain in the short time they were under my guardianship.

That monitoring schedule is still used today. I've used it for 11 years now as a headteacher; the basis of it can be seen in the following table (obviously, there are several rows beneath the headings, and I have only shown the actual first and last week of effective monitoring from autumn 2019 for illustration! Hopefully, this will show you the simplicity of it, however).

Key areas for improvement based on current data		Evidence		
Ofsted Priorities		**Evidence**		
Weekly Monitoring Schedule for Autumn 2019				
Week commencing:	**Area of SLT focus and link to Ofsted priority**	**Evidence**	**Who**	**Impact**
September 16	Are standards/ expectations set from the outset? 2b	Staff have established high expectations. Writing 'contract' is evident in all children's writing books. Editing code used and marking of writing policy is used consistently across KS1 and KS2	SLT	
December 16	*Assessment week completed: all assessment information complete, pupil progress meetings to review progress of all children. Email to governors regarding termly data.*			
ALL STAFF TO REVIEW GROUPING, PLANNING AND PRACTICE IN LINE WITH HEADLINES ABOUT PUPIL PROGRESS DISCUSSED AT THE END OF THE TERM IN PREPARATION FOR SPRING TERM 2020				

You can see how it draws together the rationale from the SDP (key areas for improvement based on current data), which feeds into the SEF, and also underpins other school improvement work in school (Ofsted priorities). We share it so that there are no horrible secrets, no nasty surprises because for us, school improvement is transparent. It is part of a journey we're all on, striving for improvement, and we will continue with it, focussing on improving for the children.

Valuable assessment versus valueless assessment?

Whilst I don't agree with SATs or national testing the way the data from them is currently used, I do think that testing and assessing children can have value. When I was first teaching many years ago, we would spend a lot of time looking at our assessments and conducting question-level analysis at various points during the year in order to inform our knowledge of the cohort of children that we had and shape some of the ways that we taught those children. Whilst I'm sure this practice still goes on, and it does at Woodlands periodically, there seems less of an emphasis on this kind of assessment than there is on the kind of assessments that are used to categorise schools and to create unhelpful league tables that have little value or use.

Equally, whilst I think Ofsted has its use to a degree (I think accountability and having your academic standards overseen by a body that is not related to a political party or the school system itself would be useful), the way it is currently configured has got no value whatsoever. It creates work unnecessarily and an unnecessary degree of anxiety for staff that pupils inevitably pick up on; it does not communicate to the community, the parents concerned or future parents exactly what goes on in a school – because how can it? An Ofsted inspection is only ever as good as the day the inspection takes place, and the reports are reductionist at best and bland documents at worst. Not to mention it is a political stick. It is only ever as effective as the people who are assessing the school and their knowledge and understanding of school systems themselves. Whilst Ofsted strives to make this an effective and transparent system, it is organised and run by human beings, to create a narrative about governmental assurance, and as long as this is the case, as we all know, human beings are fallible, and none of us are perfect; therefore, the system will always be an imperfect system.

I think that greater involvement of those in the teaching profession, in how teachers are assessed, how schools are assessed and how students are assessed, would really benefit and value the school system that we have, but I think we are a long way off that taking place, particularly whilst education is used as a political tool or weapon. We have to accept, as school leaders, that we will be assessed using the Ofsted parameters that are supported by the metrics of SATs, but what we can do is ensure that what we are doing is authentically what we believe is right whilst also using the information that we gather in our daily work to demonstrate that we are prepared for the flawed inspection system.

As I said earlier, I am not a fool or naive. I may not agree with the system that we have, and it may cause me a lot of cognitive dissonance to have to work within a system when I don't agree with it, but at the end of the day, as a headteacher who has the mental health and physical safety of the staff and the pupils at the very top of my agenda, as well as the academics and the future-proofing of the school and its finances, I have to take cognisance of those external drivers, and those external machinations – much as I would like not to. **I do not let them guide me!** Instead, I let what the school needs, what the staff needs and what the pupils deserve guide me, and then I use that to inform what I prepare for the school year and collect evidence of what we have done and why to share with everyone – Ofsted inspectors are part of 'everyone'.

Celebrating successes – cheerleading!

One of the ways I have supplemented the formal methods such as the SEF and 'Headteacher's Termly Governor Report' is to openly celebrate any internal and external successes that we have within the children and staff at school, both through my own weekly headteacher blog that I took to writing when I arrived, through X (previously Twitter) and social media and by sharing any staff and pupil accolades, awards and recognition with parents but also through nationally recognised forums such as Sky News documentaries, which share us on a wider scale. We have had the Cojos work celebrated, and this has been wonderful, and the leadership work I have done has been well received.

> Initially, I felt very apprehensive when I realised the scale of what needed to be done and it made me frightened that things would return to a time where I had little to no work-life balance. However, it is important to mention that this was before I got to know Vic and her ethos for work and the school. She is a problem solver, fixer, listener, confidant and everyone's biggest cheerleader in our school. At any point where I felt that things were becoming unbalanced, Vic was always there to turn the negatives into positives and she was a huge support who I cannot thank enough.
>
> – *Roisin*

More importantly, however, and on the topic of writing, it became about celebrating some of our perhaps previously undervalued or under recognised staff, especially those who had stuck with the school through its darkest years. One of those in particular is Laura, who perhaps did not feel valued when she came back from her second maternity leave (she is currently enjoying her third with her beautiful baby girl) and was very concerned about her job. She came into a school with me that was very different from the one she had left. She came into a school that was in a very challenging situation, with her own small children at home who also needed her time and energy.

Prior to the academic year 2022/3 commencing, Laura worked closely with the EYFS lead to discuss the implementation and impact of introducing Pathways to Write into our nursery and reception settings. Whilst she thought that this would provide a consistent approach to writing in Woodlands, the team also felt that Pathways would help to promote a love and excitement for books, reading and writing from an early age.

In order to introduce the programme gently throughout the autumn term, we, as a SLT, decided to 'pick and choose' what suited our children from the comprehensive planning resources that Pathways provide. As we are a large primary school, using a programme like this has helped us to keep EYFS closely linked to the rest of the school, ensuring consistency and a clear progression of skills. It also makes it more manageable to prepare resources for both year groups.

Once implemented in the autumn term, Laura, as per our usual routine, worked closely with the EYFS staff to refine and remodel the Pathways units to make them work for us and our school. The Pathways units have become our driver for progress at the beginning of each half term. Following this, we then tailor the learning to the interests of the children using the 'mastery targets'.

Throughout last year, due to our double RI judgement, we were able to access the support of two subject experts provided by the LA to offer support and guidance to continue to enhance and improve the teaching of writing at Woodlands and thus improve the data outcomes. After feedback from a 'book look' in December by one of those subject experts, I challenged Laura on the types of opportunities we were providing to stretch and extend our more able children whilst also supporting those children who were emerging into their year group or working well below. In response to this, Laura held a staff meeting to look at ways in which we could make adaptive teaching strategies explicit in our English books, ensuring that it was/is evident how we stretch and extend those potential 'greater depth children' (love the vernacular) and how we provide support to those 'working towards'

The introduction of writer's toolkits, vocabulary cards noting audience and purpose and proofreading and editing slips are some of the strategies now evident in books to stretch and extend those children whilst strategies such as word banks, writing frames, story maps and shared writing support the emerging writers. We also worked hard in writing, similarly to other subjects, to create differentiated knowledge organisers which introduce each unit of work and allow the children to have a shared understanding of individual expectations on them during that half term. These are displayed on their working wall as a constant reference point. This clear differentiation was easy to evidence during our inspection, and it was a privilege for Laura to celebrate with the inspectors.

Throughout the year, Laura has introduced many initiatives to enhance our writing provision to ensure the children at Woodlands get the best opportunities. Whilst ensuring our children are reaching the expected standard for writing, she has also strived to develop a love of writing across our school by arranging inspiring and creative sessions. Y5 and Y6 had a writing workshop led by a local author who talked to the children about the process of writing and worked with them to produce their own Norse myth in line with their study of The Vikings. For many of the children, this gave writing a real audience and purpose. Over in KS1, children were invited to a fun and engaging superhero writing workshop which allowed them to be creative and imaginative away from the constraints of their mastery targets. What a success story! In addition, what she has done in transforming our work in literacy, both in reading and in writing (which is really quite exceptional) has been recognised by the company that we are lucky enough to work alongside for reading and writing, the Literacy Company, as has her work in our school and the work produced by our children. Our children's work is being used as exemplification materials for other schools to be able to moderate against! I recognise that I am lucky; we have three classes in a year group and six classes in a phase at times, whilst other schools with single form entry or less, and those with mixed year groups only do not have that luxury – so our exemplification materials benefit those schools to be able to compare and contrast their work against ours if they don't have a team internally as we do.

In addition to that, Laura has been asked to write guest blogs about what we have done in our practice at Woodlands, and I know that she has been extremely successful in both engaging parents and pupils in her mission to develop reading in our school – which is now classed, as a real strength (by Ofsted but, more importantly, by us)! It will be different in every school because each school has its own unique strengths. I know that there are schools, some of which I've celebrated in my last book and publicly on X, that do focus on one aspect of being brilliant, in one aspect of what they do, and it is reading, and they are utterly world-class. We do all things well, and there are some things that we do exceptionally well, just like every other school, but I think certainly the size of our school, the intense work that has been put in during the last five years and the fact that our children now read more, and enjoy reading more, means that they can access all of those other areas of the curriculum. Most of this underpins our ability to show such good progress in all areas of the curriculum and really good engagement of our pupils in that robust curriculum.

We have had that statement fact-checked, by the way, by the wonderful Ofsted! You will know that we had our long-awaited Ofsted inspection on January 18 and 19, 2023. Inspectors always have detailed and significant feedback to share during and after the inspection; however, a report only skims the surface with a mere few hundred words allowed. This is another reason I feel they offer no real value – there we are though. At a time when many schools were (and are) dropping down a grading due to the tighter inspection framework and robust nature of inspections, I was delighted with the further detail about all aspects of the school from the feedback sessions and more than delighted about the school being awarded Good across the board – it was the golden ticket we needed!

Takeaways

■ Assessment and moderation are the 'checks and balances' needed for teachers to know that they are on the right track when compared to colleagues and also to give effective feedback to pupils.

■ Headteachers need assessment information to inform policy change and improve practice.

■ It isn't the practice of assessment or moderation that is bad but how it is weaponised.

Good reads

Blatchford, R. (2019). *The Primary Curriculum Leader's Handbook*. John Catt Educational LTD.

Kenyon, G. (2019). *The Arts in Primary Education: Breathing Life, Colour and Culture into the Curriculum*. Bloomsbury.

Ogier, S. (2022). *A Broad and Balanced Curriculum in Primary Schools: Educating the Whole Child (Exploring the Primary Curriculum)*. SAGE.

Sewell, L. (2018). *Planning the Primary National Curriculum: A Complete Guide for Trainees and Teachers (Ready to Teach)*. SAGE.

Waters, M. & Banks, C. (2022). *A Curious Curriculum: Teaching Foundation Subjects Well*. Crown House Publishing.

Warts and all
The messy business of complaints

Initially, I was not confident that I could meet professional expectations following the 2016 Ofsted inspection. The report speaks for itself, feedback felt damning and almost every area required improvement.[1] Over time and with clear leadership and planning as a whole school team, the curriculum began to take shape and show progression, assessment became clear, and we saw the improvements we hoped to see in KS2 results 2019. My confidence only further took a knock due to covid – at that point we were battling historic gaps in learning in addition to a global pandemic! When children returned to school, we knew what needed to be done. The goals were still clear, and the steps we needed to take were too. Certain feedback from external support did also knock the confidence of the team, but ways to improve were also clearly provided and the whole school worked towards these next steps each time they were given.

– Lottie

Warts and all

OK, if I haven't already done so, then I think it's really important to be clear and say that this has not been plain sailing. I need to say that there have been some huge lows. Of course, there have been some highs and some real moments of celebration, but I have to be honest with you and say it has been five long and hard years of constant and consistent efforts and hard work from everyone concerned. If you have signed up to lead a school in difficulty, or find yourself doing so, then it is to be expected. Naturally, there have been tempo changes at various points, and there have been changes in focus and direction as a result of, for example, the finances, post-Ofsted or Covid, but it is important to say there have been very low moments in this journey. This is the 'open book' section, the vulnerable section, the bit where I feel totally exposed when I tell you just how low it got; it isn't all fairy lights and coffee mornings – not even for me!

Why? Because I want to tell you that there is light at the end of the tunnel in the national climate we find ourselves in and the impact that we know negative Ofsted

DOI: 10.4324/9781003440000-16

judgements can have, I want you to find hope that people like me have managed it and therefore it is possible. I know from my many networks that the issues I share here are issues that you all feel very deeply about and which are helping create the narrative of teachers and leaders wanting to leave the profession. I may use my own personal anecdotes here, but I know that I have shared these with multiple people and have had a wave of agreement and nodding heads, shared experience and affiliation. The message? YOU ARE NOT ALONE. THIS IS NOT PERSONAL. IT HAPPENS!

For me, some of the lowest moments have had revolved around what I feel are unjust complaints. I know that even in schools that are doing well and routinely enjoy a stability we have only recently had, there are complaints, and they cause untold issues for school leaders, so it is not exclusive to our school or me, which helps a little to put it all into perspective. Now, I do think people, if they are unsatisfied, should indeed complain, be that in education or anything else – I do think there is a short book in this where collectively we could help people see that the 'how' of their complaint is as important as the 'what' that they are complaining about, but that is another story.

How not to complain

As for school complaints, I think you will come across a small group of parents in our society today who have taken the expectation of the government that they should be involved in, and have an active say in, what goes on in the child's school to an impractical and frankly unsustainable level. This is no doubt exacerbated by social media and evidenced in open social media groups across the land.

When I have looked at social media sites, as a parent and an educator (which is frequently), I have seen open warfare between people who have such polarised opinions of what should be done in a school, or educational establishment, from early years settings to university, ranging from holiday fines to behaviour issues, uniform to chargeable trips and so much more. This includes people within education, consultants and government, and also parents. To the discerning eye, this alone should be enough for everyone to see that school leaders do not have an easy job of trying to navigate the multiple expectations of their school, in line with those of government and also Ofsted, whilst ensuring children have the resilience and skills required for adult life.

Indeed, I was reading very recently about the phenomenon of 'Snow Plough Parents', for example.[2] Whilst our society is built on the premise of free speech, and we all are entitled to exercise that speech, I often think that the responsibility to act and behave in an appropriate way (the balance to this 'free speech') has somehow been lost as social media has grown and social conscience has perhaps declined.

The combination of social media growth and everyone believing their interpretation or opinion is the only one, the right one, not that it is one of many, can be toxic, and I think this can fuel the attitude of a group of parents who feel empowered to challenge educators in a way that is not always helpful; in fact, it is actually so harmful, it is destructive.

One of the most painful things that I feel many school leaders, myself included, experience is when parents have said things like, 'You do nothing for my child', 'The school does nothing', 'You have not supported me', 'You do not know what you are doing' or 'You should not be in the position you are in'. Often, this is in response to a school leader challenging the parenting style of an individual and doing so to protect the child/children in their care, for whom they are responsible, yet they appear unclear about what this means. Sometimes it is because we, as school leaders (and thus the public face of the system), do not have the answer that they have demanded or expect, believing that their case is unique and sometimes even that the world owes them or their child something special. I have no idea, nor do the colleagues I have spoken to, about this phenomenon, or where this sense of entitlement comes from, but I do know that even in these circumstances, school leaders *do* try to remain calm, compassionate and understanding, and I am certain they always try to do what is in the best interests of the child/children. We see how powerful the instinct to protect and fight for a child can be in a parent, and we respect that. But we still have our limitations within a broken system. In our school, it is not just our opinions that we share with parents when we deliver information (we never do anything maverick) but the amalgamated opinion of a whole range of professionals that we routinely seek advice from, and I have no doubt it is the same for others. We respect and have faith in the professionals from a variety of fields from whom we ask advice; as teachers, we do not have the expertise, so we have no choice but to seek it; we then merge that expertise with our own trained and professional understanding and knowledge, before making a decision and sharing it.

Specifically in our school, I know from personal experience that we have put in, and continue to put in, long hours to make things happen for children, those who are vulnerable, those with additional needs, those not even in our school yet and, of course, those who form the main body of the school. We have done all that we can, and continue to, with our limited resources, to support children with additional needs over the years, despite the crumbling services and the changes in provision outside of school, even when their parents may not have been able to.

Parents, for many reasons, sometimes struggle with the fact that their child may have an additional need or two – which we understand and empathise with. I've got relatives who are parents of children with additional needs, so I empathise with this situation on both a family level and also a professional level, but what educators, including myself, struggle to understand is when parents openly blame schools for things that are very often beyond their control. I have spoken at multiple events and have people comment on social media posts to reiterate this and how it makes them feel. It is a modern mystery. I know this may seem like a very unpopular opinion – but actually, I think it's probably a more common opinion than is commonly acknowledged when we are trying to support parents through adjusting to parenting a child with additional needs or parents for whom behaviour is a challenge to manage (more so when it is their own behaviour!), I do not understand why we become the bad guys.

Educators guide parents through every aspect, from navigating the evidence gathering for assessment, including strategies for managing the behaviours witnessed at home or school (or both) and the impact this behaviour has on other pupils, their peer-to-peer relationships and the parental expectations of the parents of other children affected; the diagnosis; and the support post-diagnosis (or, in effect, the lack thereof). It is a heck of a journey for a parent *and* a school, as is managing the changing parental expectations of what their child can do, and is able to do, in the mainstream, combined with our limitations and constraints in school about what they can offer and actually facilitate. Most schools invest huge amounts of time, energy and, indeed, care in this; staff members try to walk beside parents as they navigate 'the system', yet they are sometimes vilified by the same parents they have supported. This hurts, understandably. I know from the many and varied groups that I belong to that this is a national phenomenon that is becoming more prevalent. One can only wonder about the link between the increasing numbers of children recognised as having additional needs in our country, the simultaneous decimation of support services and the increase in complaints about schools in this area (not to mention Subject Access Requests) – but it is important to raise it.

Suspended belief!

I have felt particularly burned during my tenure as a school leader on a number of occasions following complaints, and I have had many (as I am sure most people reading this will have experienced) which, after a protracted period, have been dismissed with no further action. The things I have been accused of both doing and not doing over the years have been so grossly unfair and unjust, yet I have had no recourse. I know that this is echoed up and down the country, and my advice is, whilst having a complaint made about you can be one of the most painful learning experiences of your time in education, you must follow the process and, in the end, let it go – lest it destroy you and your mental health.

Often, complaints are around the unpleasant topics of exclusion/suspension and/or permanent exclusion. Interestingly, some parents complain that a child has *not* been suspended or excluded if their child is hurt, just as much as the parent of a child who *has* hurt another may complain that it is unfair. Whilst the descriptive language for suspension/exclusion/permanent exclusion may change, the act of imposing them as a 'sanction' and basis for them very rarely does. The systems for social support and special educational needs are overwhelmed in our country; as stated in a previous chapter, the funding is non-existent for pupils unless it is hard fought for, and in order for schools to gain funding, they must jump through several bureaucratic hoops, meanwhile trying to ensure that *all* of the children are safe, learning of the children in the class is not compromised, that the learning of the child with needs is not compromised, that *all* of the parents are happy and content, that *all* the staff feel supported and that morale is high in school. This is, as I'm sure any sensible person will realise, an almost impossible task.

There may be times when you have little choice other than to exclude. I, and many of my colleagues, have unfortunately excluded/suspended children. Extensive conversations about this have only reinforced my own views that any kind of decision to exclude is predicated on physical safety – the safety of the individual child, yes – but usually the safety of other children and staff members. I know this is at the forefront of my mind and decision-making, as it is others, when I have done it. It is never a decision that is taken lightly. Never. I also realise that it is not the answer to dealing with additional needs or antisocial behaviour communication. But in understanding the complexities around all the moving parts in the school, and meeting the expectations (or at least trying to) of all stakeholders, sometimes it is the only available option.

When children are excluded for any number of reasons, be that because they have brought in a knife, attacked other children, broken windows, destroyed resources and classrooms or hurt staff, leaders, including myself, always try to be sensitive when dealing with both child and parents. As I know no one outside of education really understands the system, I am able to explain to parents what the next steps are. Part of explaining to parents the reality of what they may be about to experience is also quite challenging. For example, if the behaviour of a child is deteriorating significantly to the point where their safety and the safety of others are compromised, the conversation I might have with the parent is that we are failing to meet the child's needs, despite all of the things that we have put in place (and for us all of those things are documented in CPOMS), the strategies, the human resources, the support networks, external advice and so on. Whilst this is never an easy conversation to have, I think it is also important to manage the parents' expectations as we travel through the journey of creating a learning experience for their child and other people's children in the classroom. I have often wondered how it would feel to be the child. I am not made of wood, after all, and contrary to the belief of some people, I do have a heart that beats rather than a swinging brick in my chest! Equally, I wonder what it would be like to be the parent of a child who is told by the school that their child's behaviour is so extreme that the school cannot meet their needs, and they are struggling – that the child may end up as a worst-case scenario (think 'left of arc' in the military world) if we cannot find a solution to keeping everyone safe, and if the situation continues to deteriorate, the child may be permanently excluded – and how that might manifest in terms of my behaviour and reactions towards the professionals giving me this information.

As a parent of a child who has been 'excluded'

As a parent, my only real experience of discussing the exclusion of one of my children was when my son inadvertently took a knife into high school. I know. He will metaphorically *kill* me when he knows I've put this in the book,[3] but equally I think it shows my pragmatic approach to many things.

One Christmas, he went to stay with his dad. He was only a young teenager, maybe 13 or 14, and someone had innocently placed in his bag (as he packed to come home) one of the gifts he got out of a cracker. It wasn't a cheap cracker. In fact, it was quite an expensive cracker. You might be surprised to know that that gift was a keyring, and on the keyring was a very small penknife. Since that day, many things have changed. Nowadays, we both have a Leatherman multitool. We both have knives that we take on our army duties, and in fact he has since trained as an All Arms Commando, so no doubt he will work with much bigger knives than those we have had in the past. However, he did not know that into his daysack, his rucksack, his school-bag, someone had placed the small keyring penknife, the blade of which was about 1.5 cm long.

During his school day, the first day back after Christmas the following week, the first week in January when I was all about my own school and welcoming everyone back, I had a call from his school to say that he was being 'fixed-term excluded'. I was horrified. My heart raced. I felt panicked for a second. WHAT HAD HE DONE! I drove from my school to his, wondering what on earth he could've done. Why would he have taken a knife to school? What was he thinking of!? I arrived at school to see my cheeky little chappy crying in the office. His head of year seemed vaguely embarrassed because, naturally, this was not a 'knife crime incident' *per se*, and my son had absolutely no previous misdemeanours, with the exception of trying to charm everyone and do as little work as possible (except in PE and engineering), as he has dyslexia and hated anything to do with writing or reading.

My child had not brought in a steak knife, a chopping knife, a meat cleaver, a stiletto knife, a machete or anything else to harm someone else/protect himself/to threaten someone. He had simply been a typical boy. A typical teenage boy (excuse my generalisation for those people who might be offended by that statement), and he hadn't checked his bag. He wasn't that keen on being organised at that time, so he wouldn't have thought to check his bag and organise his *own* possessions, flipping heck, as if! He simply went to school with it, with a few books thrown in, and one of the TAs in the class, his 1:1, in fact, had reported that he had a 'knife' in school.

In order to make a point, he had to be punished, and sanctions applied, which I completely understood. He had a clean record until that date. He hadn't got a record of violence or a history of aggression towards other students, but nevertheless, the school had to use him to make a point to other children. I accepted this. I thought, this was an opportunity where I could have kicked up a fuss and complained and cited all of the above – I chose not to. I talked to my son about the dangers of knives and about how even a small blade could kill. I told him that whether he knew it was there or not, he should have taken responsibility for his own possessions. I talked to him about how the school had a duty of care to **all** of the pupils to make sure they were safe, and someone else could have gone into his bag, taken it out and used it as a weapon – even if he wasn't aware of it. I talked to him about responsibility in general and about how he was becoming a young adult. He could no longer just drift through his life oblivious and passive, expecting everybody else to organise his lifestyle for him. And, painfully, I allowed him to be excluded.

I did compromise with the school, for sensible reasons, and agree that it should be an internal fixed-term exclusion rather than an external one and that there were mitigating circumstances, including the size of the (so-called) weapon, who had put it in his bag, his simple foolishness in leaving it in there and also the fact that he had a completely clean track record. But nevertheless, I wanted to uphold the standards that the school was trying to instil, and I wanted my son to learn a lesson about self-reliance, organisation and a sense of community responsibility towards his peer group – in a 'safe-to-fail' environment. He was understandably upset. I took him home about half an hour before the end of the day so that he didn't have to face other students (perhaps his peer group, perhaps other parents collecting children), just to try and save his self-esteem from more harm because he was a teenage boy who was crying in school. The school permitted me to take him home half an hour or so early and allowed me that time to then discuss with him the plan of attack and the reason why I was not challenging the school's punishment for him.

I compare this attitude to the attitudes of parents I have experienced and whom my networks talk to me about, and sad to say, the headteachers I know (and I, myself) have not always been afforded the same level of respect by the parents of the children we have been responsible for that I personally offered to the leaders of the schools of both of my own children – and this is painful. I am not being treated as I would treat others. But this is real life and not the cliché world of memes and the rarefied world of moral imperatives.

When parents show little respect for schools, leaders, staff or the other pupils in school, it is difficult enough, but when they use leadership decisions to then complain about schools, I feel it sometimes becomes more of a personal attack. What is worse? When representatives from the governors (both complaints and appeals committees), perhaps the LA on Ofsted's behalf, perhaps even as far as the DfE, are forced to spend time investigating only to find there is no basis for the complaint, and leaders have no recourse to hold the parents to account for their behaviours, their attitudes or their actions and perhaps time they have wasted, well, that is hard for school leaders. Essentially, parents can complain to anyone they choose to try to ruin you, your reputation and your life, but you must remain impartial and professional. Bottom line up front: there's nothing you can do about that other than breathe through it and lean on your team. Chris, my current chair of governors, illustrates the pressures:

> In the 5-year school improvement journey, dealing with Ofsted inspections and parental complaints was difficult. Being prepared was a big part in coping with all of the difficulties. Reading everything and trying to absorb as much as possible.

What you can do to mitigate potential vexatious and spurious complaints

Here is my only recommendation – keep meticulous paperwork. Our CPOMs records have been absolutely instrumental in improving the measures I have taken to support children, their parents and our staff, and also to gain funding and to effectively indicate to external stakeholders the needs of our children. Those records have also supported me, and others, when we have been accused unfairly of various different misdemeanours. CPOMS minimises the time spent searching hard-copy filing systems, redacting documentation for GDPR reasons and creating an e-copy that can be encrypted and emailed. It is a genius system.

Whilst it is highly unpleasant, and in some ways soul destroying, to have allegations made against you, it will happen. Provided your decision-making and paperwork are robust and underpinned by excellent systems, which do take time and effort, and again, show the same attention to detail and consistency that academics and finances take, then you can be assured that the process is there to protect you. Having faith in the process – the complaints process, the appeals process and your own paperwork – is absolutely key to maintaining any kind of mental health equilibrium during a complaint situation. In addition to having extremely good paperwork and robust processes, all agreed and understood by your governors and your staff, and shared with your parents, is having a supportive team.

I have made no secret throughout this book, throughout all of my social media presence and throughout my school day-to-day practice that teamwork is **everything**. Without an effective, supportive, robust team prepared to support one another (and challenge where necessary), you cannot survive as a head. Whenever I have made exclusions, and on the very few occasions that I have made permanent exclusions, I have ensured that I have met with my entire SLT many times beforehand to coach them through the conversations around it and also for them to challenge me or offer solutions I may have missed. On one occasion, our chair of governors happened to be in the school building during a situation and observed us having a conversation about whether we could meet the needs of a particular child before we made the final decision. This meant that I was not making the decision from a personal perspective; it was not reactionary, but it was made from an informed, professional, diverse and challenging perspective. There was no other decision that I could've made at that time. This was reinforced and backed up by the rest of my team. This meant that subsequently, when I received complaints and I had to deal with them, I knew I had not made those decisions alone.

In the dark hours, in the early hours of the morning, when you lie awake replaying events and scenarios (yes, you will have done it or will do it), when you question your ability, your sanity, your professionalism and yourself, you can rely upon the words of your team, who have all supported you throughout the entire process. Possibly also throughout the complaints process that may follow. Paperwork, procedures and your team are what will get you through.

How to complain

In keeping meticulous paperwork, I am supported when complaints are made against me. It is also what informs very comprehensive complaints where we need to make them against others. This is also a vital part of the warts-and-all process – the way that you complain and the way that you handle a complaint are all the same. If you can be pragmatic, if you can evidence-base everything, and if you have the evidence to challenge or refute challenge, then the stress of both creating a complaint and dealing with a complaint is massively reduced. There have been odd times when we have made quite significant complaints to, and about, the LA, and these have never been pleasant. Provided that you have the processes in place, and your governors are on board and support you because they are aware of what is going on and kept in the loop, then, again, all you can do is trust the process.

One of the things that I have learned as a headteacher is that you are always on your own when it comes down to it. Without governors, you are vulnerable. Without a union, you are even more vulnerable. If you are lucky, then both will back you. We should all be paying into a union so that, should we end up in court, we will have financial backing for legal fees, if nothing else.

However, I do know that some complaints about school leaders that involve taking advice from a union are not always easy – sometimes unions are as confused as school leaders are because they have never dealt with such a complaint. There always has to be a first, and this precedent setter is the one from which others benefit in future. I am not prepared to berate unions because I think they do their best in terms of supporting school leaders, but they do not act in isolation and are informed by a list of people who perhaps could do/have done better, know/known better, and these people are almost beyond your sphere or reach as a school leader: members of the LA, Ofsted and indeed the DfE, for example. They do not necessarily know or understand schools or the particular issues they face as well as the staff do. I know that none of you will be surprised at reading this, but you will have no doubt come across the case in the newspaper in the summer of 2023 in which a teacher was forced to resign from her post due to a complaint from a parent being made to a national (cough, cough) newspaper. Rather than investigate this complaint and support the professional *before* taking action, this person was vilified, persecuted and made to leave her post. Yet, following a substantial long investigation, she was then found to be innocent! This was too late to save her mental health and well-being or her job. This, combined with the Ofsted narrative still under scrutiny following the Ruth Perry tragedy, and coroner's enquiry findings, is a stark reminder about how truly alone you are as a head.

And everyone wonders at a recruitment and retention crisis.

One thing to note about this: if ever you are a governor, as well as a teacher or a headteacher, if ever you end up working for the DfE or the LA, this is where you can support a colleague. Where there is evidence to prove that they have **not** done what they're being accused of, where there is no evidence to prove they have done what they're being accused of, then have the courage of your convictions to make sure that that person is given the protection that they deserve.

Owning your mistakes

In terms of complaints, there are some occasions when the complaints are perfectly justified, and these are the times that you should be using the information on your systems and your paperwork to evidence the fact that you have got courage, moral courage, and that you are not hiding anything from the people who are making the complaint to you or about you.

If this is a parent, this can be quite challenging because there is an expectation that you will protect your staff members but also that you will follow due process and make sure that you behave with integrity. This means making authentic apologies and sharing information with parents that may be quite difficult and challenging. Where I have had to do this, I have been brutally honest with staff, and I have explained to them what the process would look like and the potential outcomes. This has included, amongst other things, management instructions and disciplinary actions; however, those things have **not** been shared with parents. What **is** shared with parents is the process and the investigation and the outcome and usually a very heartfelt authentic apology. I always have a governor with me to deliver this information, and I am *always* honest.

When you choose to live and work with integrity, it is never an easy choice; bear with me, it means you must tackle issues and have challenging conversations that, frankly, you would rather not have. Whilst the choices might be easier when you do live in integrity, in terms of what underpins them, the delivery of those decisions is what can be quite tricky. You have to be prepared to go against the grain, to swim against the current at times and to hold your ground when everyone else has conceded theirs. Part of that, again, is relying upon your team and your record-keeping – having the team behind you, having them challenge potential outcomes of decisions and then subsequently agree on a team decision on the way forward. Be that with your governors and your SLT for huge decisions or just your SLT for internal operational ones, this is really important. An example of this is when the governors and the SLT stood firm in their decision-making in terms of opening the entire school post-lockdown one in the summer of 2020. We wanted to open the school in a safe way. The way our school was configured is different from every other school. This is standard, from buildings to numbers to cohorts, but with three classes in every year group, the way we had to manage Covid and the impact on individuals, staffing, cover for people who were ill, bubble closures and so on, we knew that opening wholesale immediately after the lockdown could be catastrophic in our school and our area. We knew the number of people who were dying locally, and we did not want to place people at risk, particularly our staff members.

Therefore, we pushed until the very final moment with our LA, who at that time was threatening us with action should we not open, and we chose the best and the most pragmatic way to open our school for as many children as we could, as safely as we could and as quickly as we could. We kept our parents informed, many of whom were very happy with what we were doing, some of whom were dissatisfied with what we were doing. However, we kept them informed. We gave them a clear rationale – which had been agreed upon by governors and the leadership team – and we supported our staff and pupils throughout that process. We were lucky we did not lose any staff or pupils to Covid – who is to say what would have happened had we not done what we did? We will never know.

What we do know is that we also chose on the first day after Christmas, in January 2021, when we should have had a staff training day, not to open our school the following day. We agreed, following the decision of the entire staff, that we would take action, legally supported, union-backed and employment-law reinforced action, that we would not open the school. Therefore, during the day, staff spent the training day, well, training! Meanwhile, SLT spent the day planning for and informing parents about what was going to happen. None of our pupils returned, and all remained safely at home.

Interestingly, at the end of the day, the government then decided that they would also tell schools not to open the following day, and we all went into a second lock-down. We were vindicated for our decision-making; we did the right thing and pre-empted a late surge of political common sense again, not bringing together pupils after the Christmas break, who then could have ended up unwell, ensuring that we maintained safety for the entire community. Moreover, my unwavering support for the views of the staff ensured that my care and concern for them was evidenced again. When the teacher unions supported strike action, I supported the rights of staff to strike and was closing school anyway. Our children did not have a break in their time at home because they did not come in on the first day back after Christmas as many schools in the country did, and that decision was both tricky and made without government backing, without LA backing, but based on integrity, morality and the right thing to do. It was not easy. Some of the phone calls that we made that day proved quite challenging. In the end, we were justified and vindicated by the late government decision, but that won't always be the case. I say, again, doing the right thing is never the easy option.

To sum up

In terms of summarising the 'warts-and-all' chapter, I would say it's difficult to extrapolate one factor that was the worst.

There have been many times when I have lost sleep or suffered anxiety about issues in school, but usually, by bringing the problem to the team and giving them my first idea, a shot across the bow, we always come up with a better idea. I love the fact that my team challenges me and challenges one another, and that we have now built a relationship after five years, where nobody takes this personally, and our outcomes are always in the best interests of the children and the staff.

You will never escape the 'warty bits'. As a school leader, it is always how you handle the warty bits that shows the kind of leader that you are. There is no easy way of navigating them and there are no easy and quick solutions to navigating them. Often, they leave you feeling bruised and battered for quite some time afterwards, sometimes even mentally and emotionally scarred. What you can then do is share all of these experiences with others in the hope that your misfortune becomes somebody else's avoidance of the same problem. Hence this book. Some of the things that I've done, like online clinics for finances, online support chats for people going through HR issues and so on, enable me to pay back some of the support that I have had from having a larger team to people who have a much smaller team, or who may not have had that support in their school.

I would say (but the caveat as I am a cynic now) never rely upon the LA or your MAT solely – always rely on your own integrity and also ensure that you seek advice from a range of different people whom you trust and also from specialists. Don't place your fate in the hands of one individual. I have found that it's never the right thing to do in life, and it certainly is not the right thing to do in terms of school leadership. Your union is there to protect you, but they can only do that if you've got the evidence in the systems within your school that you will have established in order to provide them with the evidence and the information that they may need. At the end of the day, you will be fighting for yourself, your own professional name and your own integrity when your back is against the wall – and always enter any situation with that at the back of your mind.

> I work part time and at the time we began this journey I had a young child at home who was not yet in pre-school education. The task was daunting and learning how to manage and juggle home and school commitments was hard. I will be honest and reflect that at times my own mental health has not had an easy ride due to work pressure and school-based anxiety triggers (moderations, observations, scrutiny). This is something as an individual I have and continue to work on myself and learn to develop coping strategies for.
>
> *– Jen*

Having said all of that, and having been through all of the different things in our school that we've looked at and managed over the years, the final chapter will bring us onto all of the opportunities that all of this has brought us. Ending on a high!

Takeaways

- Agree on robust policies with the governors.
- Stick to the policies.
- Keep meticulous paperwork.
- Lean on your team.

- Find pressure-release activities that are good for physical and mental health.

- Always be in a union and advise others to do the same – if for nothing else other than legal protection.

- Make authentic apologies when they are due.

- Never meet with anyone alone.

Notes

1 https://files.ofsted.gov.uk/v1/file/2640049.
2 https://www.choosingtherapy.com/snowplow-parenting/#:~:text=Snowplow%20 parenting%20%E2%80%93%20sometimes%20referred%20to,they%20have%20a%20 clear%20path.
3 He does actually know. I wouldn't do that to him without consent!

Good reads

Barton, C. (2023). *Tips for Teachers: 400+ ideas to Improve Your Teaching*. John Catt Educational Ltd.

Feely, M. & Karlin, B. (2022). *The Teaching and Learning Playbook: Examples of Excellence in Teaching*. Routledge.

Lemov, D., Lewis, H., Williams, D., & Frazier, D. (2022). *Reconnect: Building School Culture for Meaning, Purpose, and Belonging*. Jossey-Bass.

Lemov, D., McCleary, S., Solomon, H., & Woolway, E. (2023). *Teach Like a Champion Field Guide 3.0: A Practical Resource to Make the 63 Techniques Your Own*. Jossey-Bass.

Sternad, D. & Kobin, E. (2023). *Develop Your Leadership Superpowers: 50 Key Skills You Need to Succeed as a Leader*. Econcise.

Wilson, R. & Peacock, A. (2020). *It Takes 5 Years to Become a Teacher*. P and R Education.

16 All good now
The world of possibility!

By working towards the OFSTED framework and working with people who could share best practice, give feedback and suggest improvements the school did make significant improvements. Systems were tightened up, consistency was in place and the children were achieving better outcomes. The culture shifted to that of a united team with the same shared vision but this may have been more due to the high expectations of SLT who were driving us forwards to have a shared vision and giving us more autonomy increasing our engagement and sense of accountability. The constant loom of Ofsted and observations from external people was extremely nerve wracking and effected my physical and mental health. But through it all our supportive team and SLT team kept us motivated, backed us 100% when things got tough and we were able to come out of the other side stronger than ever.

– Emily

All good now!

Well, where to begin with this 'box-up' chapter?

Basically, I'm going to start by stating the obvious: we're all good now!

We are all good.

The funny thing is, the few hundred words contained in a bland Ofsted report do not tell the story of the three hours of verbal feedback and the notes we made during it. Nor do they tell the tale of the daily lives of staff and pupils in our school. Three inspectors came to see us for two days. I sent them our SEF and the SDP; I sent them evidence of the LA subject leader monitoring and the ASIA monitoring. I know they looked at our website, probably for weeks, and also all of our social media sites to triangulate what I said in the documents that I produced for our school, which they had the night before their visit. I was excited to welcome them. I wanted the closure to the chequered past that I knew a visit would bring and the gate opening that it would allow into our future. I knew that we could be at risk of a political manoeuvre; after all, the national agenda is to force schools

DOI: 10.4324/9781003440000-17

to academise; given our double RI history, there was every possibility we would simply fall between the political cracks, and yet – I felt quietly confident that ours was a super school and that we were indeed in very good health, having been loved back to life. I am not 'anti-academy', by the way, just anti being forced.

What isn't in the Ofsted report? Verbal feedback!

As the SLT, you will sit in the verbal feedback, and staff will not, nor will governors (who do at least get a potted version). Take copious notes so that you can share the deeper feedback with key stakeholders!!!!

In terms of quality of education, inspectors met with early reading leads, maths, geography, science and history subject leaders, in addition to art/DT, PE/Cojo and music subject leaders. All subject leads could explain the rationale and sequence for progression in their subjects and were proud to show the work of children in their subject. They commented on the strengths of the way the cohesive curriculum is planned across school, which included well-sequenced long-term plans, revisiting skills periodically to ensure they were embedded, exceptionally well-planned lessons and systematically implemented positive training opportunities for all staff. This supported the narrative of Ofsted during and following both monitoring visits they made to school during the pandemic in which they commented on the ambitious curriculum and the determination of staff to continue to train and engage in CPD, even during successive lockdowns.

Regarding the foundations upon which the curriculum is built, they commented that subject leaders were able to give lots of examples of research that was undertaken and used, assessment statements matched planning and the tracking system used was clearly effective. The way the school had embedded and routinely conducted cyclical monitoring (as discussed in Chapter 14) and adapted the practice to suit the developing picture within the school, they said, was commendable. From early years through to Y6, the work is excellent and is ongoing in terms of seeking out improvement and adaptation, and this has become simply the way the school operates with significant benefit to all staff and pupils. We are never complacent; it is not in my nature to be, and this now percolates through school at a much more sustainable pace, I grant you! One award-winning Alternative Provision headteacher (with whom I delivered a session at the Schools and Academies Show at the ExCell in London recently) commented that she thinks I 'normalise excellence'. Perhaps she has a point.

Consistency was celebrated across the board, from leadership expectations to planning, from monitoring to implementing assessment – the inspectors noted that all subject leads have time to monitor their subject rather than it falling to the deputy headteacher and me, and inspectors agreed with the leadership team who said that the next step would be to measure the impact of the wider curriculum and tweak assessment as appropriate now that we have enjoyed a post-Covid year of uninterrupted teaching and can work on evidence gathered during that year.

The most wonderful part of the feedback, of course, was the children and what the inspectors found when talking to them. All pupils spoken to said they were very sure they were being challenged, and this was triangulated with what the teachers shared and what was found, and we continue to find regularly in books. Children demonstrated how they had taken on their own research – developing as independent learners, developing study skills and autonomy and becoming rounded members of the school.

Inspectors commented that leadership and management are real strengths of the school. This was apparent to the previous three inspection teams over the last five years and was commented on at the last full inspection in April 2019 when the school received its second RI (its first under me as new headteacher, as you already know). That report was a little unusual in that, although the school remained RI, leadership was given a 'GOOD' rating – which was evidently ratified by HMI. The strong governing body, having embraced the expectations and training I initiated at the start of my tenure and who have since been empowered to continue to be pro-active, are very knowledgeable, invested and know the school well. They are able to talk about the school from all angles – for example, curriculum development, subject leader roles, parental complaints and staff workload. Governors spoke with authority about the development of subject leaders and how the curriculum had been designed – because they are fully involved in the process! They were also able to discuss standards and challenges, and this was evidenced not just during the inspection but over time, in governor minutes. Governors are fully aware of statutory duties, especially the current national focus on attendance, and are fully supportive of the school as part of its high-functioning and embedded leadership system.

Supporting vulnerable children is a real strength of the school. I was glad they saw this. In large part, this is a result of the non-class-based SENDCo, Alice, and learning support mentor, Clare (AKA Clarice!), whom you read about in Chapter 6. The SENDCo works relentlessly with outside agencies and has created and embedded clear recording systems/processes resulting in direct positive impact on the lives of and outcomes for the children, and they were shown multiple case studies to evidence this. All aspects of SEND practice she has implemented are really strong, and it was on this basis that I nominated her for a national teaching award, for which she subsequently gained a Silver (have I said?) – what a legend.

All aspects of school are 'strongly good', they said (we chuckled because what this meant was anyone's guess); they also said that any barrier to a child's learning is effectively identified and mitigated by working closely with a range of agencies. English as an additional language (EAL) is very strong and based on research to support parents, school leaders and teachers in order to enable the best outcomes and maximal progress for children with EAL.

PP support systems are in place to support children and track expenditure, and this feeds into evaluative processes seen elsewhere throughout the school where value for money is assessed against pupil progress and development; well done to our Sharon, the deputy head.

Inspectors, upon talking to parents at the gate and also reviewing Parent View, established that the vast majority of parents are supportive, pupils felt safe and are encouraged to be the best they can be. Thankfully for the SLT, the governors and I, they also said that the school is considered well led and managed!

Personal development is another real strength of the school. School is passionate about equality and diversity, and as such school is a demonstrably inclusive place where it is ok to be different. Children have a good awareness of British values and why they are important and, moreover, a strong sense of morality because the Social Moral Spiritual and Cultural (SMSC) Curriculum is firmly embedded – not just mapped onto the curriculum overview but seen regularly in other areas where there are clear outcomes.

The school, they said, provides many opportunities to discover and develop wider skills and talents! Children (especially Y5 and Y6) were very articulate during the inspection and willing to share considered opinions, demonstrating that they are respectful citizens and are challenged to reflect and learn from mistakes made in school in a safe environment that enables them to grow. We also wrote national materials, with clear progression and curriculum links for Cojos, yet one of the reasons we did not gain an outstanding in this aspect was that we do not track pupils' activities and talents, or expertise outside of school.

Relationships and sex education (RSE) is part of the statutory curriculum in place, as is religious education (RE). RE is where children can talk about different religions and how their understanding of them is developed progressively over time. This is not only part of the statutory curriculum but also underpins several social activities that support inclusivity and celebrate diversity – e.g., World Diabetes Day or World Downs Syndrome Day. The school also enjoys an inclusive social community, helpfully supported by a proactive PTA, which, I am delighted to tell you, will hopefully be opening a community coffee shop on the grounds very shortly!

Behaviour and attitudes of pupils throughout school were, and are, excellent. Pupils, despite the expected numbers within a large school and the number of pupils with additional needs whom we support, were polite, calm and orderly when moving throughout the corridors. Most notably, during unstructured times, their peer-to-peer interactions were commendable. The issue that inspectors focused on, preventing an outstanding judgement in this aspect, and something which again I had highlighted as a focus (because it is a national focus), was attendance. Although broadly in line with national statistics, there were some notable exceptions, e.g., in the EAL and PP subgroups, in which attendance was lower than national standards. Although the school is following strict national guidance, which has been very unpopular and caused us some headaches, and we do fully engage with parents, Ofsted felt we still need to do more to increase attendance figures and also to monitor the impact of current attendance monitoring practice. I have my views on this.

Outcomes of the inspection in terms of early years provision echoed again the school's views and focus this year. Indeed, last year, I planned and began a painting project with the site maintenance team throughout the EYFS and a refurbishment of the internal environment to match the refurbishment of the external environment that has taken place over the last 18 months. This is now complete, and parents and staff literally rave about it being so gorgeous. If I decide to make a career change, I think perhaps interior design might be an option. As I review this, I am beyond excited that Cool Canvas came into our school and transformed two whole outside areas for our EYFS and SEND children and plans are afoot for more developments!

UP!

Woodlands is a school that has been on the up for five years and continues on that trajectory! It has been an absolute pleasure and privilege to be a driving force for good in the school and the community – to enhance the employment and life experiences of the staff who have worked in the school, as well as the academic, social and character-building experiences of the children we have served. Our plans will no doubt continue to evolve; my mind never switches off, and I am blessed with a team of thinkers with creative minds, but I want us to continue to be a community social hub, to welcome families with small children to our baby/ toddler group; to support the families of children who are neurodiverse; to support and challenge children to achieve and attain in a positively affirming, safe and rewarding environment; and to give everyone in our school aspirations and goals they can rise to achieve.

The school, our wonderful school, where I am so blessed to be a custodian for a short spell in history, was as good the week, month and year before Ofsted came as it is now, six months later. Yet the judgement we received removed all the barriers we had been unable to navigate. Because we are 'GOOD', we now get to exploit all of the opportunities that I have been setting the conditions for during the last five years because I have not just been trying to fix the school; I've also been trying to pave the way for a future legacy.

I am excited by the fact that I've worked hard over the years to share our best practices and to share all of our experiences with others, and now to build on that, I'm being asked to do talks up and down the country, both in education and in the military context to share leadership experiences that we have had.

However, before you throw the book down in disgust and think, 'What a self-absorbed witch!', I could not have done any of that had I not built a team and had their support and backing. I hope the book exemplifies that whilst I am a catalyst and an instigator, an idea generator, and I will always lead by example, I have developed a team of people who have done much of the work I have begun. I have been outward facing as well as inward focussing and inward working. I can now talk about financial audits, our manual of financial internal procedures, PP, special needs, assessment, tracking systems, training, consistency, the curriculum, early years, teaching and learning, HR, performance management, governance, complaints, school development plans, parental communication, Ofsted, the environment, behaviour management, culture, relationships – you name it, I can talk about it.

I can only do that because I have walked the walk, sometimes leading my team by the hand, sometimes being supported by others to walk the hard yards. We have definitely walked those hard yards on many occasions over the last five years, as you will have gathered. So what? The 'so what' for me is profound.

Opportunities

Having been through the process of inspection, we had the outcome that meant we got the 'green light' to open an EYFS special needs provision for non-verbal children with ASD, which we, as I review this, did! It was so successful, we are planning to do it again for cohort two, in just a few short weeks. This will involve us building on the capacity that we've already created in terms of special needs, and it will develop the new part time SENDCo into a more senior role in our school. Alice, already a senior leader, has since taken on the role as assistant head, which will help her future career progression. The enhanced special needs provision has future-proofed school financially and ensured that not only those children with additional needs come to our school, and we provide for them the most wonderful learning experience and environment but also their siblings can come, too, because the historical drop in numbers in our school means we've got space throughout the school for siblings to join us!

We also planned to open a nursery and a preschool – as I write, has been open almost a school year. Previously, we could not afford to do this – not only that, but we did not have the staffing capability. Having built on all of that good practice in early years and developed the environment, we are now in a position to be able to double the size of the nursery we opened last September and operate at a small loss financially, but also to ensure that parents now have a one-stop-shop in our school for children from two to 11 years old, no matter their needs.

We also opened our own wraparound breakfast, after-school and holiday club last September. Again, this was essential for our staff, who may have been doing additional jobs to supplement their finances and who have been able to earn money in our school during the holidays, in the evenings and in the mornings. This has future-proofed school so that we didn't have to lose our excellent staff to higher paid jobs due to the cost-of-living crisis in our country. It also means that the staff working with our children in the wraparound club actually know them, and this enhances the behaviour expectations we have in our school and the provision for children by people who are aware of the day they have had.

Our PTA plans to open a community coffee shop and a second-hand uniform shop in the space vacated by the previous preschool provider. I CANNOT WAIT for this and to see how it grows.

When I think about the potential that we now have, the future is bright, and it is tremendously exciting. As a school leader, it is rarely about 'you' and more often about what parts of 'you' can bring out the best all around you for the greater good. Superfluous questions about my future don't even register – I have no idea about the future. Interestingly, as a school leader who has worked in a school in crisis and had the good fortune to be able to turn that story on its head, people ask if I am working to become a CEO, I am not; working on getting an MBE/OBE, I am not (far too outspoken for that!); working on getting outstanding given how close we came, the answer is not an Ofsted outstanding, but simply continuing to do the best job we can, with what we have. I do not lack ambition; I am simply happy doing my job.

Outstanding? The inspection talked about attendance and the fact that we need to focus on that; personally, I think it's a bit of nonsense. There is absolutely no way that we could do any more in terms of supporting our families to bring children in and get them attending regularly. This has been a focus for Ofsted in our school because we had a small number of children, in a very small cohort of our school, who were extremely unwell, and therefore, attendance overall was affected by illness – so, to me, it is not appropriate to talk about attendance defining what we have to do to improve. We don't see the benefit in terms of the money coming into school; the LA gets that! We provide the staff to process attendance fines and take on board the multiple issues generated by fining parents, the cost to the school and the time of staff in following up, and yet it is the LA that receives the money. This is something that needs publicising so that parents no longer see this as punitive action by the school wishing to profiteer from its parent body. To me, this is another systemic issue that needs to be dealt with by the government. I completely understand the attendance and absence indicators related to safeguarding, and this is a desperate topic that should be at the forefront of everyone's mind, but statistics dictating judgements and outcomes, I think, are illogical at best.

Legacy

When I think about my legacy, because I won't be in our school forever – heck, I won't be around forever – I think about the compassionate ways of working that staff have hopefully learned from me. I hope that they will at least have taken one positive away from their experiences in Woodlands under my headship. I hope that the parents, by and large, have had a positive experience and know that each day, we have all come to school with one focus in mind: creating a place for their child to thrive. But most importantly, I hope in my heart that the pupils have taken on board all the learning that they've had the opportunity to experience in our school, formal and otherwise, because the final legacy has to be the future, and it is them.

> The school culture has a huge impact on wellbeing, workload, and school improvement. Working closely as a team, challenging each other and sharing work load helps immensely. Whilst my dad was ill and sadly passed away this year, I was overwhelmed by the support I had from my Headteacher, SLT and so many caring colleagues.
>
> – *Annica*

I think about my colleagues who have passed away far too young last summer, the summer of 2023. Louise and Helen. I want to celebrate the work of those brave women and many headteachers like them who simply want to put community and pupils at the heart of everything that they do.

I am blessed to work within a number of networks, and I think this is the secret to how we will continue in our future work, all of us as school leaders. I said at the start, and I'm now saying at the end, collaboration, networking and supporting one another rather than competing with one another has to be the future for us all.

The future is bright for Woodlands, and where we can help others, we will. Where YOU can help others, you always should. School improvement is far more than just Ofsted. School improvement is really making a change to the lives of the people that you serve: your staff, your pupils, your parents and your community.

Good reads

Bethune, A. (2023). *Wellbeing in the Primary Classroom: The Updated Guide to Teaching Happiness and Positive Mental Health.* Bloomsbury.

Bethune, A. & Kell, E. (2020). *A Little Guide for Teachers: Teacher Wellbeing and Self-care (A Little Guide for Teachers).* SAGE.

Brown, B. (2015). *Daring Greatly: How the Courage to Be Vulnerable Transforms the Way We Live, Love, Parent, and Lead.* Avery.

Cowley, A. (2019). *The Wellbeing Toolkit: Sustaining, Supporting and Enabling School Staff.* Bloomsbury.

Evans, K., Hoyle, T., Roberts, F., & Yusuf, B. Eds., (2021). *The Big Book of Whole School Wellbeing.* SAGE.

Waters, S. (2021). *Cultures of Staff Wellbeing and Mental Health in Schools: Reflecting on Positive Case Studies.* Open University Press.

Index

Pages followed by "n" refer to notes.

Printed in the United States
by Baker & Taylor Publisher Services

Printed in the United States
by Baker & Taylor Publisher Services